Roberto Rossellini

MY METHOD

Writings and Interviews

CONTENTS

PREFACE

Adriano Aprà, in his moving introduction, remarks on the unlike-
lihood that this book should exist. Writing was torture for Roberto
Rossellini. He could talk a blue streak, conjure up one fascinating idea
after another, seduce producers as easily as women. But he was never
able, no matter how he struggled, to put down on paper the wonderful projects he'd all but sold the night before.

Rossellini's formal schooling did not go beyond the first year of
high school. In a culture infamous for long sentences, endless quali-
fying phrases, infinite involution and extravagant vocabulary, his
Italian was made of short words and short sentences. He rebelled
against academe's attempt to ornament his voice, but he was not
uncultivated. He persevered in candor in speech all his life, just as he
persevered in candor in film, where his style steadily grew more
precise, artless, and rich. As a boy he read widely, always in bed—the
place where he would spend most of his life, one way or another. His
parents, nouveaux-riches bohemians, kept the house filled with
Rome's cultural élite—musicians, artists and literati. His sister re-
called that it was Puccini who first addressed her as an adult. Already
as a boy Roberto was admired for his talent at synthesizing complex
ideas, his inventive tall tales, and his allconquering charm—so allconquering that, as a result (the price the gods pay), he was thoroughly spoiled, unqualifiedly selfindulgent, and resentful of any
control. "Freedom" was always an obsession. His great uncle,
founder of the family fortune, had run away from home to join to

fight with Garibaldi and persisted even during the First World War in displaying an Italian flag that conspicuously lacked the arms of the ruling House of Savoy. Liberal ideas pervaded the house—belief in the ultimate goodness of people to work out things, hostility to ideologies and theories. Naturally when Rossellini started making films, the script form loomed as a blatant attempt to encase him in armor. Only in the flash of inspiration, only in contact with an immediate situation, could he function successfully and be himself.

What applied to filmmaking applied even more to life—to relating to women and men. Rossellini's charm was partly the genuineness and intensity of his interest in you. It's this personableness, directness, and immediacy, in his life but also in his films, that Adriano Aprá relates to "oral" rather than to "written" traditions in art and wisdom. One imagines Rossellini, who loved leisurely meals with friends, could have been happy as a Homeric bard, living in some mythic past that has not yet discovered writing, and singing *The Iliad* and *The Odyssey* to enraptured audiences.

Such performances, historically, would have been partly improvised; partly in sync with familiar patterns, as folk songs still are; and full of incidents, characters, and actions that audiences had known since childhood. No performance would be the same, and none would ever be written down, not for centuries.

But then something monstrous would occur. The "happening," the spontaneous musical theater that had existed only as a momentary, immediate and direct contact between you and the artist, would die. All that would remain would be words written in library books.

Death would mean survival, but only as a ghost. Oral tradition, for all its obvious ephemeralness (how many songs are lost? how many thousands of years?), was yet a powerfully alive reality for every boy and girl, woman and man. It formed hearts, minds, and lives. In this respect it resembled the media of today, except that it was personal and immediate and momentary. It was contemporary, whereas "written tradition" comes down to us in "texts"—and haunts us as the wisdom of ages. "I believe all ideological patrimonies should be part of our culture and formation," said Rossellini, "[but] not as doctrines to which we're tied by sentiment and habits dictated by orthodoxy."[1] Written texts, akin to commandments chiseled in stone, pre-define life, reality, good and evil for us before we are born. And Italy has a great deal of stone. Etruscans, Greeks, Romans, Byzantines, Arabs, Normans, French, Germans, Spaniards, and Americans, Paganism and Roman Catholicism, Communism and Fascism and myriad species of monarchy, oligarchy, and democracy, have vied there for mind-control for centuries. The living world is always mostly young people, as Rossellini said, "but it ends up being dominated only by the dead, because through orthodoxy it's the dead alone who dominate us, not the young."[2]

Rossellini was sixteen when Mussolini came to power, thirty-six when Mussolini fell. He remarked how difficult it was, growing up and living in a Fascist regime for twenty years, to break out of the constrictions of thought the era imposed—or even to perceive that the constrictions existed. "The moment you're inside a mechanism, you don't understand things very well; we were incredibly ignorant."[3] Youths like Rossellini were not uncommon at the time: rich hippie playboys who chased girls and raced cars and openly derided the regime, the Church, and established society in general. They might, like Roberto, also escape to Naples and sleep on parkbenches from time to time. Not until Mussolini fell and the Germans occupied Rome were they compelled to confront life seriously.

Some, when they realized how monstrously Il Duce had duped them, were obsessed by the contradiction. How is that Italians, with their wealth of written tradition, had so easily accepted Fascism?

One reply, by Antonio Gramsci, was also a call to action. Italy's culture was defective, he said, because it was too "mandarin." Those who were educated or read books were a tiny minority, isolated from ordinary people for centuries, whose culture, as a result, was artificial, superficial, lacking deep roots in the national and popular soil. The

1 Quoted in Gian N.G. Orsini, *Benedetto Croce: Philosopher of Art and Literary Critic* (Carbondale: Southern Illinois University Press, 1961), pp. 76 & 80.
2 In Pio Baldelli, *Roberto Rossellini* (Rome: Samonà e Savelli, 1972), p. 261.
3 Transcript of tapes recorded by Rossellini for Daniel Toscan du Plantier, c. 1976, Adriano Aprà collection. These tapes were the basis for the posthumous book, Roberto Rossellini, *Fragments d'une autobiographie* (Paris: Éditions Ramsay, 1987).

only way to insure a just society for the future lay in the assumption of hegemony by an authentic culture. This meant an end to the exploitation of the peasants and workers who made up the bulk of the Italian population.

Gramsci's solution was popularized during the same period in which Rossellini, De Sica, Visconti, and others were making the films that a few years later were labelled "neorealist"—*Open City* and *Paisan*, *Shoeshine* and *Bicycle Thieves*, *La terra trema*, *Bitter Rice*, etc. The notion of filming nonactors in real locations doing things that actually were happening to them—to ordinary people—seemed to promise results less bookish and more "real." Just as folk music rejuvenates classical music as an authentic representative of national culture, so people's films would authenticate cinema, and with it, Italian culture.

But, rather than an authentic bard arising from the folk, what actually happened was a series of violent clashes between the way the filmmakers perceived reality and the way everyone else did. Communists, Catholics, Liberals, moviegoers of all classes united in execrating neorealist films. The government tried to stop their production and exportation; censorship was imposed more rigorously than under Fascism.

Everyone wanted films to promote their notion of how the world should be. There was much disagreement. Everyone, filmmakers included, conceived films as propaganda mechanisms for the very same written tradition that they wanted to rejuvenate.

But Gramsci's solution was not the only one. Benedetto Croce, Gramsci's guru, disagreed with his disciple. Fascism had been an aberration, not an inevitability, and anyhow was one of the less subtle mechanisms of mind control. The problem lay deeper, in the reluctance of each of us to take off the blinders that traditions impose on our perceptions. Anything said in the collective voice of the folk (the voice of tradition) would necessarily be prosaic, and therefore false. But poetry, truth, is individual. There is something fresh, primitive, naïve, and creative in every human encounter with the world, and poetry is our emotional expression of our encounter.[4] The conven-

---

4 I am indebted to David Roberts, *Benedetto Croce and the Uses of Historicism*, Los Angeles: University of California Press, 1987.

tional truism—that individual expression must conform to collective speech—was an abomination to Croce, who insisted that *only* individual expression possesses concrete reality (actually exists), and that "language," collective speech, is a fiction, a mere abstraction. Every poetic utterance creates its own language; words and rhythms are used in a unique way every time a poet achieves expression. "There is no such thing as the true (logical) sense of a word," Croce said. "The true sense of the word is that which is conferred upon it on each occasion by the person forming a concept."[5] The only "real" language is poetry, individual speech, and poetry is not a "sign" referring to something other than itself: it contains its object within itself. "Born as poetry, language was afterwards twisted to serve as a sign."

Truth, then, can be found not in texts, but only in direct experience—instinctual, unreflected, impulsive, and frequently out-of-sync with the collective voice and written tradition, thus apparently arational. An authentic bard can only be an authentic bard, and can only truthfully express the collective and correct written tradition, by being authentically him- or herself. And then she or he will be a revolutionary.

Rossellini may never have read a line of Croce or Gramsci. But he inherited a radically Crocean attitude from his father, his mentors, and the coterie that supped and argued in his father's home. For Rossellini, all human progress results from those who have the courage not to conform. "I'm always for the 'crazy' people," he said. "My aspiration, my great dream, is that each person be himself, with all the risks this entails, including the risk of being crazy . . . If you're authentically yourself, you have such a load of honesty that it must per force lead to something.[6] From a very humble position you can face everything and you can revise the whole conception of the universe."[7]

Rossellini is referring specifically to Francis of Assisi (*The Flowers of St. Francis*). Yet all his movies are about people who manage, through conviction and little else, to revise the whole conception of

5 Quoted in Gian N.G.Orsini, *Benedetto Croce*, op. cit., p. 77.
6 In G. Menon, ed., *Dibattito su Rossellini*, Rome: Partisan, 1972, pp. 77 & 80.
7 Unpublished remarks to students at Yale, c. 1974, my collection.

the universe. Garibaldi *(Viva l'Italia!)* set out to conquer kingdoms with a thousand student protesters. Louis XIV launched the totalitarian state by endlessly prolonging a masked ball. Saint Paul convinced almost everyone that God had spoken to him. When we watch Rossellini's six-hour *Acts of the Apostles* we are struck that the world adopted (Christianity), not from any reasoned position found in books or newspapers or institutional structures, but from "oral tradition," from no other authority than one person at a time accepting the *conviction* of another. The oral tradition is more than words, *much* more. It creates true language, imposes new poetry, revises the whole written tradition. Poetic speech is infectious, sexual.

I'm not at all convinced by Rossellini's puritanical condemnations of "art" as seductive, castrating, fascistic, mind-controlling, etc. Nor by his attempts (aping André Bazin and French phenomenologists) to define his own films as just showing "things as they are" or as just "informing." Nor by his redefinition of Shakespeare and Molière as "scientists" rather than (shudder) "artists." Such prattle should not be taken too seriously. When Rossellini was inspired, his films are infectious and sexual; when he was not, they are nothing. Fortunately, he was inspired more often than not. And once one accepts his style, even in its most advanced stages, as in *Acts of the Apostles,* where to most people it *still* seems even more amateurish and sketchy than *Open City, Germany Year Zero,* and *Voyage in Italy* used to seem; once one accepts his style, his films share with Murnau, Vidor, Renoir, Ford, Mizoguchi, and Ophuls the quality of using every facet of cinema with total and precise expressivity.

One perceives that the distinction is less between the *forms* (written or oral) that authority takes, than between its *personae.* Rossellini makes "orthodoxy" sound almost as bad as *1984,* or maybe worse. Yet nothing more totally shapes life to an orthodoxy than does a great work of art, wherein all experience is from the artist's attitude (and his culture's). Rossellini spoke of St. Peter's as the "summation" of the Renaissance.[8] But there is an operative difference between a work of art that represents an orthodoxy, and an orthodoxy which works of art represent. The first demands a distance and invigorates our

8 Toscan du Plantier tapes.

autonomy; the second is successful when it is transparent. Rossellini's fear lest art be seductive and controlling is really fear lest art be bad art. His famous definition of neorealism—he said it was a "moral attitude"—was also, obviously, his definition of art. Poetry, Croce maintained, is not possible without a moral personality in the artist; the moral conscience is the foundation of all poetry—and *more:* of the only "truth" humankind will ever possess. What annoyed both Croce's opponents and Rossellini's was that such "truth" was less group orthodoxy than private revelation. Yet the "moral" imperative to see clearly must place orthodoxy continually in question.

As a boy, Rossellini thought he could escape orthodoxy and find poetry in sex, cars, cocaine, and Naples. At age sixty he found himself reenacting the drama of his own father who, equally unschooled and equally determined little by little each day to "demolish" his ignorance, had set himself, each night after work, to reading the great books, taking copious notes, and creating new texts of his own. Some of Roberto's new texts were written essays; most were films—*Viva l'Italia!, The Age of Iron* and *Man's Struggle for Survival* (histories of technology and culture), *The Acts of the Apostles, The Rise to Power of Louis XIV, Socrates, Blaise Pascal, The Age of the Medici, Descartes, Anno uno, The Messiah*—almost fifty hours of movies showing what he had learned, implicitly asking "Where are we going?" Only death, at seventy-one, halted the torrent of film.

Father and son had both confronted the paradox that momentary insight into "things as they are" is not enough. The only real escape from orthodoxy is knowledge.

Tag Gallagher

WRITING, READING, VOICE

To reopen a discussion through cinema is impossible. Cinema is too expensive. There are other means that are less expensive and more effective. We can carry out a discussion, an investigation much more thoroughly, and sort out, examine, and discuss general ideas much more effectively outside of cinema. Books are still the bases of everything. Since a film cannot be made without the contribution of the public (it is very expensive merchandise), we have to begin our discussion in a different way—and then continue it with the help of cinema. We could, for instance, start with literature, and then return to a public that has been gradually formed by literature. And we must have the courage to be didactic . . . As for me, I may not leave cinema, but it will no longer be my main activity. Still, I feel much more at home in cinema than anywhere else. It has been terrible for me to start writing. I have had to restart from zero and remake myself from scratch. I've had to acquire a technique, a language. It's not funny in the least, but I had to do it because all my discourses were becoming vain . . . [I devoted myself] mostly toward the essay. That's where I have to start from. Very loosely structured essays. I see this as a means to insert myself into the world, so as to have a chance to study it and understand it . . . In writing one can broach much larger issues . . . First of all, I want to try to see the world in which we live with new eyes, and to understand how it's scientifically ordered. I want to see it. Not emotionally or intuitively, but with as much precision as possible, and in its entirety.

Rossellini made these declarations to *Cahiers du cinéma* in 1962. The same year he made his last film for the cinema: "Illibatezza" (Chastity), an episode in *RoGoPaG*.[1] At the start of "Illibatezza" there is a citation from Alfred Adler:

> Man today is often oppressed by an indefinable anguish. And midst his daily travail, the unconscious proposes a refuge to him where he can be protected and nourished: the maternal womb. For the man of today, henceforth deprived of himself, even love becomes the whimpering search for the protecting womb.[2]

In "Illibatezza," refuge in the protecting womb is illustrated through the instrument of cinema: a home movie of the girl he's in love with that the protagonist projects onto himself. The anguished man of today, Rossellini tells us, finds in cinema—understood as protecting womb—a refuge not only from love, but from life itself, in which he is no longer able to orient himself.

The cinema Rossellini speaks about, and that he abandons, is not just the classical cinema of tale and enchantment, of allusion and illusion, of mise-en-scène and montage. It's also his own cinema, which years earlier he had consciously posed in opposition to classical models. And, more generally, cinema as apparatus: the movie theater, the projection machinery, the darkness, the protecting womb: cinema as manifestation of the unconscious, cinema that separates us from life's reality even as it reveals it on the screen in blinding immediacy. Consequently, Rossellini is rebelling against love for the cinema; even against love for the films of the French new wave. Godard may write, in his fulgurous paragraph on *India* (1959) that that film is beautiful like "the creation of the world," but Rossellini will reply years later, on the last page of his posthumous *Fragments of an Autobiography*:

> It's always the same story over and over, the same double misunderstanding again and again. On one hand, the total incomprehension of the money world. On the other hand, aesthetic vagaries and glorification by disciples, which is even more dangerous. In either case, impasse.

Hard words, radical, difficult to accept: because even if Rossellini

---

1 Rossellini returned to the big screen twelve years later, with *Anno uno* and *The Messiah*. But this attitude toward cinema had not markedly changed.
2 Translated from the Italian.

has managed to abandon his cinema, he nonetheless continues to talk
about it. But he writes from experience. He had come back regener-
ated from India in 1957, had thrown himself into cinema again, and
as a result had been better able to give it up in 1962. Rossellini's
declaration of his need to write in 1962 is surprising, given his
well-known idiosyncratic opposition to scripts: a written form of
cinema, a pre-writing of cinema. What was his intention? In 1971,
introducing his made-for-television *Socrates*, he affirms:

> Socrates didn't leave even a single written word. Which is another of
> the chracteristics that make him a man absolutely modern. Because his
> wasn't a case of laziness but of choice. Socrates was against writing, and
> it seems to me that his attitude furnishes an element of thinking that's
> rather contemporary. Writing immobilizes and freezes thought, makes
> it stable, definitive, thus dead. Written culture is an authoritarian
> instrument: it admits no contradiction, it doesn't concede any possibil-
> ity for dissent or reply to those who enjoy it. Oral culture is instead
> dialectical, mobile, continuously becoming: an instrument to collective
> communication and, we say, democratic . . . Today we have other
> instruments that can renew oral culture: audiovisual means. We can get
> back to the dialogue.[3]

Is Rossellini contradicting himself, when he says he wants to try
writing, he who so admires Socrates?

If an anthology had been compiled in the early 1960s, it would have
been a collection not of written texts but of transcriptions of oral
texts: interviews; public announcement (which, though signed, read
as though penned by journalists or publicists); conference transcripts
(originally oral); open letters (soliciting replies). Even "Dix ans de
cinéma," the one apparent exception, was not written but taped in an
interview and then assembled by *Cahiers'* editors; and the very fact
that it was never completed adds to its immediacy as Rossellini's first
attempt at autobiography.[4]

Similarly, Rossellini's cinema appears opposed to "written culture"

3. L. Tornabuoni, "Ventotto domande a Rossellini," in *Rossellini: Socrate per la TV,*
Appunti del Servizio Stampa della Rai, no. 38, August 1970. Reprinted in Sergio
Trasatti, *Rossellini e la televisione* (Rome: La Rassegna Editrice, 1978), pp. 149-60.
4 See pp. 58–77. "Ten Years of Cinema" was a series of three autobiographical essays,
signed as though written by Rossellini, that appeared in *Cahiers du cinéma* in 1955
and 1956.

and designed to reconquer the aliveness of "oral culture." When Rossellini deals with photography, in *La macchina ammazzacattivi* (1948), he depicts it as an instrument of the devil (literally!) that turns people photographed (even though just bad people) into stone, "freezing" life—an obvious metaphor, at least to me, of the sort of cinema he's opposing. In "Ingrid Bergman," the episode he did for *Siamo donne* (1952), he produces a sort of cinema that destroys its own magically seducing apparatus by having Bergman speak and look at the camera: a camera that's no longer mechanical: cinema that anticipates television. In *The Human Voice* (1947) in contrast, a film eminently "oral," in that it consists of Anna Magnani talking continuously on the telephone, Magnani's voice is *too* seducing; it's a voice from the maternal womb, to whose power of fascination the man on the other end of the phone line reacts by fleeing—hanging up. But in *The Flowers of St. Francis* (1950), which is the film about brotherhood and at the same time about the distance between people (a "distanced" film), the monks at the end separate from Francis like emanating waves to spread the message: television again.

There are many other examples of Rossellini's ambivalence about "oral" versus "written" cinema: the perfect narrative construction of *Open City* (1945) that was maintained despite the well-known difficulties of production; the studio lighting that is so attentive to the play of light and shadow on the faces and walls in *Europe '51* (1952) and even more in *Fear* (1954); the mise-en-scène that's dictated by the writing-voice in *Jeanne au bûcher* (1954); and, after the voice of purification that narrates *India*, the dilemmas of theatrical cinema recur with *General Della Rovere* (1959), an extreme meditation on the actor and his mask, with the vampire woman of *Vanina Vanini* (1961). Even among his television films, *The Rise to Power of Louis XIV* (1966) observes power through power's mise-en-scène by Louis.

Alongside these last investigations into "written" cinema, *Viva l'Italia!* (1960) affirms the "oral" cinema toward which Rossellini now incessantly inclines. But it is quite different from the oral cinema of *Paisan* (1946), *Germany Year Zero* (1947), *The Miracle* (1948), *Stromboli* (1949). These films represent a cinema that in "voice" preserves the immediacy, the warmth, the accent, the dirt. It's an oralness that Rossellini learned from Vidor, Renoir, and Pagnol. But for him it's still too seducing, still too easily transformed from medicine to poison. It's the feminine voice that is still the hero and doesn't permit him to voyage freely over the world. Thus with *Viva l'Italia!*, a masculine, paternal film, Rossellini inaugurates a new attitude, a new style, which surpasses the problems both of the "written" cinema of mise-en-scène and montage, and the "oral" cinema with the too immediate, too seducing voice. In *Viva l'Italia!* and the subsequent (*very* talky) films for television, there is an "oral culture" of a voice that was once written words, and that, in passing from writing to speech, has lost its immediacy, its dangerous emotionality. It's a "dubbed" voice; other people's voices are imposed in a monotonous manner onto bodies that talk; and the characters "cite" words that preexist in written form, in the source texts and in the "scenarios" in which Rossellini has transcribed them. This "oral culture" of Rossellini's is above all that of the apparatus which transmits his films: television, which "looks far" and has come forth out of the protecting womb of the dark auditorium.

This "written voice," which synthesizes rationally what was originally synthesized emotionally, is born from a changed attitude toward reality. Rossellini no longer limits himself to looking at the reality present in Italy or Europe or even in India. Now he has to investigate past reality, which clarifies the present. We cannot know past reality directly, with the sharpness of looking at it; we can know it only as mediated through the information transcribed in books. Rossellini's "written voice" is born from reading: so many books on history, biology, anthropology, and science that pile up on his bed for his lazy perusal. Film is his way of visualizing and synthesizing—as his beloved Comenius instructs to do—the information accumulated in so many centuries of history to help the anguished man of today to come forth from the refuge of the maternal womb, and orient himself in the vast far-offness of the Earth, the stars, and beyond.

"My discourse is purely oblationary," he will say. Like Socrates, "the man who does not write" (but perhaps also a bit like Plato, who has to write in order for oral culture to be handed down to a civilization of written culture), Rossellini doesn't impose, he offers; his discourse is maieutic: neither mother nor father, neither emotion nor authority, neither the protecting screen nor the castrating education. He erases himself behind the camera, he doesn't exhibit the travails of pregnancy. He reserves the pregnancy for those who see and listen, in order that there may grow within them the seeds which his encyclopedia has made germinate.

"Trying to make myself write has been terrible." If Rossellini really did begin writing in 1962, the texts have not, to my knowledge, been published. He may have written only notes. There are many unpublished pieces among his papers, and even a book, *La comunicazione dall'anno uno all'anno zero* (Communication from year one to year zero). But I believe all of these were written in later years. I believe he wrote mostly for himself, to organize what he was reading, to synthesize. And this is what he did in the articles and books he eventually published. And alongside this writing, there was still the voice: still more interviews, public announcements, conferences, and open letters. But while the transcribed voice constrains him at times to the tiresome task of still talking about cinema (particularly revealing are certain "difficult" interviews where his interlocutors try, seriously, to interrogate him in greater detail about his films), his own written texts go far beyond cinema's little universe.

I have perhaps betrayed him by fishing up old things in which he is still speaking about his films. It's difficult to get detached. I only hope, by following in these pages the long trajectory that led him from cinema to television and beyond, to make you feel the inebriating fascination of this going far off.

Adriano Aprà

MY METHOD

"WHO WERE YOU?"

MARAINI: When were you born?

ROSSELLINI: May 8, 1906.

MARAINI: Where?

ROSSELLINI: In Rome.

MARAINI: What did your father do?

ROSSELLINI: He was in construction. He owned a construction firm.

MARAINI: What about your mother?

ROSSELLINI: She was a housewife.

MARAINI: Do you have any brothers or sisters?

ROSSELLINI: Yes, there are four of us, two brothers and two sisters.

MARAINI: Did you have an easy childhood?

ROSSELLINI: Yes, I did.

MARAINI: Was it happy?

ROSSELLINI: Yes, it was very happy.

MARAINI: Why?

ROSSELLINI: Because our home was full of joy, as well as fantasy. A boundless fantasy which my parents never tried to hold back, quite the contrary, they encouraged it.

MARAINI: How did it manifest itself?

ROSSELLINI: In all sorts of ways, in the games we played as well as in the weirdest projects. Our family was not exactly traditional; it didn't try to preserve a certain heritage. In fact we weren't even able to keep our fortune. We consumed it all in no time.

MARAINI: How was your relationship with your father?

ROSSELLINI: It was very warm.

MARAINI: Did you admire him? Did you love him unconditionally?

ROSSELLINI: Yes, I did, a lot and unconditionally. My father was a businessman but he was also an intellectual. He wrote a few books that I still read with great pleasure.

MARAINI: Was there ever any major disagreement between you and your father?

ROSSELLINI: No, never. We had a few minor arguments, over my first big crush or my lack of commitment in school. Nothing serious.

MARAINI: And what about your mother, did you get along with her?

ROSSELLINI: My mother was terribly nearsighted, very shy, and extraordinarily witty. It was impossible not to get along with her.

MARAINI: Were you closer to your father or to your mother?

ROSSELLINI: To both, but in very different ways. I felt great tenderness for my mother and the deepest admiration for my father. He was an exceptional man.

MARAINI: Did you get along with your siblings?

ROSSELLINI: Yes, perfectly.

MARAINI: In other words, your family life was quite pleasant and untroubled. When did you first start feeling at odds with the world?

ROSSELLINI: The moment I was born.

MARAINI: Usually the first conflicts occur within the family. But that was not your experience. I imagine your relationship with the outside world was a little harder.

ROSSELLINI: I have never gone through any real drama. Yes, I have gone through some painful times, and some dangerous times as well, but no real dramas. Everything has always seemed fairly easy, and logical.

MARAINI: Do you think this is due to your happy disposition toward both things and people?

ROSSELLINI: Maybe. It's hard for me to say.

MARAINI: Can you really say that you have never suffered in your life, or at least not in any memorable way?

ROSSELLINI: Maybe everybody suffers, and I'm like everybody else. Maybe I should make an effort to remember, but nothing comes to mind. Maybe the only thing that has ever caused me real suffering was fear. I have gone through moments of terrible fear. Every time I risked too much and left myself totally vulnerable.

MARAINI: Fear of what?

ROSSELLINI: I am not practical. I am quite reckless and often dive headlong into situations where the risk is too high to be worth taking.

MARAINI: How did you feel about school?

ROSSELLINI: It was torture.

MARAINI: Why didn't you like it?

ROSSELLINI: Because it was boring, though I was lucky enough to have a few good teachers. When I went to Nazareno, the headmaster was [Luigi] Pietrobono, the famous Dantist. A little later, I had [Pietro Paolo] Trompeo in Italian literature and [Alberto M.] Ghisalberti in history. But in spite of all these excellent teachers, I still got bored.

MARAINI: Do you think school could be anything but boring?

ROSSELLINI: Sure, it should not be boring. We should reform everything. One day we might. Who knows.

MARAINI: What interested you most when you were a boy?

ROSSELLINI: Cars, engines, physics, and math.

MARAINI: Nothing else?

ROSSELLINI: No. Besides, I got seriously ill. Twenty months in bed with the Spanish flu. That's when I started neglecting my studies.

MARAINI: Do you consider this illness an important event in your life?

ROSSELLINI: I remember it as a period of extraordinary happiness. Everybody was taking care of me, pampering me. I felt wonderful. I see it as a very productive period from every standpoint.

MARAINI: How so?

ROSSELLINI: It helped me find a new direction for my life.

MARAINI: When did you start thinking about the movies?

ROSSELLINI: See, my father built the Cinema Corso, the first modern movie theater in Rome. He built it over the ruins of an old movie theater called Lux et Umbra. Right above Cobianchi, no less. And that's when I started going to the movies every day. I had a card that allowed me to get in free whenever I wanted to. Not that I was crazy about cinema, but I liked it all right. At the Corso I started meeting people involved in the business. When my father died and, in just a few months, we found ourselves reduced to poverty, I had to get a job and naturally turned to film.

MARAINI: Did you have other plans before that?

ROSSELLINI: Of course, all sorts of plans. Going to the moon, becoming a great racer. All sorts of things.

MARAINI: In other words, you were quite open.

ROSSELLINI: More than open. During my long illness I spent a great deal of time in the mountains to take care of a light form of tuberculosis, an aftereffect of the flu. Having nothing to do except feel free and open to all sorts of possibilities helped me a lot.

MARAINI: It was a period of meditation.

ROSSELLINI: Yes, a period of meditation, relaxation, and self-satisfaction. But it helped, it did me a great deal of good.

MARAINI: What was your character like as a boy? Were you aggressive, meek, sullen, generous?

ROSSELLINI: I was definitely aggressive. I am not so sure I was generous. I was quite prodigal, given to squander, even too much. I have always been quite reckless. I have no measure. I live enthusiastically.

MARAINI: Day by day?

ROSSELLINI: No, not day by day because I like to make very precise plans for the future. But I have a tendency to burn all the bridges behind me. It's a serious flaw. Particularly when one begins to have a certain amount of responsibility, loads of children, as is my case.

MARAINI: So, you started working when your father died. How old were you?

ROSSELLINI: Quite old. In 1932. I was already twenty-six.

MARAINI: How did you exactly start? What did you do at first?

ROSSELLINI: I was a sound-effects man. I had fun inventing new noises. For instance I found out that a newspaper rubbed against a door produces a marvelous sealike effect.

MARAINI: Did you immediately get a good salary, or was it hard at the beginning?

ROSSELLINI: I was paid fairly well. In the milieu I was seen as a young man full of hope and promise but not to be trusted. What was hard for me was this lack of trust, this fear of my abilities. Then I started writing screenplays for other people. In other words, I was their slave. Then I went into editing and dubbing.

MARAINI: So, you did just about everything one could do in cinema.

ROSSELLINI: Yes, I guess I know all the tools of the trade firsthand. But that was a period of great enthusiasm; cinema was a completely new field to discover.

MARAINI: Whom did you work for here in Rome?

ROSSELLINI: I worked for a company called ICI, I think, It belonged to [Luigi] Musso's father, you know, the car-racer. [Roberto] Dandi was there. But you are too young to remember these names.

MARAINI: Then what?

ROSSELLINI: Then I started making shorts about animals.

MARAINI: Why about animals? Were they commissioned or was it your idea?

ROSSELLINI: It was my idea. I love animals. And I liked to make documentaries. I have always had a taste for documentaries, not in a banal sense, but as research tools.

MARAINI: When did you make your first film?

ROSSELLINI: In 1940. It was called *La nave bianca* [The white ship] I had gone to Taranto to make a documentary on a battleship and came back with a film. Of course, later it was reworked and touched up by everybody. But that's always been my destiny. There have always been people ready to salvage what I had done.

MARAINI: Who? The producers? The distributors?

ROSSELLINI: Anyone who did not agree with what I was doing. Insofar as I am concerned one of the reasons for the crisis in cinema today is its refusal of any experiment. To do well an industry must have a research department, otherwise it can't but fail. Cinema doesn't see this, in fact, it opposes it outright.

MARAINI: You mean to tell me that your films were tampered with because they were experimental?

ROSSELLINI: I have never been able to do what I wanted to do from beginning to end. In cinema, my desire to speculate has always been stronger than my desire for survival.

MARAINI: Does this sort of tampering still go on?

ROSSELLINI: Yes, it still does. Or rather, it did until not long ago. Now I am my own producer so no one can push me around.

MARAINI: Which of your films do you like best?

ROSSELLINI: None. Once I am done with a film, I cannot see it again; it no longer interests me.

MARAINI: This seems to be part of your character, that is, it seems to go along with your lack of interest in the past and the burning of bridges. Is this how you are also in your private life?

ROSSELLINI: Yes, I am always looking forward. Novelty stimulates my curiosity. The past bores me.

MARAINI: Do you fall in love easily?

ROSSELLINI: I am a monogamist. When a relationship dries up, I move on.

MARAINI: And every time you want to start a family, have children, buy houses, make plans for the future.

ROSSELLINI: Yes, every time I get thoroughly involved in the whole thing as if it were the first time.

MARAINI: How many times have you gotten married?

ROSSELLINI: Three times.

MARAINI: And how many children do you have?

ROSSELLINI: Seven. If one is involved in a daily struggle, one doesn't have the time to turn back and look at what he has already done. One has to keep moving forward.

MARAINI: There are people who have a very intense relationship with their past.

ROSSELLINI: The past is a very useful experience, or, at least it should be, though I have my doubts about it.

MARAINI: Do you see many changes in your stylistic evolution or do you feel you have remained essentially the same?

ROSSELLINI: What I call style rests mostly in my search for something to tell.

MARAINI: So, you do not give much importance to formal research.

ROSSELLINI: I'm interested in discovering things as they are.

MARAINI: In other words, you believe in a rationally recognizable reality. Do you think that the study of psychology might help in the understanding of humanity?

ROSSELLINI: Yes, I do. I firmly believe in psychology.

MARAINI: What interests you most in a film, besides the story?

ROSSELLINI: More than the story, the ambience, the characters, things. When I started working in cinema, for instance, a movie was just another form of narrative, a love story. That was that. I have never been too keen on straightforward love stories.

MARAINI: Is there a film among all the ones you have made that was particularly hard, or that you wish you had not made?

ROSSELLINI: A film is always a sketch. It does not allow you to change your mind and do things over, the way a book does. At the moment I am writing a book, and you can't imagine how I like working at a table, with calm, without having to rely on anybody else.

MARAINI: Are you writing your autobiography?

ROSSELLINI: No. It is a sort of focalization of all the problems I have never had the time to confront, so it is only partly autobiographical. Films, however, are always and only sketches. All one can do is make the sketch as vividly real as possible.

MARAINI: Do you see any shared feature in all the films you have made? A predominant theme, maybe, that you can trace through all of them?

ROSSELLINI: I wouldn't know. I like to understand things. With my films I try to cast some light on the main issues of our times.

MARAINI: What are the issues that most interest you?

ROSSELLINI: For the time being I have found plenty of stuff in history. The history of men and women, of course, not that of kings and wars. Studying history one comes to the realization that people have always been the same.

MARAINI: You don't believe people can change?

ROSSELLINI: Yes, culture evolves and changes a civilization. But human psychology remains more or less the same. Human behavior doesn't really change.

MARAINI: In other words, in history you look for those human aspects that have always existed.

ROSSELLINI: Yes, the permanent ones. Madness and wisdom, for instance, which, in different combinations can produce either courage or fear. As far as I am concerned, human life isn't worth living if it isn't a constant adventure. In my films I try to persuade everybody to live adventurously.

MARAINI: Is this your artistic belief?

ROSSELLINI: It is my goal.

MARAINI: Do you consider yourself a religious person?

ROSSELLINI: No. My mother was religious. My father less. In any case, I have no affiliation with any church or any religious orthodoxy.

MARAINI: Have you ever been interested in politics?

ROSSELLINI: Yes, since I was a child. I felt the first stirring of a political conscience when I was eight. I had gone with my grandfather to buy a flag. I remember entering the shop and my grandfather saying: "Give me a flag but with no frill."[1] That "no frill" made me understand that there is something that's called politics that's made of

1 The "frill" in question refers to the arms of the ruling House of Savoy. Rossellini's grandfather was a republican.

particular ideas and emotions. I remember another occasion, the day Mussolini showed up on the balcony of the Hotel Savoia (the first balcony of his life), on via Ludovisi, right across the street from where I lived. It was late evening and the spotlights illuminated the whole length of the street from via Calabria on. Below us, there were several black shirts and Mussolini announced the advent of the first Fascist government. We kids were standing at the windows of our foyer, all happy and excited. My father got home at that moment. He unlocked the door, and without even glancing at what was going on in the street, said: "Remember, kids, black's good at hiding dirt."

MARAINI: Have you ever joined a party?

ROSSELLINI: No. I believe one must be alive at all costs. Any form of orthodoxy terrifies me because it makes me feel dead. Doctrines and disciplines are often necessary, but I have always dreaded them. Today we live a very young life, we are always involved in one movement or another, and in change. Yet, politically we are still dominated, through orthodoxy, by the dead. It is a terrible paradox. The dead should be part of our culture, of our knowledge, but they should not oppress us with their dogmas.

From Dacia Maraini, E tu chi eri? Interviste sull'infanzia, *Milan, 1973, pp. 95-103.*

BEFORE *OPEN CITY*

AN INTERVIEW WITH FRANCESCO SAVIO

SAVIO: For a few years now you have kept your distance from cinema, though very recently you have returned to it. You challenge the role of cinema as language, or, at least, as a means of communication, and believe that television is a better medium. Nevertheless, a long time ago, I think it was 1936 but you can set me straight if I am wrong, you started making films. What were you looking for in cinema then, and what drove you toward it?

ROSSELLINI: Well, I don't know, I was probably looking for the same things I am still looking for now. I do not believe there is that great a difference between cinema and television. However, television allows one a much greater freedom than cinema because it does not depend on an immediate success, on box office receipts. When television is controlled by the state, moreover, it has certain social obligations which it can be forced to fulfill, or even bribed into fulfilling if it fails. The structure of cinema is much more restrictive, much more conservative, which means that to do something new, which is what matters most, is getting to be harder and harder every day.

SAVIO: When you first started making films in Italy, in that particular Italy, at that particular historical time, did you think you would be allowed to express yourself freely, or did you know you were venturing into a constraining context?

ROSSELLINI: I knew full well that it was a constraining context, that there was no freedom. Everybody knew it. But at that moment my main concern was to learn to use this new language, and in this I was definitely spurred, albeit somewhat superficially, by my youth. When you're young you do things with greater enthusiasm. Maybe even a little recklessly.

SAVIO: But what did you like about the movies? When one decides to do something it is generally in the pursuit of a certain ideal, a model of sorts. What drew you to cinema? Was it American films, French films, German films, a particular director?

ROSSELLINI: No. I did not start making films because I liked a particular film. Of course, I liked lots of things in the movies. Immediately after World War I, my father built the Cinema Corso. That's where I used to go as a boy and where I saw a great many films. In a way, one could say I witnessed the birth of cinema, with D. W. Griffith. And from the start I was aware of the difference between European films, so extremely romantic, and American films, also romantic but with other elements in them.

SAVIO: You started making documentaries, which, if I remember correctly, have nothing realistic about them, in fact they are rather lyrical, or even fantastic. Isn't that so?

ROSSELLINI: In fact, I have only made one documentary . . . under water. Or rather, I made it on the roof of my house, inside a fish tank.

SAVIO: Actually you made more than one documentary, but it's true that they don't look like anything else you have done . . . On the other hand, you were not all that young when you began your film career.

ROSSELLINI: True, I began working in cinema around 1932/33. Before that I had a nicer job, that of a son, which I liked much better.

SAVIO: In the credits of *Luciano Serra, pilota*,[1] your name appears as both scriptwriter and assistant director. I mentioned this to Alessandrini who told me that in fact you shot part of the film while he was ill or absent. Is that correct?

---

1 *Luciano Serra, pilota*, directed by Goffredo Alessandrini, was released in 1938. Made under the aegis of Vittorio Mussolini—and of the Fascist regime—the film enjoyed popular success, and was awarded (ex-aequo with Leni Riefenstahl's *Olympia*) the Mussolini Cup at the Venice Film Festival of that year.

ROSSELLINI: You must remember what cinema was like then. Its rituals were quite complex. If you didn't have a tiara on your head, a pastoral staff in your hand, a papal ring around your finger and a cross on your chest, you could not make films.

SAVIO: In other words, one had to go through a very hard and lengthy apprenticeship.

ROSSELLINI: That, and the fact that the film industry then was a closed system. A film was a sort of religious rite whose performance one could attend and follow, but to officiate in it was an altogether different story. To begin with, we had none of the advantages we have today, from 16-millimeter cameras to 8-millimeter ones. Today, if you really want to, you can do what you please. Not so then.

SAVIO: On the other hand, your first film didn't really fall within this structure. *La nave bianca* had a very peculiar character.

ROSSELLINI: As far as *La nave bianca* is concerned, I started with the idea of making a ten-minute documentary on a hospital ship. But then I ended up doing something completely different.

SAVIO: With some sort of story line which is probably the least interesting part of the film.

ROSSELLINI: That was added later. When the film was finished it got people so angry we had to reach a compromise.

SAVIO: The story of the wartime pen pal writing to the sailors?

ROSSELLINI: All that was introduced later. The film I had tried to make was simply a didactic film about a naval battle. There was nothing heroic about it since the sailors were crammed up in so many sardine cans without the slightest idea of what was going on around them.

SAVIO: Yes, but besides and beyond the naval battle, the white ship was supposed to come back and rescue all the survivors.

ROSSELLINI: True, but that is part of the story that was added later, to sweeten the pill.

SAVIO: In fact, the best part of the film is the first one, dealing with the naval battle proper. The sentimental part revolving around the pen pal is much less effective. On the other hand, *Un pilota ritorna* [A pilot returns] is a narrative film in the strictest sense of the word. What do you think of it today?

ROSSELLINI: I think nothing of it because I do not like to think about the things I do.

SAVIO: You haven't seen it since it first came out?

ROSSELLINI: Nor do I intend to. And not just that film. I don't want to see anything I have done. What's done is done.

SAVIO: Does this also include what you did yesterday?

ROSSELLINI: Yes, even what I did yesterday is behind me, done once and for all. I think it is very important to keep moving on for as long as one can.

SAVIO: Do you think this is only true for yourself and your films or do you apply it to cinema in general. In other words, an old movie is an old movie even if it is not yours but someone else's. Does this mean that since it is old it no longer interests you?

ROSSELLINI: No. I'm only speaking for myself and my own films.

SAVIO: And you don't think this is so much the result of dissatisfaction as the need to keep looking ahead.

ROSSELLINI: The result of having no base, no anchor to speak of.

SAVIO: So, you don't want to tell me about *Un pilota ritorna* or *L'uomo dalla croce* [The man of the cross]?

ROSSELLINI: It's very unpleasant for me to talk about those films today because it has become so fashionable to play the victim of some political pressure that it is quite boring. However, I can tell you that all the dialogue of *Un pilota ritorna* was changed. All of it.

SAVIO: That is, from what it was originally, from the original script?

ROSSELLINI: Yes.

SAVIO: Which was written by none other than Mussolini, Vittorio Mussolini.

ROSSELLINI: Well, it was just an idea. I like to keep all the freedom I can, I never start with what's on paper.[2]

---

2 Vittorio Mussolini conceived the story, not the dialogue, for *Un pilota ritorna*.

SAVIO: Not even then?

ROSSELLINI: Not even then.

SAVIO: And yet, *Un pilota ritorna,* seems to be a very nicely balanced movie.

ROSSELLINI: But things find their balance later, that is, if they follow a certain logic. When I started working in film, as a sort of black marketeer, there was someone I was very fond of, a scriptwriter, that is, one of the three or four who wrote all the screenplays of those times. And since I was looked at as a weirdo, someone not so stupid but definitely odd, this friend of mine helped me get work. He would pay me three thousand lira to write a screenplay, of which one thousand in advance. Back then I could live twenty days, maybe even a month, on a thousand lira. It was quite a bit of money. When I was about to exhaust the first thousand lira I'd write the first part of the screenplay so as to get the next thousand lira, and then, when I found myself again in a corner, I would write the second and last part, which meant that the entire job would take me a total of two days. The whole thing was so mechanical that it was hard to keep one's illusions about it: I have never believed in that kind of work. By which I do not mean that it shouldn't exist. Some people do it. To each his own. But as far as I am concerned, in order to work I first need to gather an extraordinary amount of information, so as to know what I am going to be dealing with through and through, after which I allow myself total freedom of action. What one would call improvisation, and, in a sense, is improvisation since I believe that a film is always just a sketch, and its value is precisely in that it is a sketch. First of all because this allows one to move on, that is, to learn to become a man. And being a man is a very difficult job that must be learned every day: and that's why we need all the freedom in this world to do it well. If one gets bogged down in one's own craft then one becomes a craftsman, not a man.

SAVIO: This is certainly true in your later films, but not so much in a

---

Rossellini is confusing memories of it with *La nave bianca.* His version of *Un pilota ritorna* was not altered; he had complete liberty. The film, like most war films made at the time, has a distinct antiwar, even antifascist, message.

film like *L'uomo dalla croce*. You say you need to know a lot about the subject you're dealing with, but seeing that film one gets the feeling that you were not all that aware of what was going on.

ROSSELLINI: What could I possibly know? Everything we heard was so indirect. When you're steeped in total ignorance, it is already something if you do your damnedest to get out of it. But in those times we lacked the means to learn more. All my antifascism, if that's how we want to call it, dates back to the day of the march on Rome, when Mussolini announced the formation of the first Fascist government from the balcony of the Hotel Savoia. We were very young, my sister, my brother and I, and so we were quite excited as we watched the whole thing from the window of our apartment. We lived in via Ludovisi, right across the street from the Hotel Savoia. I remember both via Ludovisi and via Calabria all lit up by one of those flood-lights that were used during the war to spot planes. My father got home right at that moment. Without as much as casting a glance out the window he said: "Remember, kids, black's good at hiding dirt." That was my political awakening. All I knew.

SAVIO: What happened during the shooting of the film that was then finished by Pagliero? Its original title was *Scalo merci* [Freight yard], but that was changed later [*Desiderio* (Desire)].

ROSSELLINI: This is something I have never spoken about because I hate to play the victim or the hero.

SAVIO: Tell me what happened.

ROSSELLINI: This is what happened. At a certain point in time, in Italy, a cinematographers' union was formed whose first action was that of banning two people: myself and, I believe, Ninchi, though I am not so sure, maybe it was someone else. In any case we could no longer work. This happened during the war, we were facing very hard times and I was terrified at the thought that I could not work.

SAVIO: This happened in mid-shooting?

ROSSELLINI: No, no, this happened way before the film was even started. So I paid a visit to Vittorio Mussolini, who was not a bad guy.

He was the president of this union,[3] and I told him that the union's decision was in fact an infraction of the laws laid down by his father. His father had passed the antistrike laws, which automatically prevented any lockout on the part of the employers; what had happened to me was, in effect an employer's lockout.

SAVIO: What were the reasons for it?

ROSSELLINI: I don't remember, really, I don't remember.

SAVIO: Like some sort of personal attack? It's odd.

ROSSELLINI: Exactly, a personal attack. It happened after *Un pilota ritorna* and *L'uomo dalla croce,* immediately after these two films. Why, I do not know. Reasons were always so hazy then. But the same thing is still going on now. I don't know whether you are aware of all the attacks levelled against me at the Centro Sperimentale, though nobody seems to know what might have prompted them. Still, there they are. Back then, they were expressed in a different way, so I talked about it with Vittorio Mussolini who managed to get me the permission to work. I wasted no time and jumped on a project of Peppe De Santis called *Scalo merci,* and in a month we got everything ready. But then I fell ill, I had tonsillitis, just as I was supposed to begin shooting, and so I was two days late. They had already built the sets at the Titanus, on Monte Mario. I started shooting on July 19 . . . Not a good day to start a movie.[4]

Radio interview recorded on September 22, 1974;
collected in Francesco Savio, Cinecittà anni trenta,
Rome, 1979, Vol. III, pp. 961-966.

---

3 Vittorio Mussolini has no memories of this story, nor does Franco Riganti, who organized the "union"—actually an association of producers aiming to regulate distribution—Rossellini refers to.

4 July 19 was not a good day because Rome was bombed by the Allies that day, and the railroad station Rossellini was shooting in was destroyed.

A GREAT ITALIAN FILMMAKER: ROBERTO ROSSELLINI

BY GEORGES SADOUL

Italian cinema has been the revelation at the Cannes Film Festival. If Alberto Lattuada's Il bandito *[The bandit], a strong but uneven work, was controversial, everybody admired Roberto Rossellini's* Open City.

This film, which has been successfully showing in New York for a year but has unsuccessfully sought a distributor in Paris since the beginning of this year, will at last appear on a Parisian screen. Rossellini's latest film, Paisan, *has already been announced and a few film clubs will soon show it to their audiences. Many of those who have seen it have had the sort of revelation that only cinema can, albeit too seldom, bring. As for me, I was as enthusiastic about it as when I first saw* Caligari, Potemkin, *and* Peter Ibbetson.

I am quite sure that, if Italian cinema keeps its promises, it will occupy the same position in postwar Europe that German expressionist films and Swedish cinema occupied in the twenties. With Italian cinema, everyday life invades the screen. There is no subject that Rome or Milan filmmakers won't tackle, and all their topics are current.

Next to these films, contemporary French cinema, still hiding behind history and the novel, smacks of academism, while American film is like a greenhouse plant, divorced from both nature and life.

Rossellini looks like the young Jacques Feyder, and his features have the same delicacy and gentleness as those of the Soviet filmmaker Yutkevitch.

ROSSELLINI: The idea of my first important movie came to me during the historical events that provided me with its subject—which I immediately jotted down with the help of my scriptwriter, Sergio Amidei. We started shooting the film barely two months after the liberation of Rome.

In spite of the almost total lack of film, we shot most of our scenes on location, in the same places where the events we were reconstructing had actually occurred.

In order to have the money to start the movie I had to sell my bed. Then I sold a bureau and a wardrobe with a mirror. Everything else followed suit. I had to borrow money, and quickly realized that if I gave it back on time I could borrow more. And so, with the help of a few friends I was able to get the seven or eight million lira I needed. We were even able to rent a studio for the scenes that were supposed to take place at the Gestapo headquarters.

At the very beginning *Open City* was a silent movie, not out of choice but of necessity. Back then a yard of film cost sixty lira, if we had recorded the sound we would have had to spend hundreds of lira more. Once the film was finished and edited, we asked the actors to dub themselves. And as I am a rather careless technician, I have to admit that there are a few moments where the lip movements are not in sync with the words . . .

As far as I am concerned, I don't like sets, I hate makeup, and prefer to do without professional actors. As you saw, *Paisan* was filmed entirely on location. A foundation cream is enough to alter the real texture of the skin and the lines of a face. I am going to tell you a secret: if, in my films, I have used people who had acted before it was because, more often than not, they were actors without a name, and, often, without technique. However, in *Open City* I have made two exceptions to this rule.

The role of the priest is played by Aldo Fabrizi, a comic actor specializing in monologues. He played a very tragic role admirably. This film also marks the debut of Anna Magnani, a music-hall actress, who had already held a few minor roles in operettas, but had never acted in a movie except as a smart extra . . . I don't know whether you agree with me, but I believe she is one of the finest actresses in the world.

SADOUL: I couldn't agree more. This woman, who is neither very young nor very attractive, has been for many of us—and I am thinking in particular of our friend Eluard—one of the biggest revelations at this Cannes Film Festival.

ROSSELLINI: To choose my actors for *Paisan*, I placed myself, with my cameraman, in the center of the village where I meant to shoot such and such an episode of the story. The passersby immediately gathered around us and so I picked my actors out of the crowd. You see, when you deal with good professional actors, they never exactly fit your own idea of the character you wanted to create. So, in order to create the character he has imagined, a filmmaker has to engage in a real battle with his actor until he manages to bend him to his will. Since I don't feel like wasting my energies in such a struggle, I only use casual actors. Besides, it's very hard to get a professional to work well with an amateur. So, I've given up working with good actors . . .

Amidei and I never complete our scripts before we get to the locations where we are going to shoot the film. Often circumstances as well as the performers that chance has brought us, force us to change our original plans. Even the dialogue and its intonation depend on the amateur actors who are going to utter it; all we have to do is leave the performers the time to get adjusted to the atmosphere of the shooting.

So, *Paisan* is a film without actors in the proper sense of the word. The black American you found so remarkable in the Neapolitan scene claimed he had played a few minor roles but I knew he had lied in order to get the part. All the monks in the scene of the convent are real monks. The minister and the rabbi of the American army who talk with them are also a real American minister and a real American rabbi. This is also true of the peasants who live in the marshes around Ravenna and speak the dialect of the region, just as the Sicilians at the beginning of the film speak the Sicilian dialect. The English officers are as authentic as the German soldiers I picked out of a group of prisoners. And if you thought that the young American in the Roman episode had some talent, you might as well know that the only camera he had ever faced was that of a photographer who used him for a razor-blade ad.

What strikes one in Rossellini's methods is that they resemble those of the best new movie directors all around the world. This is how, in England, Basil Wright and Paul Rotha make their documentaries, or in

America the great Flaherty, in the U.S.S.R. Yutkevitch and Zguridi, in Switzerland Leopold Lindtberg with La Dernière chance *[The last chance], or, finally, in France, René Clément with* La Bataille du rail *[The battle of the rails], and Georges Rouquier with* Farrebique.
I ask Rossellini about his future projects.

I have just signed a contract with a big American company. If I have to work in the United States it will be to shoot a film taken from a novel I find very good: *Christ in Concrete,* or, if you prefer, *Jésus Christ dans le béton.* It is the story of the construction of a building by Italian masons. There is also another subject inspired by the marriages between American men and Italian women. Fifty-eight thousand soldiers have found their wives among my compatriots. It hasn't always worked out. On the other hand I'd much rather go on filming in Italy. There are plenty of contemporary subjects. I am thinking of Naples with its hordes of abandoned children, its beggars, its thieves. One should also do something about that camp near La Spezia where all the Jews not allowed to return to Palestine have been gathered.

We talked for a long time. I told Rossellini about all my hopes for Italian cinema. But he doesn't seem to know the work of other Italian directors very well. He hasn't yet seen Lattuada's latest film, Il bandito; *he respects Mario Soldati's later works as well as his intelligence, and he speaks enthusiastically of* Il sole sorge ancora *[The sun rises again], a film about the Italian partisans directed by his friend, Vergano, and of* Sciuscià *[Shoeshine], a movie about the life of young Neapolitan shoe shine boys that De Sica has just finished shooting. I don't know whether Italian film, as burdened as French film is by hard commercial contracts with America, will be able to sustain its current impetus in the next few years, but I know that, since its liberation and its resurrection, it has given us four or five of the most original films that have been produced in the world in the last twenty years.*

"Un Grand réalisateur italien, Rossellini, qui vendit ses meubles pour tourner Rome ville ouverte, *a recruté les acteurs de* Païsa *parmi les badauds," in* L'Écran Français, *no. 72, November 12, 1946, pp. 17-18.*

GERMANY YEAR ZERO

In *Open City* I treated the problem of the occupation of a world-famous capital, the center of Christianity; it was a direct statement of what I myself saw and suffered. I deal with the problem of liberation in *Paisan*. In my opinion, there remained two great themes of modern significance, which derived from the experience of war each people in its own way had passed through: the first, the atomic bombings of Japan, the second, the destruction of Germany. As a European I chose the theme of conquered Germany and made *Germany Year Zero*. For various reasons I have not yet been able to work on the atomic bomb picture.

I made a child the protagonist in *Germany Year Zero* to accentuate the contrast between the mentality of a generation born and brought up in a certain political climate, and that of the older generation as represented by Edmund's father. Whether he excites pity or horror I do not know, nor did I wish to know. I wanted to reproduce the truth, under the impulse of a strong artistic emotion.

Although the story of Edmund and his family was invented by me, it nevertheless resembles that of most German families. Thus it is a mixture of reality and fiction treated with that license which is the prerogative of any artist. There is no doubt that every child, every woman, and every man in Germany would see in my film at least some phase of their own experience.

Germany Year Zero was financed by a major French company and I set up the general headquarters of my filmmaking group in the

French zone, but the shooting took place in all four. The Americans, British, French, and Russians tried to outdo each other in their help to me. This included hard-to-come-by food rations and lodgings, camera and other technical equipment, jeeps to carry us and our equipment, and a military escort to see us on our way.

I brought my crew to Berlin with me, but found myself short-handed. On the list of available technicians I found the name of an old boyhood friend, one I had not seen for twenty years—Count Bubi Treuberg. Count Treuberg, who had just been released from prison where the Nazis had kept him for many years, became my right-hand man, and has since joined my permanent filmmaking company.

For my cast I roamed the streets of Berlin, looking for satisfactory physical types. The boy, Edmund, I discovered in a circus, where he had been born and lived all his life with his mother, and his father, the riding master. The old father I found sitting on the steps of a public home for the aged. Curiously enough he had been an actor for silent pictures in the early 1900s. The sister attracted my attention by the expression of resigned despair on her pretty face as she stood on a food line. She was a ballet dancer in a chorus who supported her mother and herself. The Nazi brother comes from an outstanding academic family. He and his father were both imprisoned by the Gestapo.

Besides these leading players, in my wanderings I collected a Wehrmacht general, an ex-wrestler, a professor of literature and the history of art, a beautiful model, groups of boys and girls who were dying of boredom on the streets of Berlin. Most of the players had never acted before, but anyone can act provided he is in familiar surroundings and given lines that are natural.

During the shooting in the streets of Berlin I was struck by the indifference of people. In New York, London, Paris, or Rome, a motion picture camera and a filming crew are an irresistible magnet for the citizenry. The people of Berlin, it seemed to me, were interested in only one thing: to eat and to survive. This, I believe, is the fruit of a defeat unparalleled in history, which has annihilated the conscience of an entire people.

The exteriors in Berlin finished, we traveled, cast and crew, on a French military train, to Rome. Here we made the interiors in circumstances which were luxurious compared to the almost unbearable discomfort of filmmaking in battered Berlin. Our quarters in Rome were adequate; our rations, supplied in some part by the Vatican, were excellent. Many of the German players were unwilling to go back to their desolate homeland. With only temporary visas they could not openly stay in Italy so they scattered through the countryside hoping to elude the police. A few escaped, but many were caught and sent home.

Most Germans who have seen my film reacted as I thought they would, negatively. They found the story too pessimistic. A few, however, were willing to accept the grim realism of the story. Many members of the cast were horrified, when they saw the finished film, of what they had unconsciously perpetrated. Edmund, after the long strain of the difficult role, became ill and had to go to the hospital for a couple of weeks.

In making *Germany Year Zero* my goal was the same as in all work I undertake. I wanted to reproduce the truth exactly as the camera saw it for that audience throughout the entire world which has a heart capable of love and a brain capable of thought.

From the Press Book for Germany Year Zero, *Distributing Releasing Corp., 1949.*

THE *STROMBOLI* AFFAIR

BY EDGARDO MACORINI

A telephone call to Mexico City costs 11,530 lira ($ 19.22) for three minutes. A phone call to Hollywood, 8,433 lira ($14.02). A legal consultation or a business call seldom lasts less than half an hour. Multiply the cost of those three minutes by ten and then by fifteen—days, that is—add up the two totals and you will get the amount of money that was spent just in phone calls to unravel, but not conclude, a double intrigue that has drawn, albeit in different ways, the attention of both American and European movie-audiences: on the one side the triangle Bergman-Rossellini-Lindstrom, and on the other the conflict of Rossellini and RKO concerning the film *Stromboli*.

At the very start, this story had two clearly distinct aspects—the first one individual and sentimental, the second one public and professional—that were collapsed into one on February 2, at 5:00 p.m., when Mrs. Elena de Montis walked into the back door of Clinica Margherita (a private maternity hospital) in Rome. The pseudonym was of course not enough to conceal the identity of Ingrid Bergman who, being alone at home when she realized she was about to give birth, had called a cab to take her to the clinic where she was to have her child barely two hours later. That's when the American press started whipping up what was to become one of the largest defamation campaigns in journalism—one whose echoes, and questionable methods, have reached as far as our country.

Since then, the protagonists of this story, Ingrid Bergman and

Roberto Rossellini, have retreated behind a wall of silence, thus giving rise to new lies and insinuations. Rossellini has now decided to break his self-imposed silence and grant us a long interview, and the authorization to make it public, not so much to deny or challenge those rumors, as to explain to us the real meaning of the muck-raking attack launched by Hollywood against him and the Swedish actress.

"My conflict with RKO, which seems to have broken out so suddenly," Rossellini tells us, "has in fact a surprisingly distant origin. Last year, during my stay in Hollywood, where I went to finalize the contract for the filming of *Stromboli* on Ingrid Bergman's invitation, I noticed a great desire to create a scandal around my private life, which first manifested itself in a series of rumors concerning my presupposed secret relationship with the actress—rumors that were circulated just a few hours after my plane had landed, and before we had even had a chance to meet. But then I thought I had sufficiently protected myself with a contract that gave me total freedom in the realization of the film from beginning to end."

He was wrong. When Rossellini signed the contract—consisting of hundreds of pages since in the U.S. there is no juridical regulation concerning that sort of situation, so that whenever there is a dispute the judge has to reach his verdict on the basis of each particular contract, that is case by case and without the backing of a code— Howard Hughes, the new owner of RKO, asked him to let him add a paragraph that would allow the film company to cut the American edition of the film according to the censorship requirements of each state. And, since Rossellini had at first refused, Hughes had personally assured the director that such a clause was only conceived in everybody's interest, to protect both the film (against any damage that could be done it in the course of public exhibition), and the artistic and personal reputation of Ingrid Bergman. Confronted with such a professional and personal commitment, Rossellini accepted.

To judge how well-founded his trust was, all we have to do is remember that immediately after World War II, Hughes, a renowned billionaire and owner of innumerable companies including RKO, was implicated in a scandal involving some defective military equipment for which the American army had paid him millions and millions of dollars. During the investigation Hughes didn't even try to prove his innocence. Instead he simply suggested that there were other VIPs involved in the deal, including the very president of the court that was supposed to judge him. The investigation was immediately suspended.

We ask Maestro Renzo Rossellini, the director's brother, also present at the interview, about the working conditions in Hollywood where he was himself at work on the sound track of *Stromboli*. "The studios' technical facilities are far superior to ours," he answers, "but the level of education and intelligence of their managers is way below that of any of our ushers. And that's not all: intelligence is carefully screened out of Hollywood, and the production of a film, in all its stages, is fully entrusted to whoever seems to be the best businessman. Movie audiences have decreased, in certain places down to half of what they used to be, and films are produced on the assumption that the average mentality of the public is that of a twelve-year old. This is a law it's absolutely forbidden to break."

Roberto Rossellini picks up where his brother left off: "Indeed, I believe that my film was boycotted because no one could understand what it meant, the ideas that I was trying to express cinematically. An RKO executive, that is, a company committee, which therefore would have everything to gain from a sound promotion of the film, has instead released a statement containing the most absurd judgments: that Ingrid Bergman is not very 'sensual' (though the posters of the film they have decided to print to lure the public are practically pornographic), that *Stromboli* is not a real film but a documentary, and all this before the film's opening date. My version of the film, the one that's going to be shown in Europe, has been amputated of a good thirty-five minutes, it has been entirely reedited, and I have discovered at my own expense how brutal and uncivilized Hollywood's methods really are.[1] But there is one more reason for the boycotting that goes quite beyond any evaluation of my work and Ingrid's: 'We shall never forgive her, and she is going to pay for it.' This is what they have said

1 The European version of *Stromboli* is 105 minutes, whereas the American one is only eighty-one.

about her in Hollywood. As for me, they will never forgive me for the films I have made unless they manage to make the public forget them. And I am not the only victim, as the case of English cinema, literally brushed off by Hollywood, clearly proves. With the help of money, Hollywood is trying to get rid of all its most dangerous competitors. As far as I am concerned, they thought it would be easy to keep me in check since I'm small and Howard Hughes is powerful. Materialistic as they are, it never occurred to them that I would give up all my American box-office receipts in order to preserve my artistic integrity. They underrated me and clearly proved they were in the wrong. The *Stromboli* that was shown in the U.S. with my name on it is not my film. I refuse to recognize it as such and am ready to face all the legal consequences of the fact. I am a living proof of Hollywood's brutality. And I'm not at all surprised to hear that the American press, which, by the way, has made a point of underlining my precise position, has given *Stromboli* a very lukewarm reception."

Rossellini goes on talking quite calmly, as if he had finally succeeded in stripping this whole story, which has so deeply wounded his artistic pride, of any emotional import. But the moment we ask him a question concerning some recent events in his personal life, he springs up and, gesticulating wildly, starts pacing up and down the room, his shoes still bearing the mud of a day's work on *The Flowers of St. Francis*.

"Now it should be my turn to carry on this interview," he answers in a lively manner. "My private life, my feelings have been fed to the public, all twisted and deformed by the basest lies. We could have dealt with Ingrid's pregnancy in a much simpler way, but we chose not to. We thought we had made a courageous choice, though others might disagree and judge us as severely as they wish. But things here have gone much too far. Someone tried to climb over the hospital wall and through my wife's bedroom window just a few hours after she had given birth. Then they spread the rumor that I had sold information about my private life to make a profit. They even claimed that the newborn was crippled and deformed to force me to have him photographed; on the other hand, had I done so, they would have immediately accused me of exhibitionism . . ."

As we were leaving, Rossellini asked us what we thought of him: we couldn't tell him. But that evening, just before the showing of a new film we had to attend as film critics, when the newsreel exposed the birth of Rossellini's son as the scandal of the day, and the public loudly expressed its disapproval, we were glad to see that here we don't share the American passion for scandals, not even when they are reworked *all'italiana,* and that the values of intelligence still prevail. This is our answer, and our best wish, for Rossellini.

"Sono la prova vivente della brutalità di Hollywood," in
Vie Nuove, V, *no. 9, 26 February 1950.*

WHY I DIRECTED *STROMBOLI*

BY ROBERTO ROSSELLINI

One of the toughest lessons from this last war is the danger of aggressive egotism. Adopted initially as self-defense, egotism soon became second nature giving individuals invincible security, true, but also a new solitude, without hope.

For some time I matured this idea of treating, after the war dramas, this postwar tragedy—this aggressive, inhuman solitude that, rejecting mythos, transfers the whole world to inside the creature and produces the disdainful certainty that one can live without love, humility, or comprehension. Reduced to its simplest terms, it turns out to be, with a new accent but with age-old significance, the struggle between Creator and creature.

I found an actress who could bring the character to life. And with Stromboli, an island that belies all the clichés of the paradise island, I found a natural setting for the dramatic language I needed. If the protagonist was a borderline case, so was the island. So I first reduced the series of events my character was going to live through to their barest structure, and focused the tragedy on her and her torment. Then, for counterpoint, I needed nature, awesomely hostile, and people, totally uncomprehending and unsympathetic. Stromboli provided me with both, perfectly.

In other words, the structures of ancient tragedy were the only ones I thought adequate to give life to this struggle between Creator and creature.

The protagonist of this tragedy is the woman, cynical and egotistical, and opposed by that silent double chorus: people with their narrow-minded incomprehension, and nature, hostile and inclement. Ignored, unseen, but omnipresent, is her real antagonist: God.

It is against Him that the protagonist is actually fighting when, with typical perversity, she revolts against the chorus. At every step she is torn between her own feelings of proud rebellion and rejection, and other feelings of obedient submission that are dictated to her by an unknown inner voice hidden in her soul.

God, her antagonist, will reveal himself to her only at the end, after triumphing over both chorus and protagonist and leading her to the summit of despair, and after forcing her to invoke the light of Grace to come free her from her inhuman solitude.

"Perché ho diretto proprio questo film,"
in Film, *no. 31-32, 16 August 1950.*

THE MESSAGE OF *THE FLOWERS OF ST. FRANCIS*

BY ROBERTO ROSSELLINI

If, as some maintain, it is possible to trace a spiritual itinerary throughout my films, I would say that *Germany Year Zero* is the world that has reached the limits of despair because of its loss of faith, whereas *Stromboli* is the rediscovery of faith. After which, it was natural to look for the most accomplished form of the Christian ideal: I found it in Saint Francis. However, I never meant to recreate the life of the saint. In *The Flowers of St. Francis*, I don't deal with either his birth or his death, nor do I pretend to offer a complete revelation of the Franciscan message or of its spirit, or to tackle the extraordinarily awesome and complex personality of Francis. Instead, I have wanted to show the effects of it on his followers, among whom, however, I have given particular emphasis to Brother Ginepro and Brother Giovanni, who display in an almost paradoxical way the sense of simplicity, innocence, and delight that emanates from Francis's own spirit.

In short, as the title indicates, my film wants to focus on the merrier aspect of the Franciscan experience, on the playfulness, the "perfect delight," the freedom that the spirit finds in poverty, and in an absolute detachment from material things.

I have tried to render this particular aspect of the great Franciscan spirit following the model of the "Flowers," where I still find, intact, the perfume of the most primitive Franciscanism.

Historically speaking, the series of events narrated in the film rests between two fundamental moments: Francis's return from Rome after having received the permission to preach from the Pope, and the beginning of his preaching. Geographically speaking, the center of the action is the "Porziuncola."[1]

To make up for what is missing and to introduce the public to the atmosphere of the "Flowers," the film has a prologue: a short story narrated by a speaker and illustrated, on the screen, by the famous frescoes of the first painters who depicted Francis.

I believe that certain aspects of primitive Franciscanism could best satisfy the deepest aspirations and needs of a humanity who, enslaved by its greed and having totally forgotten the Poverello's lesson, has also lost its joy of life.

"Il messaggio di Francesco," in
Epoca, *no. 6, 18 November 1950, p. 54.*

1 The little chapel Francis and his followers built near Assisi.

A DISCUSSION OF NEOREALISM

AN INTERVIEW WITH MARIO VERDONE

I met Roberto Rossellini in a break in the making of Europe '51 *at the studios in via della Vasca Navale. A scriptwriter was at work on the lines Ingrid Bergman was about to pronounce. The walls of the set were freshly painted: it was not long since they had been made, as Rossellini had changed his original idea of shooting in a real interior. No one knew what scenes would be shot the next day. Rossellini himself had not decided. The producer was not there—he might well never have come throughout the making of the film. Ingrid Bergman was sitting to one side on a wooden bench, wearing a fur coat and knitting. When the order to shoot came her expression changed effortlessly, spontaneously and with complete conviction, and she threw herself into the part as only great actors can. The scene was a hospital ward, and on the director's instructions his assistant had arranged movements for white-clad extras, but when Rossellini arrived he had everything changed, in one of those sudden decisions with which he characteristically throws out every plan or arrangement. A technician who was waiting to speak to him pointed out to me that however bewildering these preparations seemed, they were in a sense quite normal: "In this film all that counts is the director's orders, what he decides spontaneously, and it doesn't matter what we think. That's what really makes a Rossellini film."*

I had already learned enough to make a first attempt to sum up the man who had made Open City. *But I was able to form a clearer idea of him, as a director and as a man, after the discussions we had that day and later on. Though I knew him only through his films, he answered my questions with complete sincerity, as if confiding in a friend.*

The subject I intended to write about was "The poetic world of Rossellini," piecing it together through question-and-answer and observation. Rossellini cordially agreed to take part in this exercise in criticism and self-criticism, an exercise I proposed to base on the actual facts.

VERDONE: Would you claim to be the father of Italian neorealism?

ROSSELLINI: I leave it to other people to judge whether what is called neorealism made a greater impression on the world through *Open City.* I myself would place the birth of neorealism earlier, especially in some fictionalized war documentaries, which I contributed to with *La nave bianca.* Then came the real war films, like *Luciano Serra, pilota,* in which I worked on the scenario, and some I directed like *L'uomo dalla croce;* but above all there were some minor films like *Avanti c'è posto, Ultima carrozzella* and *Campo dei Fiori,* in which what might be called the formula of neorealism began to emerge as the spontaneous creation of the actors, especially Anna Magnani and Aldo Fabrizi. It's undeniably the case that these actors were the first to bring neorealism to life—in the music-hall turns with strong men or Roman ballads, performed on nothing but a mat and to the accompaniment of a single guitar: in the way Magnani thought them up, or in the figure Fabrizi cut on the boards of some local theatre, these films at moments gave a real foretaste of neorealism. Neorealism arose unconsciously as dialectical filmmaking, and then acquired a conscious life in the heat of the human and social problems of wartime and the postwar years. And speaking of dialectical filmmaking, we should make some reference historically to the less immediate precursors, namely Blasetti with his "character" film, *1860,* and Camerini, with films like *Gli uomini che mascalzoni!*

VERDONE: But historical precedents aside, Italian postwar films have a certain air of realism which would have been quite inconceivable before the war. Can you give a definition of it?

ROSSELLINI: I'm a filmmaker, not an aesthete, and I don't think I can give an exact definition of realism. All I can say is what I feel about it and what ideas I've formed about it. Perhaps someone else would be able to explain it better.

It involves a greater interest in individuals. Modern man feels a need to tell of things as they are, to take account of reality in an uncompromisingly concrete way, which goes with today's interest in statistics and scientific results. Neorealism is also a response to the genuine need to see men for what they are, with humility and without recourse to fabricating the exceptional; it means an awareness that the exceptional is arrived at through the investigation of reality. Lastly, it's an urge for self-clarification, an urge not to ignore reality whatever it may be.

This is why I have tried in my films to reach an understanding of things, and give them their true value. It's not something easy or lightly undertaken, but a highly ambitious project, because to give anything its true value means grasping its real universal meaning.

VERDONE: You give a clear meaning for the term neorealism—or more simply realism—but do you think that everyone who discusses it or works on it is as clear?

ROSSELLINI: I think there is still some confusion about the term "realism" even after all these years of realist films. Some people still think of realism as something external, as a way out into the fresh air, not as the contemplation of poverty and misery. To me realism is simply the artistic form of truth. If you reestablish truth you give it expression. If it's a dead truth, you feel it is false, it is not truly expressed. With my views of course I cannot accept the "entertainment" film, as the term is understood in some business circles, especially outside Europe. Some such films may be partially acceptable, to the extent that they are capable of giving partial expression to reality.

VERDONE: What object does a realist film have that you would counterpose to the usual kind of "entertainment" films?

ROSSELLINI: The realist film has the "world" as its living object, not the telling of a story. What it has to say is not fixed in advance, because it arises of its own accord. It has no love for the superfluous and the spectacular, and rejects these, going instead to the root of things. It does not stop at surface appearances, but seeks out the most subtle strands of the soul. It rejects formulas and doesn't pander to its audience, but seeks out the inner motives in each of us.

VERDONE: What other characteristics do you think a realist film has?

ROSSELLINI: To put it briefly, it poses problems, poses them to itself as well. An American paper wrote an attack on my film *The Miracle* saying that the cinema is for entertainment and ought not to raise problems. But for me a realist film is precisely one which tries to make people think.

In the postwar period we were faced by this task, and none of us wanted to make what you might call an "entertainment" film. What mattered to us was the investigation of reality, forming a relationship with reality. For the first so-called "neorealist" Italian directors it was undoubtedly a genuine heartfelt act. Then after the real innovators came the popularizers—who were perhaps even more important, as they spread neorealism everywhere, and possibly with greater clarity. They didn't have to change anything and were perhaps better able to express themselves, making neorealism more widely understood. But then deviations and distortions crept in, with fatal consequences. But by this time neorealism had accomplished the main part of its work.

VERDONE: Do you think you have remained faithful in all your films to this concept of realism as you've now spelled it out?

ROSSELLINI: If I have been faithful to it it has been spontaneously and without effort on my part. I don't think that one should preserve one's consistency at any price. Anyone who does so isn't far from being mad. In so far as I have respected certain principles in which I firmly believe, and which are very deep-rooted in me, then you can say that I have been consistent. And I think perhaps I have, since there is a single line you can trace through all my various works—the documentaries, the early war films, the postwar films and those of today. For example, it's undeniable that you find the same spirituality in *La nave bianca*, *L'uomo dalla croce*, *Paisan*, *The Flowers*, *The Miracle*, and *Stromboli's* ending.

VERDONE: Do you regard *The Flowers of St. Francis* as a realistic film?

ROSSELLINI: Of course—even in imagining what St. Francis might be like as a man, I never abandoned reality, either as regards the events, which are strictly historical, or in any other visual aspect. The costumes, for example, are part of the "reality." They are so true to life that you scarcely notice them.

What I have tried to do in this film is to show a new side of St. Francis, but not one which lies outside reality: to show a St. Francis who is humanly and artistically credible in every sense.

VERDONE: What do you think have been the constant elements in your films?

ROSSELLINI: I don't go by formulas and preconceptions. But looking back on my films, I certainly do find that there are things which have been constant features, recurring not in a planned way, but as I said, quite naturally—in particular, their human warmth. The realist film in itself has this quality. The sailors of *La nave bianca* count as much as the people hiding in the hut at the end of *L'uomo dalla croce*, the population of *Open City*, the partisans of *Paisan* or the monks in *The Flowers*.

La nave bianca is such a film—from the first scene, with the sailors' letters to their sweethearts, to the battle itself and then the wounded going to Mass or playing or singing. It also shows the ruthless cruelty of the machine; and the unheroic side of men living on a battleship, acting almost in the dark, surrounded by measuring instruments, protractors and steeringwheels—a side of them which appears unlyrical and unheroic, and yet is overwhelmingly heroic.

Again, there is the *documentary* style of observation and analysis, which I learned in my first shorts—*Fantasia sottomarina* [A fantasy of the deep], *Ruscello di Ripasottile* [The brook of Ripasottile], *Prélude à l'après-midi d'un faune*—and took up again in *Paisan* and in *Germany Year Zero* and *Stromboli*.

I constantly come back, even in the strictest documentary forms, to *imagination*, because one part of man tends towards the concrete, and the other to the use of the imagination, and the first must not be allowed to suffocate the second. This is why you find fantasy at work in *The Miracle*, *La macchina ammazzacattivi* [The machine to kill bad people], and *Paisan*, as well as in *The Flowers*, with the rain at the beginning, the young monk be:ng knocked about by the troops, and Saint Clare standing by the hut. Even the finale in the snow was meant to have an air of fantasy.[1] And then again there is the religious quality—I don't mean the invocation of divine authority by the woman in the finale of *Stromboli*, so much as the themes I was dealing with even ten years ago.

VERDONE: Do you think then that this human warmth has always been a characteristic of your work?

ROSSELLINI: I definitely began by stressing this above all. The war itself was an impulse to me: war is a heartfelt experience. If then I moved on from this to the discovery of personality and a deeper study of character, as with the child in *Germany Year Zero* or the woman running away in *Stromboli*, this was part of my natural evolution as a director.

VERDONE: Is it true to say that in your films there is often a break between a particularly good episode like the scene with the child running through the city in *Germany Year Zero*, and other parts which are inexplicably left incomplete or at least much more hastily sketched in?

ROSSELLINI: That's right. As a matter of fact every film I make interests me for a particular scene, perhaps for a finale I already have in mind. In every film I see on the one hand the narrative episodes such as the first part of *Germany Year Zero*, or the scene from *Europe '51* that you just saw me shooting—and on the other the *event*. My sole concern is to reach that *event*. In the other narrative episodes I feel myself hesitating, alienated, absent.

I don't deny that this is a weakness on my part, but I must confess that scenes which are not of key importance weary me, and make me feel quite helpless. I only feel sure of myself at the decisive moment. *Germany Year Zero*, to tell the truth, was conceived specifically for the scene with the child wandering on his own through the ruins. The whole of the preceding part held no interest at all for me. It too was thought up around the scene with the cans of milk. And when I made *Paisan* I had in mind the last part with the corpses floating on water,

1 However, the finale was actually shot without snow.

slowly being carried down the River Po with labels bearing the word "Partisan" on them. The river had those corpses in it for months. Often several would be found on the same day.

VERDONE: Do you get inspiration when you're writing the scenario or when you're making the film? Do you believe in having a fixed scenario that can't be altered or rejected?

ROSSELLINI: In the case of a film purely for entertainment, it may be right to have a fixed scenario. For realistic cinema of the kind Italy has produced, trying to find the truth and raising problems, you can't use the same criteria. Here inspiration plays the main part—it's not the fixed script that counts, but the film itself. An author writes a sentence or a page, then crosses it out. A painter uses a red, then paints it out with green. Why shouldn't I be able to cross things out too, to remake and replace film? This is why I don't think you can have a fixed scenario. If I thought you could, I would want to be known as a script writer, not a director. But I'm not a script writer. I make films.

I think for a long time about the theme of any film I make. A scenario is written, because it would be crazy to try to improvise everything at the last minute. But the scenes, the dialogue, and the scenography are adjusted from day to day. This is the place of inspiration in the prearranged order of the film. You make your preparations, get everything ready: and I might say that it's only then, for me, that the most difficult and exhausting part of making a film actually starts.

VERDONE: What contribution do you think is made by the people who make up the company on a film?

ROSSELLINI: They are the means to an end. A director has them at his disposal like the books in a library. It's up to him to judge what's of use and what's not. The very act of choosing is a part of expressing himself. When a director knows his collaborators thoroughly, and knows what he can get out of them, it's as if he expresses himself through them.

From the time of my first documentaries I have been lucky enough to have a composer I get along with exceptionally well: my brother. I discussed my first attempts at filmmaking with him and we tried to bring the picture and the music together in the most harmonious way possible.

I have worked with some marvelous actors: Marcello Pagliero and Anna Magnani, Aldo Fabrizi and Ingrid Bergman, but also real sailors and partisans, monks and fishermen. It is to them, the actors and extras, that a large part of the success of my films is due. And since I've mentioned Fabrizi, I must make it clear that it was I who wanted him to play the grotesque character in *The Flowers* which there has been so much argument about, and I assume full responsibility for it.

VERDONE: You admit that you like films with short episodes, like those in *Paisan* or *The Flowers,* the two from *Amore* ("A Human Voice" and "The Miracle"), or *Invidia* [Envy] (from Colette's *Chatte,* and forming a section of *I sette peccati capitali* [The seven deadly sins]); and even the episodes in *La nave bianca* (in the bunk room, the battle, the white ship), *Germany Year Zero* (the child running through the ruins) and *Stromboli* (the tuna fishing and the escape)—which are all finished episodes.

ROSSELLINI: You are right. It's because I hate a subject once it begins to constrain me. I hate the logical nexus of the subject matter. The narrative passages are necessary if you are to come to the critical event: but my natural inclination is to skip them and not bother with them. This is, I admit, one of my limitations—my language is incomplete. To be honest, I would be happy making only such episodes as you've mentioned. When I feel that the scene I'm shooting is important only for the logical development of the film, and not what I'm most anxious to say, then you see how helpless I am, I don't know what to do. But when the scene is important, when it's essential, then everything is simple and easy.

VERDONE: Are you saying that it's natural that you prefer to film short episodes, or is this an excuse for avoiding making a film with a complete story?

ROSSELLINI: I've made films in episodes because I feel more at ease like that. It's enabled me to avoid passages which, as I say, are useful in a continuous narrative, but precisely because they are useful rather than decisive, are a burden to me, though I can't explain it. I am only at ease where I can avoid the logical nexus. Staying within the limits laid down by the story is really what I find most difficult.

VERDONE: What do you think is essential in film narrative?

ROSSELLINI: As I see it, expectation. Every solution arises from expectation. Expectation is what brings things alive, what releases reality, and after all the waiting, brings liberation. Take for example the fishing scene in *Stromboli*. It's an episode born out of expectation. The spectator's curiosity is aroused about what is going to happen: then comes the explosion of the slaughter of the tuna fish.

Expectation is the force behind every event in our lives: and this is so for the cinema too.

VERDONE: Can you now tell me how you began your film career?

ROSSELLINI: By chance. I had been struck by Vidor's films: *The Crowd, Hallelujah*, etc.; they were perhaps the only "classic" films I had then seen. I often went to see films because my father was the owner of the Cinema Corso. My first ventures were documentaries, made in consultation with my brother. *Prélude à l'après-midi d'un faune* is not a film of a ballet, as you might think if you had never seen it. It's a documentary about nature, and so are *Ruscello di Ripasottile* and *Fantasia sottomarina*. I was struck by the water with the serpent slithering about in it and the dragonfly overhead. It's the kind of basic sensitivity you see in the puppies on the main deck in *La nave bianca*, or the flower caught by the sailor as he disembarks.

VERDONE: How much is autobiographical in your films?

ROSSELLINI: It's no accident that you ask that. There is a lot that's autobiographical in my films. In the documentaries you can find my youthful fantasies—a hornet buzzing, leaping fish mirrored in the water. Then came the war and the occupation, and many events we look back to and would like to have experienced. *Open City* is a film about fear, the fear felt by us all but by me in particular. I too had to go into hiding, I too was on the run, I had friends who were captured or killed. It was real fear: I lost thirty-four kilos, perhaps through hunger, perhaps because of the terror I described in *Open City*.

Then there's *Paisan*. It's been said that the most beautiful scene is the last: the mouth of the Po, the water and the wind in the reeds. People expressed astonishment that I'd pictured that part of Italy so well. But I'd spent years of my childhood there. My mother was from there—I used to go hunting and fishing there.

With *The Miracle* and *A Human Voice,* Magnani became a part of my world. In *Stromboli* a stranger enters the life of a simple man like the fisherman Antonio. And there's autobiography too in the feelings of the woman in *Stromboli,* brutalized by reality and turning back to fantasy—with a longing to expand, to embrace the whole world without letting go of reality, finding inner liberation in the call to God which is the final thrust of the film. She looks at the problem for the first time, almost unconsciously. It is only in the presence of nature, of her own self, and of God, that she has come to understand.

La macchina ammazzacattivi shows my wanderings on the Amalfi coast, places where I'd been happy, places I love, where some poor devils are convinced they have seen Satan. One of them told me one day, "I've met the werewolf, I ran over him on my bicycle last night." They are mad, crazed by the sun. But they have a power few of us possess—the power of the imagination.

In this film—which like *Amore* represents a search and a crisis—I had another aim as well: to get closer to *commedia dell'arte.*

The Flowers and *Europe '51* are also autobiographical in that they express feelings I have observed in myself and in my fellow men. In each of us there's the jester side and its opposite; there is the tendency toward concreteness and the tendency toward fantasy. Today there is a tendency to suppress the second quite brutally. The world is more and more divided in two, between those who want to kill fantasy and those who want to save it, those who want to die and those who want to live. This is the problem I confront in *Europe '51.* There is a danger of forgetting the second tendency, the tendency toward fantasy, and killing every feeling of humanity left in us, creating robot man, who must think in only one way, the concrete way. In *Europe '51* this inhuman threat is openly and violently denounced. I wanted to state my own opinion quite frankly, in my own interest and in my children's. That was the aim of this latest film.

The ability to see both sides of man, to look at him charitably, seems to me to be a supremely Latin and Italian attitude. It results from a degree of civility which has been our custom from very ancient times—the habit of seeing every side of man. For me it is very important to have been born into such a civilization. I believe that what saved us from the disasters of the war, and other equally terrible scourges, was this view of life we have, which is unmistakably Catholic. Christianity does not pretend that everything is good and perfect: it recognizes sin and error, but it also admits the possibility of salvation. It is the other side who only allow man to be perfectly consistent and infallible. To me that is monstrous and nonsensical. The only possibility I see for getting nearer to the truth, is to try to understand sin and be tolerant of it.

VERDONE: What are your future plans?

ROSSELLINI: I have a great many, but I think most about *Socrate: processo e morte* [Socrates: life and trial]. Socrates is a man of today. Xanthippe represents the devil. The story should be shown in three sections: an introduction, the trial, the death scene. The introduction will be set in Athens. I picture a city strung out, as the story has it, all along a road, with a landscape of infinite perspectives. Life here is simple and primitive. The houses look like some Etruscan tombs I saw at Cerveteri: the fields, animals scuttling round the houses, cauldrons hanging from the beams, goats sharing the houses of men, leaving behind them the evidence of animal life. Under the sandals of the habitants the name of their city is written, and so it is stamped into the earth they tread. As in *The Flowers*, the costumes will be simple and timeless, in other words, costumes which don't look like costumes.

As in *The Flowers* too, the events must correspond to reality. Socrates is bound to reach the same conclusions as St. Francis, though St. Francis came to them under the impulse of his dreams and hopes, and Socrates by logic. In St. Francis it is instinct: in Socrates reason.

In our civilization—Christian, Latin civilization—we don't accept truth as given. We are full of irony and scepticism, and constantly in search of truth. We don't look at things with a materialist eye, or see only the facade: we look at things in perspective. This is how St. Francis saw things—and so did Socrates.

"Colloquio sul neorealismo," in Bianco e Nero, *no. 2, 1952, pp. 7-16. Translated by Judith White.*

I AM NOT THE FATHER OF NEOREALISM

BY ROBERTO ROSSELLINI

It has been said, written, and repeated in every possible way that I
have discovered a new form of expression: neorealism. It is probably
true since all the critics seem to agree on this point, and it is impossible
to refute a general opinion.

But I have a hard time being convinced. The term of neorealism was
born with the success of *Open City*—a delayed-action success, like a
time bomb. When the film was shown in Cannes in 1946, it went quite
unnoticed. It was discovered much later, and I am not yet sure its
message has been fully understood.

That's when I was christened the inventor of Italian neorealism.
What does it mean? I feel no solidarity with the movies that are being
made in my country. It is obvious to me that everybody has his own
brand of realism, and that everybody believes his is the best. Me
included. My own personal neorealism is nothing but a moral stance
that can be expressed in four words: *love of one's neighbor.*

"On one side there is Rossellini, on the other Italian cinema." This
is what a critic once wrote about me. It is terribly true. I am trying to
react against the weakness that turns people into the voluntary
prisoners—not to say the victims, whether out of cowardice or
carelessness—of their desire to be in harmony with everything and
everybody. Because of our idolatry of the *norm,* we live in the
constant fear of becoming the exception, since we are used to identi-
fying the person one speaks of with the person one *speaks ill* of.

And when we want to react against such a monstrosity, we must pay a very high price. Because in this domain there are no sales. I am going to tell you something I haven't yet told anybody: the plight of my life is that all the happy events—let's say all my successess—are always three or four years late. In other words, I work in the most absolute moral solitude.

You see, I am insulted on all sides. It's not a very comfortable situation, but I can tell you as brutally as I believe it: praises often offend me more than insults, because most of the time they are misguided compliments. Those who proffer them haven't understood a thing.

When I state that the film of mine I like best is *Stromboli,* I am not doing it to amuse the audience, nor because it has been generally booed. *Stromboli* is a very important film for me. I am convinced that if people don't like it they have no reason to like the other ones.

I am a very simple man swimming in a flood of myths that's been poured upon me for no apparent reason. For instance, everybody claims that *The Flowers* marks a break in my work. If it were true I would know it. But it is not easy to fight against such categorical assertions. For your information, I can tell you that when *Paisan* came out, the first paper I opened contained, by way of criticism, a description of my brain that allowed the author of the review to conclude I was mentally deranged.

Another myth: my constant improvisation! The stock image of the clown who thinks he's a creative genius!

The truth is so much simpler . . . So much more logical! It so happens that I often have the development of my scenes in my head and so I don't need to write them down. What matters most to me is rhythm. And since I am always very much attuned to the atmosphere surrounding the shooting of my films, which always brings me new ideas, the only improvisation in my work goes in the direction of a better rhythm—likely to sustain a state of tension that must end up in a final resolution which I want to be striking and brutal.

According to the latest rumor, my films are "symbolical." Now, I know all too well that the tortured communist in *Open City* can bring to mind the face of Christ on the cross, that the child in *Germany Year Zero* dies to save the world, and that Irene's itinerary in *Europe '51* evokes the Way of the Cross. But I have always planned it so that this symbolic dimension would come "after" the movie, "in addition to it," as a second, richer meaning.

It is also said that I have become a producer out of some craving for power. Do you want to know the truth, in all its banality? I am financing my own films because nobody else would do it in my place, because everybody would reject them with glee.

Cocteau, whom I saw a few days ago, made a strikingly right remark: "Once Art was something abstract and money something concrete. Today art has become concrete while money is abstract." To mention only one fact: I'm yearning to make a movie of *Dialogues des Carmélites,* by Bernanos, the French writer I most admire. It looks as if I will have to give it up since there are practically unsurmountable obstacles in the acquisition of the rights.

At the moment, I am involved in a fascinating theatrical experience with *Jeanne au bûcher* [Joan of Arc at the stake]. In this field I have no history, no past, everything is new. I have to tackle elements that I discover day by day.

You will soon see the color movie I have drawn out of *Jeanne au bûcher.* Those who have seen it in Italy have liked it. I am at least sure of this. Since the screenplay is not mine but Claudel's, I hope that this movie will mark the critics' reconciliation with my work.

I am a simple man. I'd rather not be a lonely man.

"Je ne suis pas le père du neo-réalisme," in Arts, *16 June 1954, p. 3.*

AN INTERVIEW WITH CAHIERS DU CINÉMA

BY MAURICE SCHÉRER |ERIC ROHMER| AND
FRANÇOIS TRUFFAUT

The message contained in Rossellini's later films has been so variously interpreted that we thought it might be time to hear the opinion of the author himself. The interview that he has granted us doesn't allow for any misunderstanding about the moral import of his work. Will this earn Rossellini a few more admirers? No one can tell, but his detractors will no longer be able to accuse him of being either incoherent or insincere.

CAHIERS: Jacques Rivette, a contributor of *Cahiers du cinéma,* has recently written: "On one side there is Italian cinema, on the other Rossellini," by which he meant that you keep your distance from the neorealist movement under whose banner almost all the other Italian film directors seem to have gathered . . .

ROSSELLINI: True, I have kept my distance from a certain aspect of neorealism; on the other hand, what do we really mean by such a word. You know there was a congress on neorealism in Parma.[1] We spent a great deal of time discussing the term. But it's still just as vague as before. More often than not, it's just used as a label. For me, it is primarily a moral stance from which to observe the world. It is also an aesthetic position. But its basis is moral.

1 3–5 December 1953.

CAHIERS: It is generally agreed that *Stromboli* marks a break in your work.

ROSSELLINI: It may well be true. It's difficult for me to say. Ultimately—though I don't really care one way or another—I find myself very coherent. I think I am the same human being looking at things in pretty much the same way. On the other hand, one is drawn to new themes, interests change, and with them directions. There is no point in tarrying among the ruins of the past. We are all too often mesmerized by a particular ambience, the atmosphere of a particular time. But life changes, the war is over, what was destroyed has been rebuilt. The drama of the reconstruction had to be told. Maybe I wasn't equal to the task . . .

CAHIERS: This is what you deal with in both *Germany Year Zero* and *Europe '51.* Don't you think these two movies share a pessimism that was quite absent from *Open City,* but came through in *Paisan?*

ROSSELLINI: I am not a pessimist. So far as I am concerned, it is a form of optimism to see the bad as well as the good. Some people found *Europe '51* presumptuous. Even the title shocked them. In my mind it was quite humble. I wanted to say, with great humility, what I felt about our life today. I am a father, so I have to be interested in everyday life. I was also reproached for providing no solution; but that is another sign of humility. If I could find a solution I wouldn't be making films, besides . . .

CAHIERS: And yet, when you propose a solution, as you did in *Stromboli,* the critics sneer.

ROSSELLINI: I can't understand why, but it must be my fault since I have failed to convince other people.

CAHIERS: Personally we find that the Christian ending of *Stromboli* gives the work its meaning.

ROSSELLINI: You are entitled to your opinion, but let me be the interviewer for a moment. For a few years now, film critics have showed, if not quite hostility, a certain disapproval of my later films. Is it because I deal with themes that films usually avoid, or is it because my style is not cinematographic enough? It is not the usual language, I reject craftiness, I "grope" in what I think is a very personal way.

CAHIERS: Since we like your films, and think we understand them, it is almost as difficult for us as it is for you to figure out why some people don't like them. The novelty of your style may, at first, have puzzled some of our colleagues; quite a few of them, however, have revised their opinion. For instance, many of those who didn't like *Europe '51* when they saw it in Venice changed their mind when the film came out in Paris.

ROSSELLINI: It's strange to reread what the critics have said about my early films. *Open City:* "Rossellini confuses art with journalism. The film is gruesome." In Cannes, where it was shown one afternoon, nobody noticed it, then, by and by, they began to take it seriously. Even too seriously. I remember the terrible shock I received when *Paisan* first came out. I really believed in the film; it's one of the three I like best.[2] The first Italian review I read spoke of "the director's rotting brain," and went on in that vein. I don't think it's possible to say worse things about a movie than were said about *Germany Year Zero.* Yet, today it is mentioned all the time. I find this sort of delayed response very hard to understand.

CAHIERS: To go back to your style, what makes it so baffling is the total absence of what's commonly called "cinematic effects." You do nothing to draw the public's attention to the important scenes, you remain always not just objective but impassive. You give the impression that everything is equally important, deliberately so . . .

ROSSELLINI: I always try to remain impassive. What I find most surprising, extraordinary, and moving in men is precisely that great actions and great events take place in the same way and with exactly the same resonance as normal everyday occurrences. I try to transcribe both with the same humility: there is a source of dramatic interest in that.

CAHIERS: Was your outlook essentially the same in the films you made before *Open City?* We haven't seen them.

ROSSELLINI: They didn't have much luck either, but they were informed by the same intentions.

---

2 The other two being *The Flowers of St. Francis* and *Europe '51.*

CAHIERS: In *La nave bianca,* which precedes *Open City* by three years, there were no professional actors—in a way it was a neorealist film before the term really existed.

ROSSELLINI: Yes, it already revealed the same sort of moral stance. Do you know what a battleship is? It's frightening: the ship must be saved at all costs. The men do not know what's going on, they are peasants who have been yanked away from their homes, their fields, and forced to operate all sorts of machines they do not understand: all they know is that when a red light goes on they have to push a button, when a green light goes on they have to pull down a lever. That's all. They are locked up in this kind of life. They are there nailed down to their posts, literally nailed down because if the ship is hit by a torpedo, even though part of it may be flooded, the rest has to be saved. Such is the awful and heroic condition of those poor men who know nothing at all. It's difficult to imagine what it is like to go through a war in such a ship. They go as far as cutting out the ventilation in order to prevent the gases of eventual explosions from spreading through the ship. So, that's where they are, in the stagnating heat, behind steel armor, stuck, not just locked up but really stuck, and deafened by a vague and incomprehensible noise. They know nothing: they must watch out for either a red or a green light. Now and then a loudspeaker says something about their homeland and then everything falls back into total silence . . .

CAHIERS: What about the film you made after that, *L'uomo dalla croce?*

ROSSELLINI: . . . Same issue. Men with hope, men without hope. It's something very simple, but that was the issue.

CAHIERS: Since you believe, and we agree with you, that there are no two distinct periods in your work, then one must admit that both *Open City* and *Paisan* have profited from a misunderstanding.

ROSSELLINI: Yes, though it is also possible that I did not express myself clearly enough.

CAHIERS: But if you did in those two films, then it is quite unlikely that you did not manage to express yourself clearly in the ones that followed. We prefer to think there was a misunderstanding. The

Christian idea was not as evident before *Stromboli*. Some critics have been bothered by this overt expression of your Catholicism.

ROSSELLINI: Lots of Catholics have been bothered by it.

CAHIERS: It has been eloquently proved by Cardinal Spellman's banning of *The Miracle*.

ROSSELLINI: As far as I am concerned, *The Miracle* is an absolutely Catholic work. I found my inspiration for it in a sermon by Saint Bernardino of Siena. It's the story of a saint called Bonino. A peasant sets out to work in the fields with his two-year-old son and a dog. He leaves the child and the dog in the shade of an oak tree and goes to work. When he comes back he finds the child dead, his throat torn open, the marks of teeth all around the wound. In his paternal sorrow, he kills the dog and only then notices a large snake and understands his mistake. Painfully aware of the injustice he has just committed he buries the dog among some nearby rocks and carves an inscription on its grave: "Here lies Bonino (the name of the dog), killed by the ferocity of man." Several centuries elapse, a road goes by the grave. The travelers who stop to rest in the shade of the oak tree read the inscription. Eventually they start praying, asking for the intercession of the unhappy man buried under those rocks. Miracles begin to occur, and so frequently that the people of the region decide to build a church with a tomb where they plan to transfer Bonino's body. Only then do they realize that Bonino is a dog.

You can see how the story of *The Miracle* resembles the original. Here we have a mad woman afflicted by some sort of religious fixation. However, besides her fixation, she also has a real deep faith. She can believe anything she wants. Some of the things she believes in, I admit, may seem blasphemous, but her faith is so huge that it rewards her. Her action is absolutely normal and human: she nurses her child. Some Catholics have been favorable to the film, others have been afraid lest the film be misunderstood. Then there have been those who have accused me of bad faith.

CAHIERS: The same misunderstanding has greeted all the films that have followed *The Miracle*. In France it is certainly not out of religious dogmatism that the Catholics have remained reserved: here, the Christian press has admired the Sulpician imagery of *Monsieur Vincent* out of discipline, and the blasphemy of *Les Orgueilleux*,[3] out of paradox.

ROSSELLINI: Maybe I didn't make myself all that clear. Had I included ten more details in all my films, everything would have been crystal clear. The fact is that I cannot include those ten details. There is nothing easier than shooting a close-up: but I don't shoot close-ups for fear I might leave them in. Whenever I have a private screening of my films (with a very small audience, some twenty or thirty persons) people come out looking terribly shook up, their faces streaked with tears . . . The same people go see the same film in a theater and they hate it. It has happened to me a thousand times.

You have no idea how many people, women in particular, have told me: "Mr. Rossellini, we are all expecting you to give us a great film. But please stop showing us all these terrible things. Please give us a great beautiful film." "A great beautiful film" is difficult to make. I don't think I can do it, and maybe never will. People are afraid of real issues. The political struggle has become so heated that people are no longer able to judge things freely. They react only according to their political ideas. The world is ready for a great transformation. I do not know what it will be but I have hope, though things don't seem to be going in the direction I would choose. Still, I am sure the world is ready for something. Take *Don Camillo*,[4] for instance: I'm not talking about the quality of the film, which in no way explains its immense success. What explains it is that the film gives the illusion that everybody can get along. I am sure that it's possible to find some form of universal agreement, but not in that way. It would be much too simple. Shockingly so. In Italy we have been going through a political period represented by the common man: a happy-go-lucky attitude of total noncommitment. I don't think that's the right solution. I think man must enter the struggle with a great deal of compassion for everybody—oneself, others—and a great deal of love,

3 *Monsieur Vincent* by Maurice Cloche (1947), inspired to the life of Saint Vincent de Paul. *Les Orgueilleux* [The Proud and the Beautiful] by Yves Allégret (1953).
4 *Don Camillo* [The Little World of Don Camillo], an adaptation for the screen of the novel with the same title by Giovanni Guareschi, was a popular success throughout Italy during the 1950s.

but also with utmost resolution. I am not speaking of an armed struggle. I am speaking of a struggle of ideas. One must have the courage to set oneself up as an example. I know it can be very embarrassing, and it requires a great effort. It is easier to forget everything, much more pleasant, and that's why *Don Camillo* has had such a great success.

CAHIERS: Many film directors pose as champions of freedom, but they have trouble imagining it. Theirs is a very abstract freedom.

ROSSELLINI: Whenever the word freedom is mentioned, it is invariably followed by this clause: "freedom, yes, but within certain limits." Even the most abstract freedom is rejected as too beautiful a dream. That's why I find an immense strength in Christianity, because I believe that freedom is absolute, really absolute.

Yet, today people want to be free to believe in a truth that has been imposed upon them. There isn't a single person around who's looking for his or her own truth. This is what I find extraordinarily paradoxical. Point a finger at their nose and say: "This is the truth," and they are perfectly happy. They want to believe you, they follow you everywhere, they are capable of everything to believe in your truth. But they never make the slightest effort to find it on their own. Throughout history, this is what has always happened. The world has moved forward only when there has been real freedom. Real freedom has shown up very seldom in history, and yet people are always speaking of freedom.

CAHIERS: Is this what you are trying to convey in *Europe '51?*

ROSSELLINI: Do you know how I got the idea of that film? I was shooting the film on St. Francis and was telling Fabrizi about the "Flowers." After listening to me very attentively, Fabrizi turned to his secretary and said: "He was a madman." And the secretary said: "Absolutely." That's what gave me the first idea. I also found inspiration in an event that occurred in Rome during the war. A merchant in Piazza Venezia sold fabric on the black market. One day, as his wife was helping a client, he cut in on them and said: "Madam, please take this fabric, I am giving it to you as a gift because I do not want to be part of this criminal activity. I think the war is horrible." Obviously, as soon as the woman left the shop, the merchant got into a big argument with his wife who proceeded to make his life impossible at home. But the moral issue was still in question: as his wife kept pursuing her criminal activity in spite of his moral objections, the merchant turned himself in to the police: "I did this, this and this, and I need to pay for all these things," he said. Whereupon the police sent him to a mental hospital . . . His psychiatrist told me something very disturbing: "I examined him and realized that his only problem was moral. I was so upset that during the night I thought about it and told myself: 'I must judge him as a scientist, and not as a man. As a scientist, I must determine whether this man behaves as an average man.' He did not and so I sent him to the insane asylum." This is a true story so I will not mention the name of the great scientist. I have often talked about it with him, and every time he has told me: "I must dissociate, in myself, the human being from the scientist. Science has its limits: it must calculate, see, measure, and base itself on what it has achieved, on what it knows. As a scientist I must forget entirely what lies beyond the limits of science."

In a century dominated by science—and we all know that it is imperfect, that its limits can be terrible—I am not so sure how far we can trust it. This is the subject of my film. My project was very clear: Saint Francis, the story I have just told you, and Simone Weil inspired it.

CAHIERS: They say you want to make a film about Socrates.

ROSSELLINI: I have always had this dream: Socrates, the judgment and the sentence, but where can I find the right actor?

CAHIERS: And what about *Voyage in Italy?*

ROSSELLINI: That is a film I like very much. It was very important for me to show Italy, Naples, that strange atmosphere so imbued with a very real, very immediate, very deep feeling: the sense of eternal life. It is something that has completely disappeared from the world. An extraordinary thing happened to Eduardo de Filippo. When he was writing his play, *Napoli milionaria,* he would wander around Naples to gather material. One day he heard that a local family was putting on show a black child who had presumably been born to them. He went to see the show. At the door, the husband was collecting five lira from all the would-be spectators. They walked in and saw his wife with the black child in her arms. When Eduardo walked out, as he is very well known in Naples, the husband asked him: "Are you satisfied? Did you get a good look?" And de Filippo apparently replied: "Look here, you jerk, aren't you ashamed to charge people five lira to show them how your wife made a fool of you with a black man?" The fellow then took him to one side and told him: "Just between you and me, we wash the child every night!" It was a poor Neapolitan child! Since corruption was everywhere, corruption was on demand. It was a poor family that had to live. They had followed the general trend!

That amazing innocence, that purity, that refusal to participate in the filth of the world: all this was miraculous. Do you remember in *Paisan?*—I apologize for referring to myself but this issue is very important to me—When the black soldier is falling asleep, the child tells him: "Be careful not to fall asleep or I'll steal your shoes." But the black soldier falls asleep anyway, and the child steals his shoes. It is fair, it is normal, it is this extraordinary game that sets the boundaries of morality.

During the war, in Naples, I saw something fantastic. In that city there are stores—they call them *bassi*—on the second floor of residential buildings whose first floor is occupied by regular people. It is very pleasant to get out into the street and start chatting; it's the greatest joy in the world. In any case, on the first floor of one of these buildings there lived a family of sixteen people: the youngest of the fourteen children was three years old, and the oldest eighteen. They were all involved in the black market, and all their pockets were full of money. Do you know what they bought with all the money they had made? They did not buy themselves clothes, or shoes. They bought themselves coffins, marvellous coffins trimmed with silver. What was the meaning of such a thing? These poor people went through a terrible life, knowing they meant nothing at all, with one hope, the hope of an eternal life, the hope to go meet their maker in a dignified manner, as real human beings. It was very moving. Some say it is paganism. It was not paganism. It had a much deeper meaning.

Besides, one should never forget that Naples is the only city in the world that can boast of a regularly recurring miracle: the miracle of San Gennaro, September 19. And San Gennaro had better not botch it! Because if he does, he gets insulted. Awful things can happen! It is all because of that powerful faith that keeps everything together.

This is the heroic side of men; nothing else. I remember something my wife said when she started to speak Italian: "You Italians are really strange: you always say that something is beautiful or ugly and never that it is good or bad." Indeed, we say a beautiful dish of spaghetti, not a good dish, a beautiful steak, not a good steak. If this is how we speak then it is also how we see life. This is Italy in a nutshell . . .

CAHIERS: What role does improvisation play in your films?

ROSSELLINI: In theory, I shoot according to what is planned, though I keep some freedom for myself. I listen to the rhythm of the film. This may well be what makes me obscure. I know how important it is to wait in order to reach a certain point, so I don't describe the point, but the wait, and suddenly I reach the conclusion. I can't do it in any other way, for when you have the point, the core of the thing, if you set out to enlarge this core, to dilute it, expand it, it is no longer a core but something that has no longer any shape, any meaning, any emotion.

I've received Claude Mauriac's book.[5] The other evening I was reading what he has written about *Stromboli*: he says that I have put some documentary footage in the film, which was bought and edited in: like the tuna fishing sequence. That episode is not at all a documentary. What's more, I shot it myself. I tried to reproduce the endless wait in the sun, and then the terribly tragic moment of the kill: a death that explodes after an extraordinary, languid, lazy, I would even say benevolent, wait in the sun. That's what mattered, from the character's point of view. Claude Mauriac is a very precise, intelligent man, why would a critic like him say something like that? He should have got his information right to begin with.

CAHIERS: You have a reputation for shooting without a script and improvising all the time . . .

ROSSELLINI: That's partly a myth. I carry the "continuity" of my films in my head, and, what's more, my pockets are full of notes. Still, I must admit, I have never really understood the need to have a shooting script unless it is to reassure the producers. What could be

5 *L'Amour du Cinéma*, Paris: Albin Michel, 1954.

more absurd than the left-hand column: medium shot—lateral travelling shot—pan and frame . . . It's a little as though a novelist were to break down his work into discrete grammatical units: page 212—imperfect subjunctive; then an indirect object . . . and so on and so forth. As for the right-hand column, that is reserved to the dialogue: I don't improvise it systematically, it's written a long time in advance, and if I don't give it out until the very last moment, it is because I don't want the actress or the actor to get too familiar with it. I also manage to control my actors by rehearsing very little and shooting very fast, without too many takes. I count on the "freshness" of the interpretations. I shot *Europe '51* in forty-six days without using more than fifty-three thousand feet of film. For *Stromboli* the figure is even lower. Admittedly there were 102 shooting days, but we were confined to the island, handicapped by the unpredictability of the weather, and great variation in wind and sea. As for the fishing sequence, we waited eight days for the tuna to appear. In short, I work exactly like everybody else, only I do away with the hypocrisy of the shooting script.

CAHIERS: We are impatiently waiting for your film of Claudel's *Jeanne au bûcher*, which you were going to shoot in Cinemascope.

ROSSELLINI: Yes, but I was unable to. It is just in color, Gevacolor. I am very happy with the result. It's a very strange film. I know it will be said that my involution has reached its maximum limit, that I am digging my own grave. It is not a filmed play, it is pure cinema, and I would even go as far as saying it is neorealism as I have always intended it.

CAHIERS: What are your future projects?

ROSSELLINI: I am going to make a film in Germany with my wife, based on a story by Stefan Zweig, *Fear*. I want to show the importance of the avowal, of confession: the woman is guilty and can only find freedom in confession.

"Entretien avec Roberto Rossellini," in
Cahiers du cinéma, *no. 37, July 1954, pp. 1-12.*

TEN YEARS OF CINEMA

BY ROBERTO ROSSELLINI

I

After the War

In 1944, immediately after the war, everything was destroyed in Italy. The cinema was no exception. Almost all the producers had disappeared. Here and there of course, there were some who were making attempts, but their ambitions were extremely limited. Therefore one enjoyed an immense liberty; the absence of an organized industry favored the least routine enterprises and all initiative was good. It was this situation which permitted us to embark on work of an experimental nature. Anyway, it soon became clear that these films, in spite of their experimental aspects, were on the way to becoming important at a cultural level as well as from a commercial point of view.

Under these circumstances, I started to shoot *Open City*, for which I had written the scenario with some friends at the time the Germans were still occupying the country.[1] I made the film with very little money, which we raised in small sums as we went along. There was just enough to pay for film stock: no question of paying a laboratory to develop it. There was, therefore, no chance to see the "rushes" before the end of the shooting. Sometime later, having found a bit of money, I put the film together and showed it to some movie people, critics and friends. Most of them were very disappointed.

---

1 According to the writing credits of the film, these "friends" would have been Sergio Amidei, Alberto Consiglio, and Federico Fellini.

Open City was first shown in September 1945 with the help of a small festival, and those spectators who were in the auditorium whistled.[2] You might say that the critical reception was frankly and unanimously unfavorable. It was just at that time that I proposed to many of my colleagues that we found an association modeled on United Artists,[3] in order to avoid the "deforestation" which would certainly come with the reorganization of the Italian film industry by producers and businessmen. But no one wanted to be associated with the director of *Open City*, who by all appearances was no artist.

That was the atmosphere in which I made *Paisan*. When it was shown at the Venice Festival the reception was disastrous. At the Cannes Festival in 1946, for want of anything better, *Open City* was presented as an official entry by the Italian delegation, which nonetheless had a profound contempt for the film. It was shown in the afternoon and, if I recall the press of the time correctly, it was hardly a big news item.

Then, two months later in Paris, both of my films provoked a surge of enthusiasm, something which by that time I no longer even hoped for. Their success there was so great that the cinema people in Italy had to reconsider their opinion of me, only to abuse me anew when . . . but let's not anticipate. A little after that, Burstyn, the producer of *The Little Fugitive*,[4] brought out *Open City* with well-known happy results.[5]

The Word "Commercial"

Italian films thrust themselves on the entire world at a moment when the American cinema was undergoing a fairly serious crisis. That crisis

2 In Europe, unlike America, whistling signifies displeasure.

3 The original United Artists Corporation was founded in 1919 by Mary Pickford, Douglas Fairbanks, Charles Chaplin, and D.W. Griffith, with the object of producing and distributing their own, and the productions of other directors so that the artists could control all aspects of filmmaking.

4 *The Little Fugitive* (1959) was directed by Ray Ashley; it was an independent production with a very small budget. As Rossellini points out later, the film was widely distributed after its success at the Venice Film Festival.

5 *Open City* was a huge success throughout the world. In America, for example, it was widely distributed and played in cinemas and towns not usually given to screening foreign films. Its commercial and critical success led to a small flurry of semidocumentary films in pseudo-neorealistic manner in America.

was perfectly understandable, for it was the result of what happens to
national production when the ideas which gave it its vitality are worn
out. American producers did not want to face facts, but the crisis was
nonetheless quite real. The disaffection of the public accentuated it,
but the producers lazily blamed television. It was difficult for them to
confess that they themselves had caused the crisis.

The Italian cinema became stronger and reorganized itself, but not
in the way I had wanted. Italian films were made very cheaply, and so
recouped their costs easily, particularly because of the foreign markets. The American market was especially important; when *Open
City* and *Paisan* were distributed there, they were received in triumph
by critics and a rather specialized audience. The receipts for Italian
films in the United States were modest compared to those of Hollywood's own super-productions, but they were enormous if you remember the low cost of neorealist films. Nevertheless, Italian
producers were weak and didn't like the films; they wanted only to
make once more those films they called "commercial." My friend
Jean Renoir recently told me that the word "commercial" in the
minds of producers does not correspond as one might think to
potential profits, but to a certain aesthetic. Producers of "big" films
believe they have made a commercial film even if they never get back
their expenses; those same producers will maintain at the same time
that *La strada* is not a "commercial" film.[6] It was inevitable that the
Italian cinema would again fall into the same old aesthetic as the
Hollywood industry; it was, after all, reorganized and directed by the
old money-men who had returned after running away during the war,
or by new ones who were motivated by the same ideas.

The Crisis of Italian Cinema

One should never forget the presence of American films in the market.
These films are generally productions with a medium budget, very
well-made and well-received by the public. The American cinema has
one of the best national markets for getting back the cost of its films;

---

6 *La strada* (1954) was a gigantic critical and commercial success everywhere, and was
   the film which made its director, Federico Fellini, internationally famous.

it also has a powerful and direct commercial organization throughout the entire world, which is to say that it makes as much money as it is possible to make from a film, like squeezing a lemon to the last drop. Obviously, then, the battle between the American and European cinemas is hardly equal; competition is hardly possible. As I see it, the only chance for us is to make films intended for a much smaller audience, to reduce costs as much as possible, and to think carefully about how best to launch an avant-garde film (by which I mean a film made outside the usual formulas) in every market, including America. It is too easy to forget that on the other side of the Atlantic there is a public composed of connoisseurs, of specialists, which is extremely important. That public comes to see films which have something new to say. If an Italian neorealist film brings in from its American distribution no more than $100,000, $50,000, or even $30,000— thanks to "art cinemas" for example—that is already a considerable return considering the low budgets of such films.

It seems to me there is only one real reason for the crisis in the Italian cinema: the producers believe that if a neorealist film which costs pennies can bring in so much money, then a super-production with a budget ten times as big will bring in ten times as much. This is, of course, a stupid line of reasoning; you can't make films on such an idiotic basis. Another absolutely mad idea: dubbing Italian films into English and attempting to distribute them as in America. Failure is assured.[7] The policy of the Italian film industry—far more than in the rest of Europe—is to copy Hollywood formulas. The result is simply that costs are driven up so high that even foreign sales are insufficient

---

7 In this case, Roberto Rossellini was less than a great prophet. Dubbed versions of commercial Italian films have done well in the United States, and even less-commercial films often play outside the large cities in dubbed versions. In the last two decades, the practice has been to avoid making an "original version" at all. Films are often shot silently in Italy, with soundtracks in various languages laid in afterwards. A second method still, but less widely used, is to shoot each scene in each language. A third is to shoot an "international" version, with each actor speaking his own language, and to dub the film into other languages. Rossellini changed his mind about dubbing later in his career, and even accused critics who objected to the practice of being "cinematic fetishists." His own last film *The Messiah* (1975) was dubbed into the language of whichever country it was to be released in, with Rossellini himself supervising each version.

to recoup expenses. The reasons for this are rather complex, but I will try to analyze them a bit later.

The cinema which plays such an important role in everyday life is also an art: commerce which becomes, at least sometimes, an art. Everything remains to be discovered. That is the great good luck of a filmmaker; that is what should inspire him to work on the level of every other form of artistic expression and not to lag behind. The public is curious, and it is that curiosity which should be satisfied. Take, for instance, *The Little Fugitive*. It happens to be an American film which was released in the United States with no great success. Then it was a huge success at the Venice Festival. The critics and public were so enthusiastic about the film, which had been consigned to the margins of the usual distribution process, that it became a financial success in Europe, as well as in America where it was rereleased.

The Art of Waiting

Personally, I don't believe that in the course of my career I have ever been reduced to compromise. I have, of course, always kept outside the normal production system. From what happened with *Open City* I learned that in order to defend myself and my work I would have to suffer criticism and attacks without flinching. When the Italian film industry was reorganized, the industrialists at the top immediately wanted to lop off the heads of all those who were out in front. That is a normal fact of life and happens all the time; they found it necessary to make everyone equal by reducing them to the lowest possible level, and to make everyone start over again in the ranks. I think it is because I would not give in to this that the attacks against me have been more violent than against the others.

The fact that I am my own producer allowed me to make my films very fast and with a very modest budget. I think that is the only solution, and I find it works very well for me. Time is what costs most in the cinema, but what is that time used for? Usually to satisfy the finicky instincts of the director, of the cameraman, of the actors, of God-knows-who. I have been in this profession now for twenty-five years and I have always been shocked by what happens when the rushes are projected. Everyone appears to be filled with wonder and admiration at seeing something on the screen, and that something must be indubitably good in order to astound the financial "sleeping partners" who are there to see their money transformed into images. Everyone is happy at the projection; everyone is pleased at seeing each shot, at the superb sequences. Then you edit together fifty magnificent bits and—surprise!—the film is a disaster. It is no longer anything, and everyone looks stupefied. People seem to have a complex about technique: they turn on the radio, tune in to a music station, and then take themselves for Toscanini!

Beautiful shots! That is the one thing that makes me sick! A film must be well-directed; that is the least one can expect of a filmmaker, but a single shot need not be beautiful.

The only thing that is important is rhythm, and that cannot be learned; you carry it inside yourself. I believe in the importance of the scene; it resolves itself, it completes itself, at a certain point. In general, directors love to develop that point. As far as I am concerned, I think that is an error dramatically. Neorealism consists of following someone with love and watching all his discoveries and impressions; an ordinary man dominated by something which suddenly strikes him a terrible blow at the precise moment when he finds himself free in the world. He never expects whatever it is. What is important for me is the waiting. That is what it is necessary to develop; the blow, the fall, must stay intact. Take, for example, the tuna fishing sequence in *Stromboli*. For the fishermen, it is all just waiting under the sun. Then they suddenly shout "They're coming! They're coming!" They have thrown out their nets, and suddenly the water is alive and death is striking the tuna. That is the final point of the scene. In the same way, there is the death of the child in *Europe '51*. There had been a failed suicide; the child is recovering and all is calm; then suddenly, like a blow, at the moment you would no longer possibly expect it, he dies.

Naturally, this waiting manifests itself in the movement and rhythm of my films, since my work consists of following the characters. Usually in the traditional cinema a scene is constructed like this: an establishing shot in which the environment is defined; the discovery of an individual in that environment; you move closer to him (medium shot); then a two-shot; a close-up, and the story begins. I proceed in a manner which is exactly opposite to that: I always begin with a close-up; then the movement of the character determines the movement of the camera. The camera does not leave the actor, and in this way the camera effects the most complex journeys.

The Direction of Actors

It is too often believed that neorealism consists in finding an unemployed person to play an unemployed person. I choose actors solely by the way they look. You can choose anyone in the street. I prefer nonprofessional actors because they have no preconceived ideas. I watch a man in life and fix him in my memory. When he finds himself before the camera, he is usually completely lost and tries to "act," which is exactly what must be avoided at all costs. There are gestures which belong to this man, the ones he makes with the same muscles which become paralyzed before the lens. It is as if he forgets himself, as if he never knew himself. He believes he has become a very exceptional person because someone is going to film him. My task is to return him to his original nature, to reconstruct him, to *reteach* him his usual movements.

II

Germany Year Zero

I have already explained that the worldwide success of *Open City* and *Paisan* started in France. In 1947 I found myself in Paris with the idea of asking the French Government for permission to shoot a film in Berlin about Germany after the Armistice. Thus *Germany Year Zero* came into being as the third panel of the triptych on the war.

I arranged the finances with *Union Génerale Cinématographique* and, without any preconceived ideas, I left for Germany, not to shoot, but to get an idea for a scenario.

I arrived in Berlin in March, by car, at about five in the afternoon, just as the sun was going down. It was necessary to cross the entire city to get to the French sector. The city was deserted. The grey of the sky flowed back into the streets, and from about the height of a man one could look over fallen roofs. To find the streets again under the ruins, people had cleared away the rubble and piled it up. Grass had begun to grow through the cracks in the asphalt. Silence reigned; each noise intensified the silence. A sickish sweet odour of rotting organic matter exuded from the piled-up rubble. It was as if we were floating over Berlin. I started off down a wide avenue. On the horizon, a huge yellow advertisement was the only sign of "life." I slowly came up to this immense sign which was attached to a stone block in front of a store with a tiny facade. It said "Israel Bazaar." The first Jews had come back to Berlin; it was the symbol of the end of Nazism.

The four occupying nations were very hospitable and permitted me to wander everywhere, so that I returned to Paris with a very clear idea of the film in my head. In every country, more-or-less "funny stories" are related which can tell one a good deal about life in that country. At that time this story was being told in Germany. A man arrived in Berlin and someone put him up. The first morning he was asked if he had slept well. "Yes, in spite of those trains which kept passing under my window." "But you must have been dreaming; there are no trains." "But there are. I heard the steam and the water pumps." The host took the guest to the window and showed him there were no trains. The following morning, the guest was awakened by the same noise. He got up, looked out of the window, and saw old women in men's clothing clearing away the rubble. As they passed bricks to one another along a line: "Danke schönen"—"Bitte schönen"—"Danke schönen." That is the sort of story which gives you a proper point of view.

The Germans were human beings like all the rest. What was it that could have carried them to this disaster? A false philosophy, the essence of Nazism; the abandoning of humility for a cult of heroics; the exaltation of strength over weakness, vaingloriousness over simplicity? That is why I chose to tell the story of a child, an innocent, who through the distortion of a utopian education was brought to the point of committing a crime while believing he was accomplishing something heroic. But a small ethical flame still burned within him; he killed himself to escape his sense of moral disquiet.

Finally, I was able to make *Germany Year Zero* exactly as I had intended. Whenever I see the film again now, I come out of the screening upset; I think my judgement of Germany was right, not complete, but right. For all that, and contrary to all experience, *Germany Year Zero* was badly received. It was then that I began to ask myself some questions.

The world of the cinema had reorganized itself, and had returned to its prewar habits and styles. *Germany Year Zero* was judged according to the prewar aesthetic, even though *Open City* and *Paisan* had been admired for what they had done in terms of a new style. The political world had also reorganized itself, and the film was judged politically. The critics of *Germany Year Zero* taught me what the respective journalists (or more likely the editors of their newspapers) thought about the problem of Germany, but they gave me nothing useful on the level of film criticism. At that moment I found myself in a dilemma: either prostitution or sincerity.

I Chose Sincerity

I have already said that I believe cinema is a new art and has the potential for making many discoveries. It is that potential which makes being a film director intoxicating. It was in that spirit that I made *A Human Voice* from the play by Jean Cocteau.[8]

The cinema is also a microscope in that it can take us by the hand and lead us to the discovery of things the eye alone could never perceive (be it close-up, small details, and so on). More than other subjects *A Human Voice* offered me the chance to use the microscopic camera. The phenomenon to be examined was Anna Magnani. Only the novel, poetry, and the cinema permit us to rummage through a personality to discover reactions and motives for actions.

This experience, pushed to an extreme in *A Human Voice,* was useful to me later in all my films, since at one moment or another in shooting I feel the need to cast the scenario to one side in order to follow a character in his most secret thoughts, those which are perhaps not even conscious. It is also this "microscopic aspect" of cinema which made neorealism; it is a moral approach which becomes an aesthetic fact.

8 *Amore* is made up of two stories: *A Human Voice* with only Anna Magnani and a telephone in the cast, and *The Miracle* with Magnani and Federico Fellini.

When I had finished *A Human Voice* I found myself with a film forty minutes long. As we are the slaves of commercial programing, it was practically unsaleable. I therefore had to look for another story of about the same length. Federico Fellini, who often worked with me, wrote a story which I filmed under the title *The Miracle*. According to Fellini, it was taken from a Russian short story but he claimed he had forgotten both the author and the original title. When he saw that I was much taken with the story but that I was searching desperately for the original text so that I could make legal arrangements for the rights, he confessed that he had invented the story down to the smallest details. He had lied at first because he was afraid that I would find the story ridiculous.

After a time, both stories were released under the title *Amore*. The Italian critics said that *A Human Voice* was not cinema. It was certainly the only time I have ever seen critics affirm anything so unanimously.

The Miracle was the object of very serious accusations.[9] An American priest, whom I met in Italy, told me that it was manifestly clear that I had wanted to make money by exploiting blasphemy for blasphemers. He was unfamiliar with a sermon of Saint Bernadino of Siena. It concerned a saint named Bonino. A peasant went to the countryside with his two-year-old son and a dog. He left the boy and the dog in the shade of an oak and went to work. When he returned he found the child with his throat cut and with the marks of teeth around his wound. In his grief, the father killed the dog. It was only at that moment he saw a huge snake and understood his error. Conscience-stricken at his injustice, he buried the dog in the rocks close by and engraved an inscription on the tomb: "Here Lies Bonino: Killed by the Ferocity of Man." Several centuries went by, and the road passed by the tomb. Travelers who stopped in the shade of

---

9 *The Miracle*, as the film was known in English-speaking countries, was the object of a good deal of controversy. It was condemned by the Catholic Legion of Decency and denounced by Cardinal Spellman (who later admitted not ever having seen it). As local censorship boards (and local cinema owners who were afraid of "offending" their audience) followed the lead of the Legion in banning the film to non-Catholics as well as to the Catholics who, in theory, were not going to attend the "condemned" film anyway, a series of court cases came about. These resulted in a landmark legal decision that films could not be banned on the grounds of "blasphemy." By then, however, it was too late to save the film commercially, at least in the United States. It played in a few large cities, where it was often picketed by the Legion, but was never widely distributed because of the "controversy."

the oak read the inscription. Little by little they began to pray there, to ask for relief from their unhappiness. Then miracles began to happen, so many that the people of the area built a beautiful church and a new tomb to enshrine the body of Bonino. As they were transferring the remains, they discovered he was a dog.

You can see that the story of *The Miracle* is rather similar. It is about a mad woman who has a sort of religious mania, but she has faith as well, a real and profound faith. She could have believed anything she liked. I admit that what she believed was rather blasphemous, but her faith was immense, and that faith was her recompense. Her action is absolutely human and normal: to suckle her child. I believe *The Miracle* is an absolutely Catholic work.

A theme which obsesses me, and which can be found again in *Stromboli,* is that of the absolute lack of faith, the absence of a desire to fight for anything, which was typical of the postwar period. What bothers me is the sort of cowardice which brings people to gather together like sheep under the staff of some pastor or other. However, the character played by Anna Magnani in *The Miracle* is the exact opposite. She is mad, but in the midst of her mental confusion, she has a faith, deluded if you like, *but a faith.* Once, a politician said to me with a great deal of bitterness: "Men want to have less social justice provided they also have less freedom." It is that mentality which even today obsesses me and frightens me, in spite of certain signs lately which might indicate a return of conscience.

A Letter from Ingrid Bergman

It was at this time that I received some concrete offers to work in the United States. These offers came from David O. Selznick and were extremely attractive. Selznick, who has a very forceful personality, would have been a valuable patron for my career as a director had my goal been a "career." After long negotiations, I decided to stay in Italy. Four years later, Selznick and I became very good friends, and he is a man I appreciate for his great human qualities. One thing which held me back and influenced my refusal was simply that in Italy there is hardly enough work already and I was afraid of betraying my friends and the people who usually worked with me, in this way.

On 8 May 1946, I received a letter from Ingrid Bergman. She had seen *Open City* and *Paisan* and wanted to make a film with me. The 8th of May is my birthday. On the evening of the 7th, I got a phone call from Mr. Potsius of Minerva Films who told me that he wanted to see me in order to give me a beautiful present. I thought he was referring to my birthday, especially as I had sold him the rights to *Open City* for a mouthful of bread when it was a "bomb" and he had then profitably exploited it as a "masterpiece." The next day he brought me the letter from Ingrid. He had already read it, for it seems that Minerva had just burned all its accumulated correspondence and that he had opened all the letters without first checking to see if they were addressed to him. I answered the letter at once, and on 17 January 1949, exactly five years to the day of the first turning of the camera for *Open City,* I arrived in Hollywood to discuss the idea of *Stromboli* with Ingrid.

A big producer showed a very great interest in our project and we had long conversations over a number of breakfasts, lunches, and dinners. That is how I learned English, since the same words came up interminably over and over in our conversations. I must make one point clear: all these conversations I had with him were of an aesthetic order. He explained to me all that his great experience in the cinema had taught him, and he tried to convince me of the necessity of working with a detailed shooting script. Some of his arguments were extremely judicious, but I was absolutely opposed to the idea that it was necessary to work from a detailed script for reasons I have explained a hundred times already.

As I shoot in real interiors and unretouched exteriors to begin with, I can only improvise my direction to correspond to the settings I find myself in. Therefore the left hand column of a shooting script would be left blank even if I had to make one. Then, I choose my secondary actors at the time and place of the shooting. Therefore I cannot, before seeing them, write their dialogue. Otherwise it would of necessity be theatrical and false. The column on the right side would therefore also be left blank. Finally, I believe strongly in the inspiration of the moment.

Anyway, one evening Ingrid and I were summoned by telephone to another meeting in his office. He had called a press conference and announced the production of the film to the newspapers. Very surprised, we took our places anyway and were photographed signing a phony contract. From that day the discussions between the producer and myself took a decided turn for the worse, to such a degree, that a short time later I refused his proposition.

I felt out of my element in Hollywood, the city with the highest density of intellectuals. I hardly understood that atmosphere of contempt, wounded pride, and frenzied chauvinism. I must say anyway that I made some good friends there, but the atmosphere was directly hostile without the reasons for it—at least at that time—being at all clear to me. One day, Ingrid was invited to a reception at which she was the guest of honour. When she returned she told me with complete amazement, that on her right was sitting a Hollywood big shot.[10] This man, after trying to dissuade her from making a film with me, told her that I had come to see him a year before in Europe to beg him to take me to Hollywood, and that I was so insistent that he had to treat me very rudely to get rid of me, and that finally he had me thrown out, telling me he had no use for a guy like me. Now obviously I knew this man only by reputation. When he was pointed out to me in a restaurant in Paris last year I could only remark with astonishment that a man as sly as twenty foxes managed somehow to look smaller than even one.

At the beginning of March, having put the production of *Stromboli* on the road, I returned to Italy, where Ingrid joined me on the 9th.

III

Stromboli, Little Island

At the beginning of April, we began to shoot the film on the island of Stromboli, and, at the same time, the scandal over our private life

10 Rossellini's note: "This is the second time I have talked about a famous person without giving his name. I am not writing these reminiscences either to scandalize or to provoke controversy; for this reason, neither have I asked the reader to excuse my discretion." Nonetheless, Rossellini's reference a bit later to the man in question as being "as sly as *20 foxes*" is enough of a hint for one to guess easily the man's identity.

exploded.[11] What was the reason for all of that? Why was there a resounding scandal over a simple divorce and remarriage, especially in the world of the cinema, and, in particular, the American cinema, where divorce had for a long time been an institution which everyone treated like a routine, everyday matter? I have already said that in a general way the atmosphere of Hollywood was not friendly to me. Ingrid was an actress, I was a director; it was normal that we should arrange to do a film together. The world of Hollywood received this news as if it were an insult and a blow to its prestige.

Stromboli was a small island, very isolated from the rest of the world. There was no telephone, no electricity, and a connection to the mainland by boat only once a week. News of the outside therefore came to us very late, and we didn't realize that a scandal had burst until we saw the arrivals of journalists, photographers, and even friends—not forgetting the "experts" from the distribution company, "experts" in publicity and public relations—all come to give us their advice as to what was best for the "common interest." It was then in my life that I had the surprise of learning that in the world there were many hitherto unsuspected professions, "specialists" of the most precise sort. Every wave of sensational news doubtless had but one purpose: to frighten us. In the face of constantly repeated "sensations," the "experts" suggested only one solution: deny everything.

11 The "scandal" was simply that Ingrid Bergman and Roberto Rossellini were in love and openly living together, although Bergman was still married to Peter Lindstrom. When she was divorced, Bergman was pregnant with Mr. Rossellini's son; a little later they married. The furor which this provoked internationally is now unbelievable. The films which Bergman had made were boycotted by women's goups, by "morality" organizations, and finally by exhibitors. When Stromboli was released in a mutilated version in the United States (the centre of the commotion), however, the distributors and exhibitors tried to use the "scandal" to sell the film to a large audience (for whom the film was never intended); although the advertisements and posters blazed "Flaming Volcano! Flaming Emotions!" few went to see it. Ironically, the exploitative handling of the film kept away the discriminating audience which would have found the film more than interesting.

One of the most unfortunate results of the "scandal" and the subsequent financial failure of Stromboli, was that the series of films which Bergman and Rossellini made later were rarely released and distributed outside Europe—films which are among the finest Rossellini made and certainly the best with which Miss Bergman was ever associated.

When Ingrid and I offered to suspend production, or even purely and simply to give up the film, in order to deal with the situation after a period of reflection, when we would be at our ease, and free from all other responsibilities, the "experts" absolutely disagreed. Above all: work! Friends and "experts" busied themselves in pointing out the grave dangers that the scandal threatened to our respective careers. If they had calculated on our cowardice and hypocrisy by underscoring the danger we were running, they had evidently miscalculated. For us, Europeans, and for me who had no experience in these matters, it was difficult to describe what American journalism was.

Many American journalists are merely guardians of the established order, a militia ready to bludgeon anyone who dares to break that order. I had been struck, during my stay in Hollywood, by how the appearance of a certain newspaper, a certain radio broadcast, could make everyone hold their breath. Every day, hearts would beat rapidly when the newspaper came out, and life would stop for the broadcast. At that time in Hollywood, there was a story going around which, for all its being invented, is still revealing.

A famous lady broadcaster, as she was finishing her weekly program, saw one of her "hunting dogs" bring in a final bit of gossip hastily scratched on a bit of paper. Already a bit senile, she clamped on her glasses, assumed a pathetic voice which barely hid the sadistic joy she was feeling at being the first to deliver this dismaying news and read from the paper: "Janet Smith is getting a divorce." On this dry note the program ended, and the assistant, who was finally able to speak, explained that in his haste he had made a mistake: the item should have read "Joe" instead of "Janet" Smith. A few minutes later, Janet Smith and her husband telephoned, upset but deferential and submissive, and begged the broadcaster to retract the false report. But the scandalmonger, whose imagination was never at a loss, rather than retract—which would have been a blow to her prestige— proposed a bargain with Janet Smith from which everyone would get something. Janet's husband was to move to a hotel at the expense of the broadcaster, who several days later would then announce the couple's reconciliation with a lot of publicity. She would exalt love with all its torments and paradoxes, the boundlessness of an artist's emotions, the lyricism of their feelings, and so on. Janet Smith and her husband evidently didn't dare refuse. There was nothing to do except give in and hope. The same evening, installed in the hotel, the husband began to receive phone calls from all his friends congratulating him on finally understanding what a slut he had married. The whole affair naturally ended in a divorce, which the broadcaster took pleasure in announcing just as everyone began to think it would never happen.

Sentiments after the War

To return to *Stromboli*: what interested me in the film was treating the theme of cynicism, a sentiment which represented the greatest anger after the war. Karin gambled on the ingenuousness of the love of a poor, primitive soldier and married him with the sole purpose of getting out of the internment camp. She trades the barbed wire for the island, but once there she finds herself even more enclosed. She had dreamed of something entirely different. A strong but determined woman who had gone through all the difficulties and trouble of the war and had always pulled herself through more or less all right, she was now the victim of small, stupid things: a crude husband, a small island without vegetation. She is doubly a prisoner in that she is pregnant. For her, being pregnant is stupid, humiliating, ignoble, and bestial. She therefore decides to leave, but at the top of the volcano she must climb over to get to the small port on the other side of the island, in the midst of hostile nature, broken by fatigue, bowed down by a primitive terror, in animal despair, she unconsciously calls upon God. "My God" is the simplest appeal, the most primitive and the most common that can escape from the mouth of someone overcome with suffering. It can be a mechanical invocation, or an expression of a very high truth. In one case as in the other, it is always the expression of a profound mortification which might also be the first glimmering of a conversion. This is the construction of the film. It wasn't difficult to figure out my intentions, I would even have explained my intentions, if people just took the trouble to read the Biblical verse which is printed on the screen after the credits of *Stromboli*: "I will answer those who ask for nothing; I will be found by those who seek me not" (*Isaiah* 65:1).

Many people were dead set against the film, particularly the ending, for diverse reasons. All of them joined together, however, to demonstrate that I was a cretin. The film was mutilated in America. I have not seen what "they" did, but I understand that thirty-five minutes are missing, that there is now a "lyrical" commentary on the action, and that at the end it seems Karin has the intention of returning to her nice little husband who is waiting for her at home.

When the shooting was finished, I made a cut of the film very quickly so that the American studio people would have an idea of how to edit their negative (I kept a second negative myself). The copy which I had not had time to perfect was then released in Europe. It seemed absurd to me to show the film in a version that had been so hastily edited. Still, I had to go to court just to obtain what is normally asked of us as directors—a bit of thought about the editing and a bit of advice in order to make the necessary modifications. All of that was refused me. I would perhaps have obtained satisfaction if it had been possible for me to pursue the long legal process. I only won the case as far as the Italian version was concerned; in the end, this version differed only slightly from the one released in the rest of Europe, but it was drastically different from the American version.

Stromboli won the *Prix de Rome* and although a number of critics defended it, the majority attacked it violently. What I had felt and suspected when *Germany Year Zero* was released, was now very clear to me. The critics were reacting politically and were no longer even bothering to hide it. A limited group, politically involved, infatuated by the cinema, but amateurs nonetheless (there are too many amateurs in film criticism) had with the aid of a particular terminology created a critical movement which looked attractive from the outside and had a strong following in Italy, especially among journalists without taste, intuition, or sensibility. In this way, they were able to seize upon a popular critical vocabulary in place of making intelligent critical judgements.

That is why I also attribute political reasons to the reversal of critical opinion today which has benefited *Open City* and *Paisan*. I think that this group by its activities and by creating an enormous critical confusion, has contributed in large measure to the current crisis in the Italian cinema, feeding the divisions between filmmakers, by encouraging producers even indirectly, to persist in commercial or would-be commercial productions.

A Small "True Incident"

To illustrate what I am talking about, I will tell you a small "true incident" that seems significant to me. A very important film man who shared the ideas of this critical group wanted to collaborate with me. He invited me to revisit the swamps at the mouth of the Po river where I had shot the last episode of *Paisan*. It was November, cold and raining. "Cigolani," whom I had hanged in *Paisan* seven years before,[12] was very happy to see me again. One day as we walked on the banks of the Po, which was rapidly rising, he said to me: "What do you bet that this year the Po is going to overflow the banks on the other side again, and that those sons-of-bitches are going to have the benefits they had from the last flood?"

What had happened was that the year before the Po had overrun the other bank, and the people who lived on that side, after getting through the tragedy, had benefited from all sorts of assistance which had practically changed their lives, while those on the unflooded side of the river got nothing and were forced to continue living in the same conditions they always had. When I told this story to my filmmaking friend and would-be collaborator, his eyes clouded over and he accused me of wanting to make a progovernment film.

Men usually adopt a political or moral position by choosing it from the range of "truths" with which they are presented. This choice is rarely made from personal conviction, but is the fruit of chance, of worry about getting ahead, or from a desire to live peacefully. Once committed to a cause, they are obliged to defend it and prove it has been worth devoting their lives to. That is generally how movements of public opinion are formed, and how philosophic, aesthetic, and moral movements win followers. Everything is sacrificed to consistency to the point of maniac pigheadedness, which kills all liberty and all imagination.

To return to the release of *Stromboli:* ranged against a small nucleus of defenders and myself, was a hostile front composed of the

---

12 "Cigolani" was a professional who played the partisan in the last episode of *Paisan;* in the film the character he played was hanged.

critical group without precise ideas, the defenders of justice and morality, sensational writers and journalists, and other general social nuisances. All were duly represented. From this confrontation came all the epithets that were used against me: communist and proclerical, anarchist and devout, imbecile and clever. My films were judged to be sublime and ignoble. They talked as much about my evolution as about my involution. Then a certain newspaper joined in this chorus of judgements and I was able to read all sorts of remarkable things, each more unbelievable than the one before. *The Miracle,* for example, was said to be the product of perfect Communist technique which was intended to "divide and rule," and the film was an insult to all Italian women. After they had finished with the work, they started on the man. They said that I was the "head of a gang directed by Mao Tse-tung which had the sole goal of destroying the brains of American filmgoers," and that I was either head over heels in debt or was living "like a Renaissance prince." The judgments that I have collected whether hostile or adulatory, were varied, funny, and often very eloquent. I have only given examples of the most ridiculous ones as I prefer to forget the most serious injustices.

Freedom of the Press

I remember that when the Allies either "liberated" or "invaded" Italy they distributed "occupation lire" on which were printed the four basic freedoms to which everyone was entitled, among them the freedom of the press. I will always defend the freedom of the press, even if I have been inconvenienced by it. Nonetheless, if my experiences serve for anything, as I sincerely believe they do, I must tell an anecdote which illustrates the morality of a certain type of newspaper.

At one time in our lives, my wife and I were literally besieged by press photographers. For four months Ingrid and my son could not leave the apartment. The photographers did everything to violate our privacy. What they wanted was one particular photograph. One night, at about one in the morning, the doorbell rang. The maid, who was frightened, asked through the door who was there. They answered that it was the police. She opened the door and two men, one carrying a camera, pushed their way in. She managed to push them back out to the landing and called down the porter for help. He came out on the stairs and demanded how they had got in without his knowledge. The two "journalists" evaded his blows and escaped the same way they had come in, by scaling the fence at the entrance to the courtyard.

There was only one way to put an end to the siege: to publish the photograph they were seeking so desperately. I finally decided I wanted some peace and took the photograph myself. I gave it as a gift to the press agency which had bothered us the least and which had often gone so far as to deplore the behavior of the others. The siege was lifted, but not without an accumulation of bitterness. A rumor circulated and finally came back to me that I had sold the photograph at a very high price. I thought at the time that the story had been invented by the rival agencies that had been frustrated.

Three years later, I told this entire misadventure to some friends in Paris. They were a very sympathetic couple; he was the director of a large daily newspaper. He told me that his newspaper had published the photograph, having acquired it at an exorbitant price. The agency had justified the incredible price by saying that it had been necessary to pay me a fortune for it!

"Dix ans de cinéma," in Cahiers du cinéma,
*no. 50, April/September 1955, pp. 3-9 (I), no. 52,
November 1955, pp. 3-9 (II), and no. 55,
January 1956, pp. 9-15 (III). Translated by David Overbey.*

THE INDIA I HAVE SEEN

AN INTERVIEW WITH CLAUDE BOURDET

Do you want to get to know India? India with its three hundred and eighty million inhabitants, its five hundred and fifty-eight thousand villages, its eighty cities with a population of more than one hundred thousand souls, its States, each larger than France, and its seventeen languages, some as different as Russian and French? In Bombay, I've just paid a visit to an old friend who, for six months now, has been trying to get to know India, to discover it for himself and reveal it to the world. He has just covered twenty-five thousand kilometers of land in every possible direction, by plane, train, van, and at times even on foot, armed only with the collective eye of a movie camera, and the intention to show the world the India he loves so passionately, the India he has discovered with a freshness of soul that never fails to move his fans. The friend in question is Roberto Rossellini, and to my mind his experience of India is one of the most fascinating ever.

I found him in the apartment of some Indian friends, hiding away from all the muckrakers who have followed him all the way up Malabar Hill, a quarter of this city that's oddly reminiscent of the rococo areas of Cannes and Nice. The large Bay of Bombay, lined with modern buildings also recalls the Promenade des Anglais, in Nice. One must plunge into the heart of the city to find the more crowded neighborhoods, teeming with humanity, and the sacred tree, and the temple at the end of a narrow alley . . .

Rossellini, all dressed in hand-woven cotton like the Indians he is filming, looked much thinner, no doubt because of the overwhelming heat, and maybe also the mindless persecutions of which he is so often a victim. But his eye sparkles when he speaks of this enormous country, its inhabitants, its jungles, its animals.

BOURDET: In a few words, Rossellini, what is India?

ROSSELLINI: Only a journalist could ask such a question! On the other hand, you are perfectly right, this is the sort of question that should be answered.

And so Rossellini starts looking for an answer, a short definition to satisfy the tourist I am. Suddenly, he finds it, and his hands—the hands of a cold Italian, spare in movement—make a gigantic gesture, worthy of a Neapolitan.

India is a stomach. An enormous stomach with an enormous digestive tract. That's what India is. It has digested all the religions of the world and has made them its own: the original paganism of the Dravidian nations whose indianized idols decorate the Southern temples, the Hinduism of Aryan conquerors which might have been the gastric juice that has allowed such an extraordinary assimilation, Buddhism and those two other Hindu reforms, that of the Jains and that of the Sikhs, the Christianism that came in from Asia Minor during the first century of our era and then returned with the Portuguese, the Mazdeism of the Parsees chased from Persia during the Moslem invasion . . .

And here Rossellini stretches his arm toward a vulture that's slowly circling right above a clump of proud trees under whose branches hides the Tower of Silence, where the Parsees of Bombay, following an age-old usage, expose their dead.

And then there was Islam. This gigantic stomach has assimilated all its conquerors: the Aryans, the Moslems, the Mongols . . . and the English. And what is truly extraordinary is that all these cults, all these races have stratified next to one another with little or no antagonism.

In Delhi, in the old Mosque of Koutab, built in the thirteenth century, I had seen how Moslem architecture had blended with the older ruins of a Hindu temple. The pillars of the two buildings joined and crisscrossed, and one could imagine pilgrims of both cults coming together to pray on either side of the wall. I mentioned this to Rossellini.

It's still going on today. Not far from where I am currently shooting, there is a Buddhist temple. In a corner, there is a small Hindu altar. I asked the bonze how come it was there. "This is a very poor area," he told me. "They have no temple here." But who officiates for them? I asked him. "Oh, I do," he said, smiling.

I also tell Rossellini about the statue of Queen Victoria, sitting enthroned in the middle of Delhi's large views, and of avenues with English names, such as Allenby Avenue or Kitchener Road, etc. Rossellini tells me:

I once asked them for what reason they kept English names and statues. "It's part of our history," they answered me. Naturally, they do change a few names, and pull down a few statues, but little by little, gently, so as not to upset anyone. Why should India, now independent and one of the most powerful nations in the world, bother to preserve this British heritage which is only one more cultural layer to add to all those already piled up by history? Clearly such a moderation bespeaks prodigious wisdom.

BOURDET: Do you believe it is religion that has created this climate of tolerance?

ROSSELLINI: Maybe, or maybe it is the people who have infused their own nature into their religion. Is it religion and its doctrine of transmigration that have determined the extraordinary relationship that exists between the Indians and animals? Or rather, is it the life of this frail humanity surrounded by a luxuriance of both flora and fauna, the constant proximity of man and animal, that has given rise to the idea that there must be a continuity between man and animal? Gandhi, in his perfect humility, has asked: "Why should we be the only creatures to have a soul?" Starting from here, the curiously logical Indian spirit had to come up with the idea of all the stages through which a single soul moves either up or down from the lowliest animal form to the highest, and finally to the human form.

BOURDET: When one thinks about animals in India, obviously one thinks of the cow, the "sacred" cow. I have seen a few lying in the middle of the street, skinny and peaceful, and the flow of carts, cars, and plain pedestrians, all going around them.

ROSSELLINI: Here in India there are some twenty-five million bovines, which, of course provokes the sarcasm of most Westerners. Indeed, they are too many, and indeed it might be good if the Indians ate a little more meat, but we should beware of all these preconceived notions. First of all, there are not fifty million committed vegetarians in India. If lots of people here are vegetarians, it is not so much out of choice as because of their poverty. On the other hand, popular wisdom tends to react quite forcefully against any form of mental regimentation. At Gandhigram, in the South, where Gandhi's zealots have decided to transform the liberal teachings of the Mahatma into some sort of vegetarian fascism, a dissenting villager has reacted against this sort of collective contentment by putting up a restaurant whose door is surmounted by a huge sign stating: "This is a restaurant for carnivores." But the cow, in this country of scanty crops where, until now, only the rain of monsoons could produce a harvest (and when monsoons are irregular it means famine), this animal which manages to find enough to survive in the barest stubble fields, still provides not only milk for the children, and the muscle to cover the longest distances, but also fuel. You must have seen, in the villages, those large stacks covered with clay and containing cowpats—the only fuel of hundreds of thousands of villages.

BOURDET: Does the villager's consideration for animals, his respect of different forms of life, extend as far as to include wild animals?

ROSSELLINI: Well, it is often difficult to determine what's domestic and what's wild. One day, as I was about to begin shooting in a jungle village, I asked where I could find some wild animals. "Take the road at dusk." I was told. "The road to where?" I asked. "The road, the road, you'll see," the villager answered. And so that evening I had the extraordinary experience of motoring down the jungle road in the midst of a real procession of all sorts of animals which I could fend off only by hooting the horn: thousands of birds, monkeys, antelopes, and every now and then a long snake winding its way across the road, bears sauntering along its edges for hundreds of meters, a panther . . . All these animals were on the road for the same reason I was on the road: because it was the easiest way to go from one point to the next. And for some, to gather the fruit and grains that showed more clearly than in the tall grass.

BOURDET: What about tigers, and wild elephants?

ROSSELLINI: I lived in a village where, before going home, I often had to wait for the local tiger, which liked to take a stroll right around my house, to leave. Tigers attack humans only when they are either sick or wounded, and unable to catch faster prey.

I had gone to watch Rossellini film the story of a tiger chased from its own home by the construction of a factory. It was a female, and since she could not abandon her cubs she had often attacked both men and children. As the workers of the factory were about to kill it, an old villager who knew the tigress well having often come across her in his walks, chased her away with loud shouts and burning branches so that the townies wouldn't kill her. She had the right to live since she had killed people only when forced to it. This is not a legend either, but a true story which Rossellini had heard in a village.

As for the elephants (I have devoted a whole episode to them), it's incredibly difficult to know whether they are domestic or wild. In a village, I know an elephant that was often set free in the evening so that he could go pay a visit to his wilder colleagues in the jungle. A chain around his foot prevented him from going either too fast or too far. And every day, the poor mahout had to go look for him. But once found, the elephant never made any trouble to go back. Its domestication essentially consisted in performing, without even trying, some hard chores that he found very amusing, in letting his mahout go fetch him some three hundred kilos of leaves which he should have otherwise gathered himself, and in allowing the same mahout to wash, curry, and scratch him for hours on end. It is quite delightful to watch those huge animals obligingly offer their "master" all the nooks and crannies of their vast surfaces to groom. I really couldn't tell you what a tamed elephant is unless it is an elephant that has tamed its mahout.

BOURDET: And you have filmed this?

ROSSELLINI: Yes, it's the story of two couples: an elephant and his sweetheart, and a poor mahout who has no time to spend with his own sweetheart except for the few moments his large, selfish friend is willing to spare him.

BOURDET: What you are describing for me is a prepatriarchal society. What happens when modernity irrupts into one of your jungle villages, or into other small hamlets with their dry-mud huts, like those I've seen on the outskirts of large cities?

ROSSELLINI: In the first place we must understand that the average villager, both in the jungle and in more cultivated areas, has no fear or admiration for our civilization. In fact, he seems to feel a great deal of scorn, both serene and full of irony, for what comes from the city, and, particularly, for anything resembling a government. He has seen so. many of them! That of the Brahmins, that of the Buddhist emperors, that of the Moslem and Mongolian conquerors, that of the English and now that of Nehru. To them, government means the tax collector, the sovereign's leech, an unbearable but inevitable evil, sidekick of another village canker, the moneylender, the usurer. Peasants look at both these people, their smooth talk, and insatiable greed, with a five-thousand-year-old reserve of skepticism.

BOURDET: Still, this defensive posture, as you see it, seems to me terribly fatalistic: it's at one with the caste system, this "each in his place" where each function is defined by heredity, and everything, though tempered by skepticism or spite, is accepted with resignation. How can such a civilization change? How can they wish for something different?

ROSSELLINI: Indeed that seems to have been the main problem: a material transformation of the country was not going to be enough, its fatalism had to be changed too. To transform things from top to bottom wouldn't have meant much; any other reform coming from high up would have been swallowed up and digested just as it had happened with the rule of the Buddhist emperors. The alarming problem was how to change five hundred and fifty-eight thousand villages with all their inhabitants. This is what we have been trying to do since 1952, following Gandhi's example.

BOURDET: Spinning wheel in hand?

ROSSELLINI: You mustn't be sarcastic, and you mustn't look at all this with the eyes of a Westerner, a citizen of an industrial, underpopulated country. The spinning wheel is just an accessory. I repeat it: it wasn't just a question of changing one village but five hundred and fifty-eight thousand. Villages that had been sleeping for thousands of years, waking up only briefly during the rains of the monsoons. The rest of the time there was no water, and no harvest. And yet the enormous and evergreen banyan tree seemed to indicate there was water somewhere deep down. And the water of the only well in the village seemed to be inexhaustible, enough for the twenty-five hundred inhabitants of the village to drink and wash with. There were seventeen castes, or sub-castes, each with its own jealously guarded activity. Even the lowest one, that of the Untouchables, had its own specially reserved tasks. When there was a need for money, or the harvests were particularly bad, one could always turn to the usurer who'd squeeze you a little drier the following year. Why change anything since that was the way things had always been?

One day, in 1952 or '53, a young man arrived at a village. He was twenty-six or twenty-seven years old. He came from the city. He had crossed the jungle. He said he was a Gram Sevak, or a "village worker." "Another tax collector, another guy who wants our money," the villagers thought. But this young man hadn't come to take anything away from them. Rather, he wanted to make them understand they could help themselves, and wanted to show them how. After a few months, he had managed to earn their trust. He had shown them there was water underground, and that all they had to do to have it was dig for it; he had shown them that there was some pottery clay not too far away, and that they could set up a cooperative brickyard and, by and by, transform their homes of clay and dry mud into brick houses; that with the water of the new wells and simple norias they could irrigate the fields and have two or three harvests a year instead of one; that since the precious cowpats could not be used as fertilizer, they could instead resort to green manure; that it was possible to spin and weave with less rudimentary machines, and that woven fabric, and even silk or golden ribbons, could be sold in the city. This is what the Gram Sevak has done. Have you ever seen a community development area?

BOURDET: Indeed, I have seen one of those renovated villages. It was still in a wretched condition, but it already had several wells, a few weaving shops that seemed to be working all right, and a few brick houses that had come to replace the otherwise rather unattractive mud-houses. And, above all, it had a population of young men and women who looked full of energy and interest.

ROSSELLINI: Don't believe for a second that it all happened by itself. Obviously the Gram Sevak who had produced such a change was worthy of his name. Unfortunately many of them come to a village with an attitude of condescension and officiousness. When they fail, the village is even worse off than before. And then there is the usual lack of understanding, petty jealousy, and bitter feuds among the clans that dominate the village. And centuries of fatalism to get over. In spite of it all, mistakes and other reverses notwithstanding, the villages are changing. What counts is not material results, still minimal and precarious, but the change in outlook, the fact that the villagers have discovered that they can change their lot. This is what counts. Whereas five years ago it was the hardest thing to get the villagers interested in any form of progress, now they are the ones who push forward, who spur the Gram Sevaks, who ask them questions to which they often have no answers.

BOURDET: But, honestly, Rossellini, how far do you think it can go? As I was going around I had the nagging feeling that, first, very few villages have been touched as yet, and, second, none of this has in any way affected either the caste or the property system.

ROSSELLINI: Up to now, one hundred and ninety-two thousand villages out of about five hundred and fifty thousand have been touched. These are, of course, the official numbers. No reason to doubt them, but in most cases only the surface has been scratched. Nevertheless, the movement is expanding and more rapidly than the government's capacity to fill the required posts. In some regions, however, it has met with total failure. In the state of Travancore-Cochin [present-day Kerala], for instance, as it is openly admitted by a very courageous book, *Kurukshetra*, published by the administration of community projects. This book explains how down there there is an already highly developed, educated population, which, due to an almost total absence of real villages, is living in natural communities with immense problems of poverty and unemployment that cannot be solved by educating the peasants since they are already much better educated than anywhere else. However, in the rest of India, the movement is spreading quite rapidly, and in a few years it will have reached almost all the villages. At that point, three hundred and eighty million Indians will open their eyes to their problems, to problems in general, even those that cannot be solved at a local level.

BOURDET: What do you have in mind? Industrialization? An agrarian reform? A political revolution?

ROSSELLINI: I'm telling you, everything starts from the village. The enormous Hirakud dam, inaugurated on January 13, with a reservoir that has formed a lake of seven hundred square kilometers, was built for the most by a real army of many thousands human ants, women in particular, who carried away the rubble in wicker baskets.

BOURDET: Indeed that would seem to be the best way to employ such an enormous amount of humanpower.

ROSSELLINI: I wouldn't be too sure. This is another Western idea. Huge dams, like Hirakud, are indeed quite useful, and the second five-year plan anticipates that half of the irrigation works will be of this kind. Nevertheless, a maximum utilization of manpower and a minimum utilization of capital, material, and machinery is more often than not achieved through local works, such as wells and other minor irrigation plans. As a result, during the first five-year plan, only a quarter of the three million hectares of land were irrigated by means of dams and other major works, while the remaining three quarters attained the same results with wells and other simpler solutions. In the next plan, the proportion will change to fifty-fifty. But the most important thing, which I've tried to show in the episode of my film devoted to Hirakud, was the sense of pride such a mammoth operation had awoken among the workers I interviewed—pride that the subordinate managerial staff of the administration were often unable to understand. Both these vast plans of industrialization and the development of villages have one point in common: be it in the fields or in a factory, the villagers are stepping into the modern age.

BOURDET: What about the agrarian reform? And unemployment?

ROSSELLINI: These are indeed the two fields where progress is till somewhat behind. The agrarian reform is still very theoretical. The movement for the collection of land by voluntary gift, promoted by Vinobha Bhav, a disciple of Gandhi, has already yielded two million hectares, but of the worst kind. In the villages, the development centers have been unable to change anything in the landed property system. The book I was telling you about, *Kurukshetra*, admits, in many of its articles, that the landless peasants are those who reap the least profit from the collective effort. Often, as Carl C. Taylor, one of the editors, points out: "One wonders whether they are anything more than battalions of workers working under a subtle social pressure and with very little hope of ever improving their lot." On the other hand, it's often enough to take a walk through these villages to notice the gradual disintegration of the caste system, an emerging awareness in politics, and the mixture of interest and incredulity of the villagers (those perpetual victims) at the fact that they are now urged to vote. All this should be enough to realize that once the five hundred and fifty-eight thousand villages have started to move, all these problems will have to be tackled, including that of landed property. Maybe some reactionary Indians, steeped in their Gandhist piety, had not seen what was coming. But Gandhi surely had.

BOURDET: And what about Nehru?

ROSSELLINI: Nehru isn't afraid of anything and will go as far as he wants. I give you an example. You know that the communists have won the electoral war and have seized power on both the democratic and parliamentary level in the state of Kerala, in the South. A few congress members would like to sabotage their victory: Nehru has opposed them and has formally forbidden anyone to stand in the way of the natural unfolding of this communist experience. Such a thing terrifies foreign capitalists but not the more serious Indian politicians. They have even coined a new expression around it: "If Kerala fails the communists have had it; if Kerala succeeds the communists have had it." Which simply means that if the communists of Kerala manage to solve their problems, they will turn into something quite different from the followers of Stalin: they will become Indian socialists.

BOURDET: In other words, you believe that the Indian stomach will even manage to digest communism.

ROSSELLINI: Maybe. Whatever the case, in a country which has always tragically suffered for a total absence of constructive opposition, in a country where the domination of a Congress representing a single party, has produced the traditional abuses characteristic of the single party system (corruption and nepotism) in numerous regions, the mere emergence of the communist government of Kerala has provoked a big wave of salutary civic consciousness. When the ministers of Kerala cut their own salaries, those of the central government and of numerous other states followed suit. Nehru has known this all along and that's why he has supported the experience of Kerala, which he sees as a necessary thorn in the side of Congress.

BOURDET: Dear Roberto, you have an answer for every question and, all in all, you seem quite optimistic for the future of India.

ROSSELLINI: I've only given you a large picture of the situation. I haven't told you about all the ills and troubles of the administration: its slowness, its inefficiency, its stubbornness, its diffidence—an administration that's far worse that those of France and Italy put together. I haven't told you about the Brahmins who, having gradually lost all their privileges as the highest caste, have automatically become all-powerful civil servants simply because they can read and write. I haven't told you about a new form of discrimination, more cruel and insidious than the old caste system, the distinction between the literate and the illiterate. But I assure you that none of this matters. This remains one of the best people in the world. Dear Claude Bourdet, I'm a hard nut to crack: I have known people in just about every country, and here I have found more shit than anywhere else, and not because of the cows. Yet, I've often been moved to tears during my conversations with some Indian villagers. All I want to do is introduce them to the entire world. That's the purpose of my film. If there is anything I can do, this is it.

I left Rossellini eight days ago. Will this wonderful project, already three-quarters done, this Paisan *of the jungle, villages and towns of this huge maternal subcontinent ever see the light? Because Rossellini hasn't lost twenty-five kilos just because of the heat. It's also because of the "Rossellini affair," the scandal mounted against him by professional muckrakers and cheap rags in search of an audience, with the collaboration of rival and envious film producers, and, of course, the inevitable American journalist, out for the kill, conscious agent or occasional instrument of the Hollywood industry that never forgave Rossellini for having kidnapped Ingrid Bergman.*

What's most frightening is that here, in India, in this new nation where a brand new film industry occupies such an important place and plays such a powerful political role, the plot against Rossellini has attained a virulence and a power that would be hard to imagine anywhere else. Under the pressure of the Indian cinema bourgeoisie, a few big government figures have been trying to prevent Rossellini from completing his film. All they have to do to achieve their aim is refuse to extend his visa. Rossellini's only hope, and last trump, is Nehru and his sense of justice. Can the head of one of the largest countries in the world, the leader of a national and international politics of progress and wisdom, let such a staunch advocate of the new India fall victim to his old-fashioned cronies? Hard to believe. Rossellini's film might yet become, at a modest but most revealing level, a touchstone in the future of India.

"L'Inde que j'ai vu," in France Observateur, *4 July 1957.*

CINEMA AND TELEVISION

JEAN RENOIR AND ROBERTO ROSSELLINI INTERVIEWED
BY ANDRÉ BAZIN

RENOIR: I am preparing a film version of Stevenson's *Dr. Jekyll and Mr. Hyde* for television. Although I've transferred the story to the present day, and to Paris, my adaptation is still faithful to the original. I'm going to introduce the program with a little talk, as if it had to do with something uncanny that really happened a short time ago in a street in Paris.

ROSSELLINI: My first program for French television will be about India. I made ten short films while I was there, with television in mind, and I'm doing the commentary myself as well as providing the necessary linking passages.

BAZIN: When you're making a television film, Mr. Renoir—shooting more or less off the cuff with several cameras—do you manage to keep a sense of actuality in the direction itself?

RENOIR: I would like to make this film—and this is where television gives me something valuable—in the spirit of *live* television. I'd like to make the film as though it were a live broadcast, shooting each scene only once, with the actors imagining that the public is directly receiving their words and gestures. Both the actors and the technicians should know that there will be no retakes; that, whether they succeed or not, they can't begin again.

In any case, we can only shoot once, since some parts of this film are being shot out in the streets and we can't afford to let the passersby realize that we're filming. And so the actors and technicians must feel that every movement is final and irrevocable. I'd like to break with cinema technique, and very patiently build a large wall with little stones.

BAZIN: Obviously this kind of film can be made much more quickly than an ordinary cinema production.

RENOIR: I've just done a shooting script, and the result works out at a little under four hundred shots. For some reason, I've discovered by experience that my shots usually average out at about five or six meters each (sixteen to twenty feet), though I know it sounds a bit ridiculous to gauge things this way. . . . Anyhow, I imagine that four hundred shots will give me a film of about sixty-five hundred feet or in other words, of average length.

BAZIN: Are you thinking of showing the film in the commercial cinema as well as on TV?

RENOIR: I don't know yet. I'll probably try it out with an ordinary cinema audience. I think that television now has sufficient importance for the public to accept films "presented" in a different way. I mean that the effects achieved are no longer entirely dependent on the will of the director and the cameraman—the camera can produce effects almost by chance, as sometimes happens when you get a wonderful newsreel shot.

BAZIN: But doesn't television present a classic problem in technique— that of the quality and small size of the image? The Americans seem to lay down certain rules in shooting, the main actors have to remain inside a sort of square in order to keep the action always in the picture. . . . Do all these restrictions of the medium frighten you at all?

RENOIR: No, because the method I'd like to adopt will be something between the American and French approach. I believe that if one follows the American TV technique, one risks making a film which it will be difficult for audiences to accept on the screen. But by adapting these techniques, one should be able to arrive at a new cinematographic style which could be extremely interesting. It all depends, I think, on the starting point, the conception.

I believe Roberto would agree with me that in the cinema at present the camera has become a sort of god. You have a camera, fixed on its tripod or crane, which is just like a heathen altar; about it are the high priests—the director, cameraman, assistants—who bring victims before the camera, like burnt offerings, and cast them into the flames. And the camera is there, immobile—or almost so—and when it does move it follows patterns ordained by the high priests, not by the victims.

Now, I am trying to extend my old ideas, and to establish that the camera finally has only one right—that of recording what happens. That's all. I don't want the movements of the actors to be determined by the camera, but the movements of the camera to be determined by the actor. This means working rather like a newsreel cameraman. When a newsreel cameraman films a race, for instance, he doesn't ask the runners to start from the exact spot that suits him. He has to manage things so that he can film the race wherever it happens. Or take an accident, a fire. It is the cameraman's duty to make it possible for us to see a spectacle, rather than the duty of the spectacle to take place for the benefit of the camera.

ROSSELLINI: I think what Renoir has just said brings out the real problem of film and television. In practice, there are, strictly speaking, hardly any really creative artists in the cinema: there has been a variety of artists who come together, pool their ideas, then translate and record them on film. And the actual filming itself is very often secondary. The real creative artist in the cinema is someone who can get the most out of everything he sees—even if he sometimes does this by accident.

RENOIR: That's the point. The creator of a film isn't at all an organizer: he isn't like a man who decides, for instance, how a funeral should be conducted. He is rather the man who finds himself watching a funeral he never expected to see, and sees the corpse, instead of lying in its coffin, getting up to dance, sees the relations, instead of weeping, running about all over the place. It's for him, and his colleagues to capture this and then, in the cutting room, to make a work of art out of it.

ROSSELLINI: Not only in the cutting room. Because I don't know whether, today, *montage* is so essential. I believe we should begin to look at the cinema in a new way, and to start with abandon all the old myths. The cinema at first was a technical discovery; and everything, even editing, was subordinated to that. Then, in the silent cinema, *montage* had a precise meaning because it represented language. From the silent cinema we have inherited this myth of *montage*, though it has lost most of its meaning. Consequently, it is in the images themselves that the creative artist can really bring his own observation to bear his own moral view, his particular vision.

RENOIR: Yes, when I spoke of editing I was using a convenient phrase. I should, rather, have talked of choice . . . rather like Cartier-Bresson choosing three pictures out of the hundred he's taken of some incident, and those three are the best.

BAZIN: Television is still rather frowned upon—particularly by the intellectuals. How did you come to it?

RENOIR: Through being immensely bored by a great number of contemporary films, and being less bored by certain television programs. I ought to say that the television shows I've found most exciting have been certain interviews on American TV. I feel that the interview gives the television close-up a meaning which is rarely achieved in the cinema. The close-up in the cinema is essentially a reconstruction, something prefabricated, carefully worked up—and, of course, this has yielded some great moments in the cinema. This said, I believe that in thirty years we have rather used up this type of cinema and that we should perhaps move on to something else. In America I've seen some exceptional television shows. Not because the people working there have more talent than in France or anywhere else, but simply because, in a town like Los Angeles, there are ten channels operating constantly. In these circumstances, obviously, one has the chance of finding remarkable things . . .

I remember, for instance, certain interviews in connection with some political hearing. Here, suddenly, we had a huge close-up, a picture of a human being in his entirety. One man was afraid, and all his fear showed; another was insolent, insulted the questioner; another was ironical; another took it all very lightly. In two minutes, we could read the faces of these people, we knew who they were. I found this tremendously exciting . . . and somehow an indecent spectacle to watch. Yet this indecency came nearer the knowledge of man than many films.

ROSSELLINI: In modern society, men have an enormous need to know each other. Modern society and modern art have been destructive of man; but television is an aid to his rediscovery. Television, an art without traditions, dares to go out to look for man.

BAZIN: There was a stage when the cinema appeared to be doing the same—particularly at the time of the great documentaries, of Flaherty.

ROSSELLINI: Very few people were looking for man, and a great many were doing everything necessary for him to be forgotten. . . . The television audience is quite different from that of the cinema. In television you're talking not to the mass public but to ten million individuals; and the discussion becomes much more intimate, more persuasive. You know how many setbacks I've had in my cinema career. . . . Well, I realized that the films which were the most complete failures with the public were just those which, in a little projection theatre before a dozen people, pleased the most.

RENOIR: I can confirm that. If we were to have a competition of failures, I'm not sure which of us would win.

ROSSELLINI: I'd win; I'd bet you by a long way. . . .

RENOIR: I'm not sure. I have the advantage of age. . . . Be that as it may, take the example of my film *Diary of a Chambermaid*. It was very badly received, mainly because of its title. People expected to laugh their heads off at a film with Paulette Goddard called *Diary of a Chambermaid;* they didn't, and they were dissatisfied. In the early days of television a TV company bought this film and it is still watched with admiration by enthusiasts. Thanks to television I've made a great deal of money out of it. I thought that I'd made a cinema film; and in fact, without realizing it, I'd made one for television.

ROSSELLINI: I had an interesting experience with *A Human Voice*. I wanted to establish the film's capacity to penetrate to the very roots of a character. Now, with television, one rediscovers these feelings.

BAZIN: If cinema audiences at first looked to films for something richer than television could give them, perhaps now, accustomed to the limitation of television, they are ready to take something simpler from the cinema again. This might mean a reconsideration of the conditions of film production.

RENOIR: At present, if a film's to be sure of a sale in the French market, it has to be a coproduction. To be sold abroad, it has to consider the tastes of different audiences, and one ends up by making films which lose all their national character. But the curious thing is that national character is what attracts international audiences. So the cinema is in danger of losing both its individuality *and* its market.

BAZIN: So the answer, as you see it, is that films should be able to recover their costs in the home market, and should in consequence be made more cheaply?

RENOIR: Exactly. For instance, I hawked the script of *Grand Illusion* around all the film companies for three years and no one would touch it. But at that time they did not have the excuse of not wanting to take risks since films were paying their way. *Grand Illusion,* for instance, had recovered its costs after its run at the Marivaux Cinema in Paris. Money was easier to come by and one could afford to experiment. The trouble about the present cost of films is that you either have a sensational success or you lose a lot of money. As a result producers play safe, and when one plays safe art is no longer possible.

ROSSELLINI: I think the mistake of European producers is in trying to follow the American pattern without realizing that the whole basis of American production is completely different from our own. . . . But there may be other reasons of a moral, or even a strictly political, nature. All the mass culture media have had an enormous success; and in profiting from this public appetite the people feeding it have supplied a false culture, simply in order to condition the masses in the way which best suited certain great powers.

RENOIR: I'm not so sure of that. . . . I have a sort of faith in the immense stupidity of the men who run gigantic enterprises, I believe they are always naïve children, rushing headlong towards what looks as though it ought to bring them money. I believe that the word "commercial" haunts them, and provided they bring out a product which is theoretically commercial they are quite happy. The word, in the cinema, means a film which has no daring, which corresponds to certain preconceived ideas. A commercial film isn't necessarily one that makes money. . . .

ROSSELLINI: You once said to me that the commercial label went to the film whose aesthetic ideal was that wanted by the producer.

RENOIR: Just that: and this ideal doesn't, I think, derive from anything more than the practice of a naïve, incomprehensible religion—and one which even works against their own interests. I don't believe that the producers are powerful enough, or cunning enough, to be Talleyrands trying to remould the world in their own image.

For instance, for film production to continue as at present, it needs a well-organized, stable society. It is in the interests of the producers to maintain a certain standard of morality, since if they don't do this immoral films won't sell. But at the moment we're rushing headlong towards the production of films which undermine all the accepted rules for social survival. If you like to see Mme. Brigitte Bardot making love simultaneously with her lover and her maid, it's because you think this is prohibited. But too many films like this will make people think this is normal. Well, these people are going to ruin themselves. . . .

ROSSELLINI: Yes, the producers have ended up by creating ersatz substitutes for human emotions. Love, passion, tragedy—all emotions are deformed.

RENOIR: During the hundred years of romanticism, it was possible to score a great theatrical success by relying on the fact that the daughter of a workman couldn't marry the son of a duke. And this was because people believed in social differences. Society, by maintaining its faith in social divisions, also maintained the conditions in which such drama could succeed. . . . Each work of art contains a little morsel of protest. But if this protest turns into destruction, if the system blows up, the possibility of such drama at once vanishes. This is what is happening now. We have got to the stage of little amorous reunions such as I mentioned. The next time, I suppose, father will be one of the three, making love to the girl. Then it will be mother . . . And what comes after that? The moment will come when no one knows how to outbid the last player.

I am sure that the great quality of the early American films sprang from an American puritanism which put up barriers to American passions. When we saw Lillian Gish, who was probably going to be assaulted by the villain, we trembled . . . it meant something. Today, what can you do with the rape of a girl who has already made love to the entire town?

ROSSELLINI: In the last analysis, people instinctively construct the society they desire.

RENOIR: Absolutely. Certain restrictions are extremely useful for artistic expression, and though it sounds a paradox, absolute freedom doesn't permit absolute artistic expression. We can only hope that people will reconstruct the barriers, as they did for instance in painting. Cubism, after all, was nothing but a deliberate constraint adopted after the exaggerated and destructive freedoms of post-impressionism. . . .

BAZIN: You both seem to approach television in different ways. You, Mr. Renoir, are again looking for the *commedia dell'arte* spirit which always attracts you; and you, Mr. Rossellini, seem to be returning to the interests which made you the originator of Italian neorealism.

ROSSELLINI: Someone—I've forgotten who—said that we are living in an era of barbarian invasions. We're also living at a time when man's knowledge is becoming ever deeper, but when every man is a specialist. This disturbs me, and I'm returning to documentary because I want to hold people up to people. I would like to escape from this rigid specialization and return to the broader knowledge which makes it possible to achieve a synthesis . . . because that after all, is what matters.

BAZIN: You made *India '58* and the documentaries for television at the same time. Do you think the documentaries influenced the other film?

ROSSELLINI: In the documentaries I was exploring a precise world, and in the film I tried to summarize my experience of it. The two things complement each other.

RENOIR: I can define Roberto's position and my own: Roberto is continuing the pure French tradition—of investigating humanity: I try to be Italian and rediscover the *commedia dell'arte*.

ROSSELLINI: I'm striving to set moving a variety of enterprises, not just a single film; if you produce a range of work, you can, in a way, help toward forming public taste. It's very difficult for me to find a screen subject at present: there are no more heroes in life, only miniature heroisms, and I don't know where to look for a story. . . . What I am trying to do is a piece of research, a documentation, on the state of man today all over the world. And as I find dramatic subjects, exalting heroes, I may move toward a fiction film. But the first stage is the research, the observation, and this has got to be systematic. Think of everything there is in the world—all the folk music, the needs of radio, of the record industry. You can find heaps of things—in Peru, Mexico, Haiti—that will pay for the enterprise without tying you up in big capital expenditure.

RENOIR: I think there is another reason for our interest in television, Roberto. It may be because the importance of technique in the cinema has vanished during the last few years. When I began in films, you had to know your trade thoroughly, to have all your technical skill at your fingertips. We didn't know, for instance, how to make a dissolve in the laboratory, and because you had to do it in the camera you had to be absolutely clear in your own mind about when you wanted the scene to end. . . . Nowadays a director would waste time if he concerned himself with technical problems. He becomes something much closer to a theatrical than a literary author.

The Bayeux Tapestry is more beautiful than the modern Gobelin's tapestry. Why? Because Queen Mathilda had to say to herself: "I haven't any red, I'll have to use brown; I haven't any blue, I must use some color like blue . . ." Obliged to make use of crude contrasts, constantly struggling against imperfections, her technical difficulties helped her to create great art. If the job is technically easy, that spur to creation does not exist; and at the same time the artist is free to apply his invention to different forms. Today, in fact, if I conceive a story for the cinema, that story would do just as well for the stage, or for a book, or for television. . . .

All the industrial arts (and, after all, the cinema is simply an industrial art) have been great at the beginning and have been debased as they perfected themselves. It's the same thing, for instance, in pottery. I did some work in ceramics myself, trying to rediscover the technical simplicity of the early days, and the best I could manage was a false "primitivism" since I deliberately rejected all the developments of the potter's technique. Instead I plunged into a genuinely primitive trade: the cinema.

But the cinema is moving the same way. The people who made those fine early American or German or Swedish films weren't all great artists—some were very indifferent ones—but all their pictures were beautiful. Why? Because the technique was difficult . . . In France, after the splendid first period, after Méliès and Max Linder, films became worthless. Why? Because we were intellectuals trying to make "art" films, to produce masterpieces. In fact, the moment one can allow oneself to become an intellectual instead of an artisan, one is falling into danger. And if you and I, Roberto, are turning toward television, it is because television is in a technically primitive state which may restore to artists that fighting spirit of the early cinema, when everything that was made was good.

"Cinéma et Télévision. Un entretien d'André Bazin avec Jean Renoir et Roberto Rossellini," in France Observateur, *July 4, 1958, pp. 16-18. Original French text edited by André Bazin, Jean Herman and Claude Choublier.*

AN INTERVIEW WITH *CAHIERS DU CINÉMA*

BY FEREYDOUN HOVEYDA AND JACQUES RIVETTE

We know that Roberto Rossellini has brought back two films from his trip through India.[1] The first one, shot in 16 millimeter, is currently the subject of a TV program, J'ai fait un beau voyage,[2] *the second one, shot in 35 millimeter, is being turned into a full-length film tentatively titled* India '58. *There is still some work to do on both the editing and the soundtrack. Nevertheless, moved by our impatient curiosity, Rossellini has consented to invite us to a private screening of the working copy of the film.*

CAHIERS: Did you film the television documentary first?

ROSSELLINI: Yes, it gave me the opportunity to prepare for the film and to get to know India. At first I just wanted to see, to make a simple reportage, without any particular purpose; I didn't even have a particular cinematic product in mind. The film, on the contrary, has a clear dramatic development. In the film I have tried to express the emotions aroused by India, the inner warmth of the Indian people. I have tried, if I may say so without seeming ridiculous, to give a poetical expression to my feelings as a reporter.

CAHIERS: Is this why you have deliberately edited out of the film any sketch relating to the cities?

1 See "Rossellini tourne *India '57*" by Jean Herman, in *Cahiers du cinéma*, no. 73, July 1957.
2 *L'India vista da Rossellini*, in the version broadcast by the Italian television.

ROSSELLINI: Yes and no. I had started with the idea of including a much larger number of episodes, and I filmed all I could. I had to make a choice and confine myself to what I found most particular, to what allowed me to reach a deeper and deeper understanding of India. So, I left out all the episodes that seemed a little too explanatory or technical.

CAHIERS: Why do animals play such an important role in the movie?

ROSSELLINI: Because they are very important in India. What struck me most, coming back, is the total absence of nature in our countries. There, people live in nature. It's very important: even very modern people, as the Indian people are, live very close to nature, all the time. Nature is very present, also in the cities. No need to go to the country: nature is in the cities. Here nature no longer exists. Not even in the country. The trees one finds in the Bois de Boulogne are trees, sure, but they are not nature.

CAHIERS: Is this the reason why you start your film with a documentary sequence on the cities and end it with nature?

ROSSELLINI: Yes. I begin with a documentary because that is the reality that allows me to delve deeper into things. If I had filmed all the episodes that I had contemplated, the film would have been very long. Fortunately I met with all sorts of problems, the climate, the enormous distances. Every time we had to move it took two weeks. Our material suffered. The film melted in the heat: we had to jump from one air-conditioned room to the next.

CAHIERS: What criteria did you use to eliminate certain sketches?

ROSSELLINI: I started by doing those I considered most urgent, the ones I had no doubt about, in order to be freer later on. And I cut out all the more expository ones, the more technical, the least—I don't know, I feel uneasy using this word—poetical. There are three episodes that I deliberately put aside. The first one was a story meant to illustrate the contrast between modern and ancient India. It was the story of the widow of an industrial tycoon who had been unhappy all her life because her husband only cared about his business. But when her husband dies and his brother wants to close up shop and sell the business, the widow refuses. She feels it would be a betrayal of her husband. She sells her jewels and everything else she has to buy out her brother-in-law and keep the business going, though she knows from the very start that all her efforts are doomed to failure. She does it anyway because it is a sign, a proof of her fidelity. I eliminated this episode because it was less typically Indian than some of the other ones. It could have happened anywhere—though in India the family is very important.

The second episode focused on community projects, those national undertakings whose aim is the development of villages, the agricultural reform, etc. This is one of the oddest aspects of India: the people the government sends to the villages generally have a rather sound knowledge of agriculture, yet they are not sent as teachers but as servants, to be at the disposal of the village, and only if the village wants them. The results have been astounding. This sort of thing is very interesting but I have had to give it up because it is more important politically than poetically, and the episode involving the dam already expressed pretty much the same ideas.

As for the third episode, it was a sort of fable that took place in a mountain village where two or three hermits had withdrawn to live a life of contemplation. The silence, among those immense mountains, is extraordinary. Then, suddenly there is noise. Big trucks start travelling up and down the road that crosses the village. A hundred kilometers up the road a dam is being built, or something like that. The two or three hermits decide to leave. But the village doesn't want to let them go, and, though it draws quite a bit of profit from the recent progress (being inhabited by small artisans and weavers who are now earning their livelihood more easily selling Coca-Cola and gasoline), in order to keep its hermits decides to build a detour. And then they have to reconquer silence, which, once its sense is gone, is one of the most difficult things to reconquer. Doors, windows, the slightest things, everything is noise. The conquest was to take a long time and a great deal of patience. It was a very nice story, but a little too constructed. It was a fable, a fairy tale. And I wanted no fables in my film.

CAHIERS: And yet all your sketches have the look of fairy tales.

ROSSELLINI: Maybe, but they are first and foremost real events which I have filmed such as they were. There is no moral to be drawn out of them. They are events that are there and that show what is man, people, nature, and so on and so forth. The sketch I have just told you about had a moral, and that bothered me.

CAHIERS: The idea of noise returns in the episode about the tiger, where the sudden arrival of a generator destroys the harmony of the jungle.

ROSSELLINI: Yes, but the episode of the tiger has the advantage of being much simpler. Here we really have man and nature. The natural balance is broken, so something is bound to happen. The other sketch was a little more elaborate: it fell somewhat beyond the scope of *India '58*.

You see, in India nature is so very obvious, so powerfully obvious! I have tried to tear through the myth and look at things in their reality. For instance, the monkey man dies because there is a heat storm. It is a meteorological event so powerful that it affects men in rather dramatic ways. I had started out with the firm intention of avoiding commonplaces, which in India include tigers, elephants, cobras, etc. However, commonplaces originate in a reality which must be looked at squarely for what it is. What's most striking in India (as I point out in my television broadcasts) is the simultaneity of history. You are steeped in the most primitive humanity while living in modern times. Samples of every historical period are there, coexisting right under your eyes, at the same level. This is what has struck me most about India.

CAHIERS: Wasn't there one more episode in your initial project: the story of a woman, the head of a gang?

ROSSELLINI: I dropped that one immediately because I had come up with that idea reading the papers, in Europe. It was right for a certain kind of sensationalist journalism. There was nothing in it.

CAHIERS: And what about the story of a very rich man who suddenly decides to get rid of all his riches and go beg on the road?

ROSSELLINI: It wasn't a real sketch. I knew that that sort of thing happens quite frequently in India, but it was only a general idea: I haven't done anything with it.

CAHIERS: Did India turn out to be quite different from what you expected?

ROSSELLINI: Yes, India is profoundly different. What I mean is that on the surface it can even resemble your image of it, but not profoundly. For instance, one often speaks of Indian mysticism. And indeed, Indians are mystical, that is, they grant a great deal of importance to metaphysical life. But it is also true that they are extremely realistic, extremely concrete. They have a Cartesian mind, and at the same time are quite materialistic.

CAHIERS: Why India? Had you been thinking of it for a long time?

ROSSELLINI: If I thought about India it is because this country has recently won a great battle with the most modest means. They were able to turn nonviolence into an extremely effective political instrument. Of course the support of the English Labour Party was essential in securing this victory, but it's also true that the struggle down there was carried out according to methods that are totally unfamiliar to us. Being absolutely intolerant, we must always assert our desires or our dreams with the butt of our guns, because we have no time to let our opponents change their mind and accept, or get closer through reasoning. This is, first and foremost, what has drawn me to India.

CAHIERS: In this case, why didn't you construct one single story instead of confining yourself to a few particular aspects?

ROSSELLINI: Yes, they are particular aspects, fragments, but India is something so very complex that, if you don't take something here, and something there, from all its different facets, I don't think you'll ever be able to construct anything at all. A single story would be something very false. Don't you think?

CAHIERS: In other words you go back to the spirit of *Paisan*. Does this mean that *India* marks a break from your previous films?

ROSSELLINI: After you've walked for a while in a certain direction, you lose your curiosity, your enthusiasm. You start seizing on to new things. After all, I am still moved by the same need to understand people, individuals. Besides, some of my later movies were rather biographical. They were my own fables (at least today I can see it, if I didn't there and then). And I also felt the need to seek new sources, and since I couldn't find any here, I went to India. What I would like to know is whether seeing the film, and leaving aside the anecdotes, one comes out with the impression of a world. Because the goal of my film was to produce that impression. What method I chose to achieve that goal is irrelevant. The goal is all that matters, and only you, the public, can decide whether it was important to show that world or not. In *Voyage in Italy* it was necessary to evoke a particular ambiance. What mattered there was not so much the discovery of a country as its dramatic impact on the two characters—it was the third element: on the one side the couple, on the other Italy. In India, the premises are not anchored in a conflict. What matters is that the spectators leave the theater with an impression similar to the one I received while I was there.

CAHIERS: Why did you place the monkey episode last? Because it is the most dramatic?

ROSSELLINI: It's difficult to say because everything is based on feelings. I think that at that particular moment certain feelings become not only subtler but sharper, more impassioned. I didn't place this episode at the end because it was the most dramatic, but because it illustrates the perfect rule of Nature. The vultures are waiting, but they are not going to eat the man because he is not dead. They must wait for the death decree. The death of the man must be legalized for the vultures—part of nature—to accomplish their natural function. That's already quite extraordinary. So, when his master dies, the poor monkey, who at this point is no more a monkey than a man, feels the need to go at once to the monkeys and to the men, to go back and move on. That's a drama we all share, the struggle we all are involved in.

CAHIERS: During the screening of your film we were aware of something like a determination to pare the story down to the barest essentials. Is that so?

ROSSELLINI: Yes, it's even more than a determination. It's a constant effort. In his article on *Voyage in Italy*,[3] Rivette compared me to Matisse. It struck me and made me particularly aware of this spare-

3 "Lettre sur Rossellini," *Cahiers du Cinéma*, no. 46, April 1955.

ness. A spareness that represents a new effort for me, but when I manage to achieve it my satisfaction is boundless.

CAHIERS: In your interview with Renoir and Bazin, published in *France Observateur*,[4] you expressed an unfavorable opinion of film editing.

ROSSELLINI: Yes, film editing is no longer necessary. Everything is there—particularly in this film. Why fiddle with anything? Those who make films believe that cinema is always somewhat of a miracle. We go to a screening and see things moving on the screen: it's quite astounding. We understand what the actors say: and that's also astounding. The technical aspect of filmmaking is always astounding: I don't find it so, but lots of people do. The same is true for editing: it's a little like the magician's hat. You fill it with all sorts of techniques and then pull out a pigeon, a bunch of flowers, a pitcher full of water. Then you shake it up a bit and pull out one more pigeon, one more bunch of flowers, one more pitcher of water . . . This sort of editing bothers me; I don't find it necessary. I am talking about editing in the most classical sense of the word, of the sort one learns at the IDHEC.[5] It was probably necessary at the time of silent movies. None of Stroheim's movies would exist without editing. Stroheim would shoot up to ten versions of the same scene and then choose the one that seemed most effective. At that time they were still trying to put together the proper cinematic language—language as instrument not as poetry.

Today that's no longer necessary. Of course there is some editing in my film, but the sort of editing that has to do with the best utilization of the material I have, not with language.

CAHIERS: At the time of silent movies what was filmed had very little reality in itself. The reality of the film was the result of editing.

ROSSELLINI: And there is another important factor. Today a film camera can move. Then it couldn't. Then even the idea of doing tracking shots seemed absurd.

---

4 "Cinéma et Télévision. Un entretien d'André Bazin avec Jean Renoir et Roberto Rossellini," *France Observateur*, July 4, 1958, pp. 16–18. [In this volume, pp. 90–99]

5 IDHEC=Institut des Hautes Etudes Cinématographiques, a French film school.

CAHIERS: So, your editing doesn't follow any particular plan?

ROSSELLINI: None. I don't premeditate anything. On the other hand I have a quick eye and rely on what I see. I know that if the eye is drawn to certain things, it means that they are legitimate. I am not trying to philosophize over it. . . . But no, I really don't see any interest in traditional editing. I always try to seize things in movement. And I don't have to follow any movement through to get to the next shot. When I have shown the essential I cut: that's it. What matters is to connect what's in the image. If you examine my editing with the eyes of a filmmaker then I can see how it might bother you, but I don't think it's necessary to look at it with the eyes of a filmmaker.

CAHIERS: André Bazin mistrusted any optical effect resulting from editing. According to him, one had to show the tiger and the man in the same shot. Your film shows them separately.

ROSSELLINI: If you have to make the story more believable, then, of course, it is better to show the man and the tiger in the same shot. But if the story is already believable for other reasons, I don't see why you'd have to use a particular technique. Everything depends on what you want to do. I do not want to create a sensation. On the other hand, from his point of view, Bazin was right. If you want to create a sensation, then you can be sure that the sensation is going to be much stronger if you show man and tiger at the same time. But my story doesn't need a sensation. You remember how the episode starts: a long track through the jungle during which you hear the love song of the tigers. Maybe it wasn't even necessary to show the tigers. I show them to underline what's going on.

I never calculate. I know what I want to say and always go for the most direct way of saying it. That's all. I don't lose sleep over it. If it is said, I don't care how it is said. You assure me that my film gives the impression that everything was planned in advance. No, nothing was planned in advance, but the ideas were fast and clear. If there was a choice it was at the level of the idea. What matters is ideas, not images, if you have very clear ideas in your head you will find the most direct images to express them.

CAHIERS: Isn't that your creed as a filmmaker?

ROSSELLINI: Yes. Ideas can be expressed in a thousand ways, by writing, for instance, if I were a writer. The only advantage of a film is that it can place ten things in the same frame. No need to be analytical in the movies—though it can't be helped.

CAHIERS: Can we ask you the opposite of what we just asked you? Why didn't you make a simple documentary, à la Flaherty?

ROSSELLINI: What mattered to me was people. I wanted to express the soul, the light that's inside these people, their reality—a reality that's so absolutely intimate, unique, attached to an individual with the meaning of the things that surround him. Because the things that surround him have a meaning, since there is someone who's looking at them, or, in the least, their meaning is unique by virtue of the fact that there is someone looking at them: the hero of each of the episodes, who is also the narrator. If I had made a simple documentary, I would have had to let go of what was happening within, in the heart of these men. But even in that case, to bring the documentary to an end, I think I would have had to look into the heart of those men.

CAHIERS: In other words it is a return to the beginning of neo-realism.

ROSSELLINI: Yes, that's what it is.

CAHIERS: But, if we may ask you again, why India? Couldn't you have done what you did in Brazil, or even in France or Italy?

ROSSELLINI: Yes. I can even tell you that all this Indian adventure to me has been a sort of study for a much vaster project that I have already begun to set up.

I believe that all the means we have been using to diffuse culture have become sterile for the simple reason that we have totally abandoned the study of humanity such as it is. We have started offering stereotypes of human beings, the ersatz of feelings, of love, death, sex, morality. We deal with false problems because we live in a civilization whose banner is optimism. Everything is fine, except for a few trifles. We have built false problems that way. Like, for instance—and this is one of the clichés I find most irritating—that of youth. Youth has always been and will always be a problem. It is not a twentieth-century problem. It can express itself in different ways: kicking an old lady in the belly, for instance (though today one would probably rather spit in her face). The revolt of children against parents has always existed, from the beginning of history. Every time a new generation steps in, it has to revolt as part of its function, otherwise it would be of no use.

Today everybody's concerned with false problems while the real problems are totally forgotten. And what are these real problems? First of all we must know people as they are. We must begin with an act of profound humility, and try to get closer to people, and see them as they are with objectivity, without any preconceived idea, without any moral standard, at least at the beginning. I have a very deep respect for human beings. Even the most horrible man is worthy of respect. What matters is to figure out why he is horrible. I don't allow myself the right to condemn anyone.

Even now that the world has become so small, we go on without knowing one another. We don't know our neighbors, the people who live on the other side of the river, in Switzerland! Today, when we live side by side, it is very important that we begin to know one another. Only a profound knowledge of humanity, a real and unprejudiced analysis of the feelings, the tenderness, the warmth that one individual can feel for another individual, can lead us to a solution of all the problems we are facing today—problems that are, even technically, different from those of other times.

Maybe this is taking us a long way from our initial point, but I must explain what my moral concerns are. Abstract art has become the official art. I can understand an abstract painter, but I cannot understand how abstract art could become the official art form since it is the least intelligible. This sort of phenomenon never happens without a reason. What is the reason? It's that we are trying to forget people as much as possible. People, in modern society and in the entire world, except perhaps in Asia, have become the gears of an immense, gigantic machine.

They have become slaves. And all the history of humanity consists of innumerable passages from slavery to freedom. There have always been moments when slavery had the upper hand, and then freedom would again prevail, but seldom, and only for a short time, for no sooner would freedom be reconquered than slavery would be reestablished. In our modern world we have created a new form of slavery. And what is it? The slavery of ideas. The slavery of ideas by every possible means, be it a detective novel, a radio program, or a film. This is also due to the fact that techniques have grown more and more refined, and that the acquisition of in-depth knowledge in a specific field, necessary for social recognition, prevents people from acquiring a wider knowledge of the world. I can't remember who said: "We live in the century of a vertical barbarian invasion," that is to say, the extreme deepening of knowledge in one field, and utter ignorance in all the other fields.

Since I first got into cinema, I have heard people say that films should be addressed to a public that has the intellectual maturity of a twelve-year-old. And indeed, it is true that cinema (in general), just like radio, television, and all other forms of entertainment meant for the masses, brings about the cretinization of adults just as it immensely accelerates the development of children. That's where the imbalance of the modern world originates: from the impossibility of ever understanding one another.

This is one problem that should be addressed very seriously today: how to disseminate the knowledge of things and ideas, how to arouse people's curiosity about what they don't know. I do not believe in that kind of smiley optimism that makes a terminally-ill president appear on television all spruced up like a Hollywood star to broadcast great health and liveliness when everybody knows he's all rotten inside. That sort of optimism can lead us to the worst disasters. What are we to think of a world that believes itself perfectly happy, and which, in order to be happy, has to drink itself silly, go to the shrink, sniff cocaine, or stuff itself with tranquilizers? Tranquilizers have become daily remedies: at the slightest surge of anxiety one pops a pill and everything is fine. But life has no longer any meaning: since the meaning of intelligent life is, in the etymological sense of the word, "to understand" things "inside."

Understand: that's what we must do today, because before our eyes a new world is being born where extraordinary technological discoveries are constantly made. Of course, here and there, there is always someone who has some sense, albeit very vague, of what he is doing. Everybody else has fun, as though they were just reading a novel.

They have no idea of what is going to happen in the world. That's why lies are so widespread. More than ever, if you ask me.

Do you want me to give you an example of the power of advertising? I have read it in the book *The Hidden Persuaders*, by Vance Packard. It has to do with chocolate. Ten or fifteen years ago it was sold in large bars. Small chocolates were very rare. Then toothpaste ads took over ("chocolate causes cavities"), along with slim figures (as I am fat, I always side with fat people). And suddenly chocolate consumption fell drastically all over the world. Cocoa farmers were starving, children were suffering from dropsy, it was terrible. Chocolate was a dying industry, it had to be resurrected. The problem was tackled in the most serious and scientific way possible. It was soon agreed that the best way to get out of that bind was to present chocolate in a way that would assuage the feeling of guilt of the consumer. And that's how they started promoting small chocolates. Business immediately took a leap forward, children stopped getting dropsy, etc. . . . It is terrible, don't you think?

Today, every instant of the day, the individual is invaded by things coming from the outside, all of them threatening. In the end, everything is threatening. The slogan "Drink Coca-Cola" is in itself a threat. Do you think that today we can be happy with the world in which we live?

CAHIERS: Don't you think that the Indian world may well, one day, become like ours?

ROSSELLINI: I don't care to look that far. What worries me is that people today are facing huge problems because our entire civilization is in question. We are all bustling about trying to save things that, for all we know, are not even worth saving. It would already be an excellent starting point if people began to get to know one another. What happened in Italy, during the war, at the moment when the invaders arrived, was quite extraordinary. We were under German rule, the Fascist regime, suffering under all sorts of persecutions. Then, one day, the others arrived, as enemies. Three days later they realized we were not their enemies because we were people just like them, their equal. I remember a sentence that was in every Roman mouth: "He too, he's just a poor mamma's boy." Out of the war was born an extraordinary sense of fraternity which we managed to kill in three years. An admirable sense of fraternity.

So, why shouldn't one make the effort to go seek people everywhere, and start telling about them to other people, to show them that the world is full of friends—and not full of enemies, even if there are some enemies. Suddenly, by some accident or other, the tiger becomes a man-eater, which is not what it is by nature. Cars are also man-eaters, since every day at least fifteen people die on French roads. On the other hand, one cannot hate a car because there are accidents.

Well, as for cinema, what function could it possibly have? That of confronting people with things, realities such as they are, and to get them acquainted with other people, other problems.

CAHIERS: But isn't cinema losing its audience?

ROSSELLINI: Yes, but these contractions in audience are insignificant. Besides, one can't look at everything in relation to cinema. One must look at things in relation to the world. Today, television is also a reality, as is radio. And then there are the books that cost only ten francs. And the newspapers that cost twenty-five francs—they are a little more expensive than books and much, much worse.

This project that I am talking about must be carried out at all costs. My own personal effort might be ridiculous, useless, a flop, but at least I have started to do some television broadcasts in which I can not just provide the image but also say and explain certain things. So I am trying to contribute to the awareness of a world that's quite close to ours and contains four hundred million people. Four hundred million people is not a trifle. It's a sixth of the world's population. It has to be known.

Maybe my television broadcast will help people understand my film. The film is much less technical, less documentary, less explanatory, less didactic, but since it provides the perception of a country through emotion rather than through statistics, it should make it easier for the public to get into it. This is very important to me, and I intend to devote myself to it in the future. This is why, with the help of some friends, I have tried to set up this sort of program in France.

CAHIERS: Do you mean to shoot all these films yourself?

ROSSELLINI: Most of all, I would like to find someone to produce them. Starting with a general survey and a documentation, and then moving on to the dramatic motifs, but only to represent things as they are, remaining strictly within the ambit of honesty. Yes, cinema must teach people how to get to know and recognize one another instead of going on telling the same old story over and over again—all variations on the same themes. We know everything we can possibly know on theft. We know everything we can possibly know on holdups. Everything we can possibly know on sex: not as it really is, of course, but all its side aspects. Death? What does it mean now? Life: what does it mean? Pain: what does it mean. Everything has lost its real meaning. Again, I repeat, we must try to go back to seeing things as they are, not their plastic versions but the real matter. The solution has to be there. Then, maybe, we will be able to find a sense of direction.

"Entretien avec Roberto Rossellini," in
Cahiers du cinéma, *no. 94, April 1959, pp. 1-11.*

FROM *OPEN CITY* TO *INDIA*

INTERVIEWER: I believe that at the moment you shot *Open City* Italy was still in the war, that is, it hadn't yet been liberated. Only Rome had been liberated.

ROSSELLINI: That's right, only Rome had been liberated, and we started shooting the film immediately after its liberation. However, we had prepared the script during the German occupation. Obviously, the filming was quite hard: there were no means, no studios, even film was in short supply, we had to buy pieces of film from photographers who peddled them in the streets.

We shot the film and then gave it to a distributor. But when the distributor saw the film—I had signed a contract with him whereby he would pay a guaranteed minimum amount the day I gave him the film—he sent me a registered letter to inform me that our contract was no longer binding since the object of the contract was missing, that is to say, the film. According to him, what he had seen was not a film, and so he did not accept it. As a result, I went through a difficult period, I was heavily in debt, as I had had to borrow money to produce the film. Then someone bought it, and the film started having a career of its own, and paying off, if belatedly.

INTERVIEWER: I believe it was shown at the first Cannes Film Festival.

ROSSELLINI: Yes, at three in the afternoon, and I was probably the only spectator there.

INTERVIEWER: Success came later, from Paris, I think.

ROSSELLINI: Yes, from Paris. Then it did fairly well in Italy, and it was a success in America.

INTERVIEWER: The idea was to show the Resistance in Italy.

ROSSELLINI: Yes, I think that the idea was, above all, that of making an honest gesture, and showing things exactly as they were. This is what made it necesary to turn to what is commonly known as neorealism: we had lived, gone through the destruction of war, we couldn't afford the luxury of inventing stories; what mattered was to cast a thoughtful, serious glance on the things that surrounded us.

Paisan

This is another war movie, about the war in Italy. It ideally follows the itinerary of the Allies from their landing in Sicily through their northward advance across the peninsula. It also tells of all the tragedies war had caused and left behind. Which were: incomprehension, that is to say, the problem of language—people who met could not understand each other directly; corruption, or, at least the tragedy of misery and hunger, which entailed ruses that could easily be taken for corruption; the feeling of love; the meeting of different tendencies, ideas, religions; and finally, the partisans. The film mostly focused on the Resistance. And the stories, even though only sketched, weren't entirely invented, nor were they entirely real: they were probable. They are the combination of real events, news items, put together and smoothed over so that they could sustain the film, and allow it to produce an accurate sense of what war had been at that particular moment.

Here again, we had a very hard time shooting this movie, a movie that was also very poorly received. I remember when the film was shown in Rome, because there were a few people who liked it; Moravia, who was among them (it shouldn't be forgotten), used to go to the theater every day to introduce the movie to the tiny audience, and explain to them what they were going to see. Once again, it was in France that the movie was first appreciated, and where its success began. After which, it went fairly well everywhere else.

Germany Year Zero

Another war movie, this time dealing with the consequences of the war in Germany. Taken along with *Open City* and *Paisan,* it constitutes a triptych, at least those were my intentions (which I think it fulfills), and completes the picture of the tragedy we went through. And since the Germans for months had been our main obsession, the crux of our tragedy—when they occupied Italy after the signing of the armistice—I wanted to go see them at home, in their own tragedy, in their own drama.

I remember arriving in Berlin, as a guest of the French government, in March [1947—ed.'s note], around five in the afternoon. Everything was steeped in a greyish atmosphere. I had to cross the entire city by car to reach the French sector. I remember, as we were driving through all those ruins, seeing, in the distance, along the horizon, a yellow spot sticking out from the surrounding greyness of the landscape. By and by, we reached that yellow spot: it was a huge sign, installed on top of a tiny stone cube that had been built among the ruins, bearing the inscription: "Israel Bazaar." I really believe it was the most eloquent sign of the German defeat: the first Jew who had come back to Berlin and had opened up his little store.

The film tells the story of a boy. I wanted to show what education can lead to. It is a boy, raised and educated in a Nazi school, who finds himself facing a serious family problem: a father who is sick and starving, and a brother who is hiding at home after having fought to the end. In order to solve the problem of hunger, the boy thinks it is normal, indeed quite heroic, to kill the father, who has become useless, so as to save the life of the brother, who, at least, has fought. This boy finds no support around him, everybody is against him; still, when he tries to confess what he has done, he speaks with pride, because he has indeed behaved like a good German.

Amore

This film consists of two episodes. When I was in Paris to present *Open City* and *Paisan,* and to organize the production of *Germany Year Zero,* I met Cocteau, and since I was very much interested in the idea of having Anna Magnani act in *A Human Voice,* we shot this forty–forty-five minute film in Paris.

After which we had the problem of finding one or two more episodes to film so as to reach the length necessary for a full feature. It was hard to find a story that would relate to the other episode without interfering with it. One day, Fellini, who was my assistant director, very shyly told me a story he vaguely remembered having read, a Russian short story, of which he couldn't even remember the name of the author. Later, I discovered that it was a lie: he hadn't read anything, the story was his own idea, but he didn't have the courage to admit it. It was the idea behind *The Miracle,* the second forty-five-minute film we shot.

It's a film that has provoked terrible reactions. It has been considered blasphemous, and it has been very hard to have it shown in America and in other places. We had trouble with censorship. It was odd that it should be considered blasphemous, since that was not what it was meant to be. I remember that then, to justify what I had done, I used to tell a story, part of a sermon delivered by Saint Bernardino of Siena. One day, a peasant had gone to work in the fields and had brought along his son and a dog. He had left the child under a tree and the dog to watch over him, and had set off to work. Upon his return he had found his son with his throat cut open: the child had the mark of two teeth on his throat. The dog stood by the tree shaking all over. In a fit of rage, the peasant killed it. But after he had killed it, he noticed that, on the child's body there was a large snake, which had obviously killed the child while the dog had tried to defend him. The peasant, feeling sorry for the innocent dog—whose name was Bonino—buried it under the tree, and wrote an epitaph on its grave that said: "Here lies Bonino, unjustly killed by the rage of man." As time went by, the people who passed by the grave would stop and, not knowing that Bonino was a dog, pray on his grave. And so Bonino started making miracles, indeed, so many that one day the people of the area decided to build a church in which they meant to bury the bones of this Bonino. As they were transferring the bones of the presumed saint they realized it was a dog. Saint Bernardino used to conclude his sermon by saying that what mattered most was what was in the soul of the people who went to the saint in faith and not the fact that the saint was a dog. This film was shot in more or less this spirit.

Stromboli

This is not a war movie, though it shows a character that has just come out of the war, an extremely cynical character who puts to use the skills developed during the war as means of self-defense against the fatality of persecution. At a certain point, these very same skills become so destructive and subjugating that the character suddenly realizes there is no longer any way out, and for the first time becomes capable of a human gesture. This is a character who believes that all difficulties, all threats, can be easily surmounted with cynicism and other such ploys. At the end, when all hope of escape from the situation at hand is clearly lost, the character, in an extremely human, humble gesture, begins to cry and asks for pity. This is the whole story. I don't think I need to add anything else about this film.

The Flowers of St. Francis

This is a film about innocence, innocence as a means of combat. This is the same sort of innocence I discovered in *Paisan,* in the episode that takes place in the Franciscan convent. It is the innocence full of faith of *The Miracle.* It is the theme of this strength, of the enormous strength of innocence that I have wanted to tackle one more time in *The Flowers.* At the same time, it is an attempt at making a historical film but with profoundly real elements, in other words, an attempt to reconstruct life as it very probably, or even certainly, was then. This film was shot in this spirit.

It was not a success. It was very well received by people who love cinema, but, I must admit, it was not understood by the public at large.

Europe '51

This is a movie I should have shot in France, but circumstances prevented me from shooting it there and so I had to shoot it in Italy. The idea came to me while I was filming *The Flowers.* I asked myself: if Francis, or someone like him, came back to earth today, how would he be treated? He could only be treated as a madman. But at the same time, the film deals with other things as well: it tries to show what the problems were that were afflicting Europe then, which are more or less the same we have today. Obviously the dialectic expression of these problems has changed since then: the communists of 1951 are not those of 1962, even the Catholics are no longer the same. Things have changed, and I think that maybe this change could already be sensed in the film. If what I am saying is true—only the audiences can express a judgment—it is proof that the method of investigation and prospecting of certain problems is quite effective since the film did not mean to look into the future but rather to look at reality, at things as they were. Later that reality evolved to its logical consequences, for consequences are always logical since nothing happens by chance, and, I believe, everything depends on an underlying logic.

So, it was the idea behind *The Flowers* that led me to his film. Simone Weil was also a strong source of inspiration. I had been studying the case of someone who could be considered both a madman and a friend. A world-renowned neurologist—who shared my passion for underwater fishing—had told me a story that had quite struck me. During the war there was a cloth merchant who had gotten involved in the black market. Then one day he had woken up with serious moral qualms. He had realized that until then he had behaved basely and that he had profited by all the tragedies that surrounded him. In the throes of remorse, he had turned himself in to the police, and the police had sent him to a psychiatric hospital to get his head examined. My friend had examined him and had found him absolutely sane. And this was precisely the problem: the merchant did not behave as an average man, he behaved quite differently, therefore he had to be classified either as an absolutely exceptional person, and therefore a genius, and therefore a monster, and therefore a saint, or as a madman.

In the end, the man had spent some time in the hospital, not much, but enough to be treated. All these circumstances gave me the opportunity to make a movie that would reflect the situation of Europe at that particular moment. This is the movie that came out of that.

Voyage in Italy

This is a film that gave me a great deal of trouble, I must admit it, because when it came out [in France—ed.'s note], it was immediately mutilated, transformed; they changed the title and tried to turn it into a commercial movie, but for all their efforts, they didn't succeed. However it also gave me great joy as it brought me in contact with François Truffaut, who was then a critic at *Cahiers du cinéma*. I was in Germany shooting another film, *Fear,* and one day I received a letter from him telling me that he had seen the movie, had liked it very much, and had defended it.

In this movie I try to show what Mediterranean, Latin, people are like, how they are in fact and not as they are perceived by the Anglo-Saxons, or other Northerners, who always come to see us as if we were animals in a zoo. The film also deals with a couple. A couple whose marriage is an actual business agreement: they have formed a company. When they come to Italy to rest, on a vacation—to collect an inheritance—they find themselves alone, and since what kept them together is no longer there, they come face to face and realize they do not love each other.

Jeanne au bûcher

This is the filmed version of Honegger's and Claudel's oratorio. I had the opportunity of bringing the oratorio to the stage first in Naples, then at La Scala in Milan, then in England, then at the Opéra in Paris, then in Spain, and then in Sweden. I had staged many performances of this oratorio which I adore, just about everywhere in Europe, and so one day I thought of turning it into a movie since I have always been looking for new film techniques. This was a perfect opportunity to do an experiment, to use certain techniques that would render the fantastic aspect of the story while respecting the oratorio as it was, as I had staged it, without translating it into something cinematic.

The film exists, I made it, and if my other movies have not been commercial successes this one has been a total failure, because it was never released [in France—ed.'s note], and no one has ever even wanted to see it. This is all.

Fear

This is probably my most structured film, there is more of a story in it. In fact it was inspired by a novella by Stefan Zweig. In any case, it interested me because it dealt with Germany ten years later—of course, this is an alteration I brought to Zweig's story. It is the material reconstruction, but also the quest for a moral solution, of all the problems of those times; but it is also about the importance of confession, because it is in the ability to confess that one can achieve a certain humility, and, above all a great tolerance. This is the reason behind this movie.

This film hasn't been a great success either. It was shown more or less secretly in small suburban theatres. This is all I can say about this film.

India

Its real title is *India, matri bhumi,* which means the humus of the earth. It is probably my most exemplary film—not as a film, as an example—the one that best explains what we have said in our interviews, all I have said concerning my ambitions in film. This is a film that I have really made experimentally. I have tried to put on film what I thought in a probably theoretical way. It is an investigation, as thorough as possible given the limits of film, of a country, of a new country such as India, which has recovered its freedom, and has emerged from colonialism—at that point, India had been independent for only ten years—and of the immense effort it has taken to make it get back into gear and become a country like any other.

How is the film constructed? Part of it is a documentary, in the strictest sense of the word, though I have tried to avoid looking at all the things a tourist looks at, such as monuments, etc. My eyes have focused mostly on the streets, people, the most immediate manifestations of everyday life. And then there are a number of short stories, somewhat fictionalized but only insofar as they are probable, since they are not the fruit of fantasy but things I felt around me, stories that were more or less told to me; and so I structured my movie around these elements, these four short stories mixed with the documentary.

I don't know what you think of the movie. It was released only in Italy, and not with great success. It was made with a French co-producer who, however, never had it released in France, I don't know why.

It is a film I love because, as I said, I saw it as an attempt to do something new in the field of knowledge, of information: the sort of information that's not simply scientific or statistical but that is also a sort of document of the feelings and behaviors of men. If you want, you could say it is an ethnological film. This is all I can say about it.

Transcript of a series of television presentations to be broadcast by ORTF, in French, as part of a series that was however never aired. To judge from the context it would seem they were recorded in 1962, in Rossellini's Roman apartment.

Rossellini with Ingrid Bergman and children, Robertino, Isabella, and Ingrid Isotta

Rossellini during the shooting of
La nave bianca (1941)

Aldo Fabrizi in *Open City* (1945)

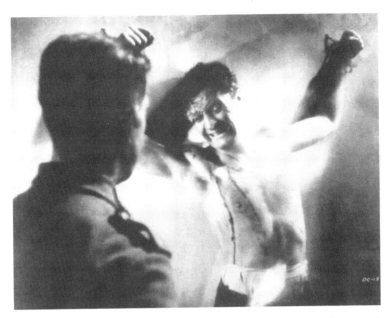

Marcello Pagliero in *Open City* (1945)

Anna Magnani in *Open City* (1945)

Alfonsino and Dots M. Johnson
in the Naples episode of *Paisan* (1946)

Harriet White and Renzo Avanzo in the Florence
episode of *Paisan* (1946)

Partisans in the Po River episode of *Paisan* (1952)

Shooting *Gemany Year Zero* in destroyed Berlin (1947)

Federico Fellini and Anna Magnani in *The Miracle* (1948)

Ingrid Bergman and Mario Vitale in *Stromboli* (1949)

Ingrid Bergman and crew members during the
shooting of *Stromboli* (1949)

The Flowers of St. Francis (1950): Francis and his "brothers"

Shooting *The Flowers of St. Francis* (1950)

Ingrid Bergman and Alexander Knox in *Europe '51 (1952)*

Shooting *Voyage in Italy* (1953)

Voyage in Italy (1953): the procession

Ingrid Bergman and George Sanders in
Voyage in Italy (1953)

Renate Mannhardt and Ingrid Bergman in *Fear* (1954)

The bathing of elephants in *India* (1958)

Rossellini and Sonali Senroy in Venice (1959?)

First row (left to right): Ermanno Olmi, Rossellini, Elio Ruffo, François Truffaut, Jean Aurel; second row (left to right): Tinto Brass, Gillo Pontecorvo, Carlo Lizzani, Francesco Maselli, and Luigi di Gianni; in Venice during a conference on "new cinema"

Vittorio De Sica in
General Della Rovere (1959)

The execution scene in *General Della Rovere* (1959)

Renzo Ricci (Garibaldi) and Paolo Stoppa (Bixio) in
Viva l'Italia (1960)

Jean-Marie Patte (Louis)
and Giulio Cesare Silvani (Mazarin) in
The Rise to Power of Louis XIV (1966)

Pierre Arditi (left) in *Blaise Pascal* (1972)

Marcello Di Falco (right) in
L'età di Cosimo de' Medici (1972)

Roberto Rossellini

AN INTERVIEW WITH *CAHIERS DU CINÉMA*

BY JEAN DOMARCHI, JEAN DOUCHET AND
FEREYDOUN HOVEYDA

This is the third interview Roberto Rossellini has granted us. Its tenor is so high that suddenly the scope of the Italian issue for which this interview had been reserved has become much too narrow. This text may, must, surprise our readers as it has surprised us after all the surprises we have already received from a work that's probably richer than any other in its solutions of continuity. In any case, Rossellini's opinions will always find a place in these Cahiers, *even when they turn away from cinema, indeed, even when they turn against him.*

CAHIERS: It would seem that in the last three or four films your work has found a new orientation. Is this deliberate on your part?

ROSSELLINI: One moves on. . . . One thing attracts another, and one moves from one to the other. I don't know whether my evolution is deliberate. I would know it only if I were writing a treatise on logic.

I have the feeling we are in the situation of working bees to which one gives a certain food to make them become what they must be. This is the dramatic aspect of the mass-entertainment arts that educate, orient, and condition us.

The other drama is that if the last century was dominated by the dream of freedom, this one is dominated by respect. The margins of discussion and judgment have become minimal. One may dare express a few opinions among one's relatives and friends, but they are generally banalities directed at things one would never openly oppose. Everything goes. There is no longer any critical sense.

Nothing scandalizes any longer. Because, either we understand what's been said (or at least parts of it) thanks to our conditioning, or we refuse to listen to it. In a society imbued with dialectic, speech could scandalize, but I don't see how it could do anything of the sort in ours.

If there is scandal, it's confined to trifles. We live in a period where sex is at the center of both life and culture. That it is a very important thing, I don't question it, but that it should be turned into the focus of thought, I find that rather odd.

And that's not all. Humans have lost their edge. We are steeped in conformism. In any given discussion, the terms of the dialogue are restricted to a very limited number of ideas. And yet we live in a world where ideas change with an extraordinary rapidity. It's an absurd phenomenon: discussion is getting more and more restricted while horizons are widening every day.

As for art, it is increasingly turning into a means of evasion. This is a sign of decadence. Where is thought in all this? I don't think there can be any greater joy than that of thinking, and I believe this joy could be diffused very rapidly if we only gave people the chance. Unfortunately, we live in a society that does its best to render people as superficial as possible, I would even say as vulgar as possible provided you don't take the term in too pejorative a sense: people are more spineless than dishonest.

I live a rather isolated life, and so am always surprised, when I come in contact with people, at the currency not just of ready-made ideas, which would already be something, but of ready-made sentences. You would think one can buy them at the Bon Marché along with other plastic objects. And what's really frightening is that the largest part of a discourse is made up of such sentences. It is a clear sign that we have been conditioned to such a degree that we are no longer capable of any joy, of any enthusiasm in discovery.

Art itself is caught in a vicious circle, cinema as well as the other arts. In literature, we can write entire chapters while contemplating our toes. Isn't it horrifying? In cinema we keep repeating the same things over and over again. The only change possible is in the choice of certain frames, in a new lighting trick. What matters is to prove that we can repeat the same story over and over again, always providing it with the same variations. This is a sign of enormous impotence.

CAHIERS: Isn't censorship a little responsible for this state of affairs, at least in cinema?

ROSSELLINI: Expression requires desire, and will. You will always be able to do what you want if you have the will and, above all, a precise awareness of what needs to be said. That's why discourses—to use a very general term—discourses of revolt are vague, whereas they should be scientific. I mean that they do not reflect an awareness, a precise knowledge of things, they lack the power of perception.

So it is quite normal that we should have built a society based on conformism, just as it is normal that whoever wants to break through the wall of norms, of conditioning, should meet with trouble.

What support should anyone who dares do such a thing expect?

On the political level nothing seems to be enough to solve the problem. On the aesthetic level, there is no scandal except when people can't find the discourse they are accustomed to hearing. As for the critical level, there is no hope for help.

If you devote yourself to research (because there are some experiments which, without being successes, have the value of a research), you automatically expose yourself to the ridicule of those who do not understand why you might want to leave the herd.

I never get angry with those who defend an idea, I get angry with those who don't have the strength to impose an idea.

One can talk endlessly about censorship, but aside from its legitimacy or illegitimacy, which is not in question here, the fact is that we live in a world which, in the name of freedom, is ready to let itself be massacred by the atomic bomb. So, we should really try to understand what this freedom means. What is it? Its foremost expression is the individual's right to vote, but the same person who has the right to vote, to decide the fate of a government, and therefore of a nation, doesn't have the right to make up his own mind, to decide whether his children can or cannot see such and such a film. In my mind that's a very clear example of the lack of freedom that we have been conditioned to accept.

I do not mean to say that this is a criminal process, what I want to say is that, through tropism, we have gradually moved in a certain direction: a way has been paved, a habit has been formed, and all out of weakness, carelessness.

CAHIERS: Don't you think that a beneficial evolution of thought might yet be possible?

ROSSELLINI: The problem is becoming so large that it is impossible to define it so quickly.

CAHIERS: But aren't these precisely the problems that you have tackled in your later films, focusing on individual cases?

ROSSELLINI: What's important is to reopen the discussion globally, and, within the context of this problem, cinema is a very small thing. The problem is general, the action must be general.

One or two individuals won't be enough to do the job. Ideas must ripen, people must become aware of things, and all this must slowly take shape in the very body of the society in which we live.

CAHIERS: The role of the artist, even though his function may be relatively limited, is precisely that of trying to tackle this problem. Most great film makers do it, be they Renoir, Fritz Lang, or you. They try to convey this message in the hope that the young might understand it and diffuse it.

ROSSELLINI: Indeed this is a way, albeit minor, of broaching the problem. But to propose a model is not the same as to confront a problem. The action must be more far-reaching. The important thing is to approach these issues from a general angle. There are a few ferments around likely to stir up things, but they are too few and far between.

CAHIERS: The profound dialectic of the modern world might well rest in the fact that whereas true individual values have found shelter in science, science keeps contributing to the collectivization of culture you were just now bemoaning.

ROSSELLINI: I see what you mean but I don't agree with you. For us, who represent the other face of the dialectic Science/Art, the solution would be to put the conquests of science to good use, but this is precisely where we find ourselves lacking. We've reached the point where, though we're perfectly capable of appreciating the advantages of writing with a ballpoint pen or of owning a Frigidaire, we're no longer able to tell stories, to invent. At a time when we're heading for the conquest of space, we laugh about it and say: what for? And yet we must all wish the world to move on and evolve. All the efforts and suffering of humanity generally bring about a development, a change which often end up being quite extraordinary.

As for us, artists, since we pretend to devote ourselves to art and its defense, what are we doing, in our field, that could be compared to the accomplishments of science?

What is our role in this immense urge to conquer?

Art has a very important role to play in the field of education, whose aim is first to get people ready to conquer something, and then to turn them into specialists. At which point we have the problem of specialization. And this is a serious problem. Everything we do today has a strictly educational goal. But I reject this kind of education. "Education," in its strictest sense, entails the idea of leading, directing, conditioning, whereas we should move much more freely in our quest for truth. What matters is to inform, to instruct; but "education" is not that important.

Naturally one needs some education, but freely, and only when the information is vast and complete. Instead, our educational methods always tend to reduce the role of information, in favor of indoctrination.

CAHIERS: Can't cinema also contribute to information, education?

ROSSELLINI: Cinema can help, but it is not The Means. If there was already a vast program of information and instruction in every domain, cinema could join in and contribute to the discourse in a more allusive form, propose new models, awaken people's emotions to the deeper value of things. But cinema cannot carry out this discourse in a direct, didactic fashion, just as it can't convey information in its totality. So we must start by dealing with general ideas.

In this we can use every possible means, but always within a global vision of things. We have to reintroduce ourselves into the general movement of humanity—in a way, we must go back to some form of humanism—instead of sitting still, chewing over things that we have already swallowed and digested, ruminating them, reswallowing them only to regurgitate them and chew them again. We must look for new pastures.

CAHIERS: Do you feel that cinema has failed its mission, which was precisely that of becoming the art of our century?

ROSSELLINI: Yes, I believe so. It has made a few attempts, even a few heroic attempts, but it has failed. More than that: among all the arts, cinema is probably the most responsible for this enormous process of conditioning and stupefaction that has been going on.

CAHIERS: But a work such as *Poem of the Sea* [by Dovzhenko, 1958], for instance, was quite effective in tackling purely general problems from the inside, through lyricism, and in showing the influence of science on our times. A film like *India* also points at the way we should follow to tackle those problems.

ROSSELLINI: The point is not to tell me about my own films, but to look at those that have represented this sort of endeavor. Have they had any success?

CAHIERS: None. Even in Russia, *Poem of the Sea* has had no success.

ROSSELLINI: We should wonder why. This is a good example of the sort of discourse that people cannot understand. Even though it is extremely simple, they cannot understand it. This is what has given me the impression that all we do in cinema is in vain, at least from the point of view of general usefulness. There are only a few people who understand: as for the majority, not only do they not grasp anything, but at times they even act offended.

We thought that cinema could do a great deal. But only propaganda films have been able to accomplish a lot in a world that has been going in a particular direction, and in which everything that's done is done in that very same direction. Within a very precise context, and according to a well-established ethic, cinema has been very effective.

It has also done quite well at popularizing things. But when it comes to sorting out and discussing general ideas I don't think cinema can do anything of the sort.

Let's speak more clearly. To reopen a discussion through cinema is impossible. Cinema is too expensive. There are other means that are less expensive and more effective. We can carry out a discussion, an investigation much more thoroughly, and sort out, examine, and discuss general ideas much more effectively outside of cinema. Books are still the best alternative.

Since a film cannot be made without the contribution of the public (it is a very expensive merchandise), we have to begin our discussion in a different way—and then continue it with the help of cinema. We could, for instance, start with literature, and then return to a public that has been gradually formed by literature.

And we must have the courage to be didactic. Now, when you are didactic in cinema you are immediately accused of being an imbecile. Nevertheless, didacticism is absolutely necessary.

CAHIERS: On the other hand couldn't cinema pull the spectator out of his conformism?

ROSSELLINI: The problem is huge. In the first place, the spectator wants a familiar product. All he can accept are small variations within the same product.

Then there is the problem of the critics. Critics, in an even more frenzied way than the general public, are accustomed to the consumption of a certain product. If we give them spaghetti, they will accept variations in the sauce, but if we give them another dish, it won't work, they'll revolt.

It is therefore useless to persist in this direction. What we must do is find another medium that may become very popular, or else one that addresses only a small élite but is capable of provoking a secondhand diffusion of new ideas. This sort of work can be done systematically, and will be accomplished all the better in that it doesn't entail any financial concern.

CAHIERS: We agree, we have to restore a certain sensibility, but the problem of sensibility has always existed and we don't think we should rely on books . . .

ROSSELLINI: I believe that cinema will be able to participate effectively in this discussion only after we have explored all our new problems with the most traditional forms, and brought them to the attention of the public.

Once we have acquired a great freedom of discourse in every field we will be able to make that discourse more systematic and more effective from a didactic standpoint, and even if only a small number of people are touched by it, those people will be in a condition to do what is needed to diffuse it. Cinema would slow down this process considerably, when in fact we need to accelerate it as much as possible. In any case, once we have recognized the problem, there is no point crying over it. We must immediately pass to action, and in the fastest, most effective way possible.

As for me, I may not leave cinema, but it will no longer be my main activity. Still, I feel much more at home in cinema than anywhere else. It has been terrible for me to start writing. I have had to restart from zero and remake myself from scratch. I've had to acquire a technique, a language. It's not funny in the least, but I had to do it because all my discourses were becoming vain.

If one were working toward the satisfaction of one's own ambitions, toward one's dreams of glory, the understanding of a few enlightened individuals would be more than enough, but when it is not a matter of personal satisfaction, and one needs to confront certain harrowing problems, then it's a different story.

If you find yourself on the terrace of a burning house and are able to write a brilliant poem on the death that's going to turn you into a roasted chicken, it's wonderful, but it is also absolutely useless. If, instead, you are able to become a fireman who, once the fire has been extinguished, is able to remember what happened, and write a sublime poem about the roasted chicken, then you have done everything you can do.

CAHIERS: You have spoken a great deal about effectiveness, on the other hand there have always been great revolutionary actions that have had no immediate effect, and have only become effective much later.

ROSSELLINI: In our accelerated times we can't wait any longer. Besides I'm very impatient.

CAHIERS: But the public is getting gradually sensitized, becoming accustomed to new things. To your work, for instance. *Voyage in Italy* is getting a better reception every day.

ROSSELLINI: I am not taking myself into consideration: me and my work, me and my public, me and the critics. That's not how I compose my discourse. I have no place in it. I am in it, if you want, but on the other side. The most important thing for me is to do. It's my greatest joy. So, in a way, I am even an egoist.

CAHIERS: In which direction are you going to concentrate your efforts?

ROSSELLINI: Mostly toward the essay. That's where I have to start from. Very loosely structured essays. I see this as a means to insert myself into the world, so as to have a chance to study it and understand it.

CAHIERS: Nevertheless, a few of your films have appealed to a very large audience. Don't you think you could again attain such a success, even if based on a misinterpretation?

ROSSELLINI: If it based on a misinterpretation it's even more tragic. Every time I have received an award I have accepted it out of kindness, but I have never participated in the ceremony precisely not to be an accomplice in misinterpretation.

Through cinema, I've undertaken a survey of humanity, and of the problems and events that touched me. Whether I have done it well or not, it has broadened my awareness of the world. But now I know I can no longer do what I want to do through cinema. It's not just a matter of knowing whether the public is going to understand me or not. It's a different kind of pressure. I have to rewrite the discourse from the very beginning, putting into question an entire line of writing as well as our entire civilization.

CAHIERS: To return to a point you brought up. Do you think cinema could be less expensive?

ROSSELLINI: We've always done our best to make it as inexpensive as possible, but in fact it has always remained as expensive as possible.

CAHIERS: Do you think that the direction followed by Rouch— whether good or bad—can lead somewhere?

ROSSELLINI: In writing one can broach much larger issues.

CAHIERS: What are the fundamental ideas that will emerge from your books?

ROSSELLINI: First of all, I want to try to see the world in which we live with new eyes, and to understand how it's scientifically ordered. I want to see it. Not emotionally nor intuitively, but with as much precision as possible, and in its entirety.

One of the major aspects of the modern world is economics. What was it to begin with? What has it become? How does it work? What are its aims? Its means? And so on and so forth. I must start the discourse from the beginning, dividing it into strictly scientific chapters.

What is physics? Chemistry? What are our political organizations? Where do they come from? How did they take shape? What are the ideas that brought them to life? How were these ideas planted? How has adaptation intervened?

The process of adaptation is very important. It's odd: whenever a new historical direction emerges it immediately sets off a huge surge toward renewal, but this surge is immediately reabsorbed into nostalgia and a maudlin attachment to the past, so that everything generally ends up in a compromise. I have nothing against this, it is human, but I want to analyze this process to see how humanity progresses.

If we wanted to write history today, and if we wanted to write the history of the men who have made history, we would write entire chapters on criminals, perverts, and madmen, and now and then, among them, we might find a few little wise men. For thousands of years, humanity has accepted this state of affairs without saying a word. Today we live in the age of science, and yet politics is in the hands of men who know nothing about science. . . .

There are a thousand things to say, and they must be tackled one by one. In other words, if a man has received a lot in his life—including the privilege of a few knocks on the head—he doesn't have to kneel in a corner of his room and sob, rather he must try to understand what's happening, that is, if he has any faith in humanity. As for me, I have enormous faith in humanity, and I want to try and see why certain things are done rather than others, why there is madness, criminality, though I am absolutely sure—since I have faith in humanity—that there is no man anywhere who gets up in the morning telling himself: "I am going to have a great day of crime!" No, he gets up in the morning and tries to be a good man, though his actions may later turn out to be criminal.

If we don't study all this in depth, nothing will ever cohere.

I believe that one good thing our civilization has given us is the possibility of carrying out a scientific investigation, to examine things thoroughly in scientific terms, that is to say with no risk of error if the investigation is carried out properly. Today we have the means to work in such a fashion, and this is where we must start from if we want to reopen a new discourse.

First of all we must take stock of the situation, and recognize the world. Then we can begin to analyze it. At which point dreams and intuition might stream forth again.

I believe this is, on a much larger scale, the same method I followed when I made *Open City* and *Paisan*. The tragedy of war was over. You had to avoid being a poet and whatever else an artist usually is, and force yourself to look around in a strictly realistic fashion. That's where I started from. Today I want to start it again, but on a much larger scale.

Every year, in every commercial company, one must take stock. Why? To know where one is. What do we do in our world to take stock of what we have acquired? Nothing.

CAHIERS: Don't you think that the problem might be how to give people new dreams, including dreams of action?

ROSSELLINI: But we must first decide what sort of dreams we are going to give them.

One of the characteristics of our society is that when we do something for people we do it to "educate" them, to direct them toward some goal instead of letting them find the road they should follow on their own. Either you believe in democracy or you don't. That's the main point.

How can there be democracy without knowledge? We must start with knowledge without which there is no freedom. The greatest ideas are, without the shadow of a doubt, democracy and freedom.

In order to promote these ideas the world must cease to be a mystery to people so that they can participate in it. So, we must let go of empiricism and turn to science. On the other hand, art can make you understand through emotion what you may be unable to understand through your intellect. You can create a lyrical primacy around science.

In any case we'll have to turn to what the French call "Cartesianism": the domain of reason, and abandon Anglo-Saxon empiricism, though it has the merit of having permitted the establishment of a scientific civilization.

Once we are in the domain of reason, it will be easy to conquer everything: freedom, democracy—not their ersatz but their reality.

CAHIERS: There is also non-Aristotelianism.

ROSSELLINI: Not for me. I am more than ever an Aristotelian. Aristotle says: "It is not true that free time is the end of work: work is the end of free time." Which simply means that people's natural time is free, while work is an obligation, what one owes to society, to the family, etc. But people's vocation is free time, and this free time must be useful. It can be useful only if man can devote himself to the study of science, philosophy, or literature.

One of the plights of humanity is that people are useful to society as consumers. They are a cell in the digestive tract. This consuming humanity must try to find a different horizon.

CAHIERS: A unitary vision of the world might have been possible at the time of the Greeks, but today . . .

ROSSELLINI: We can try, as the Encyclopedists did. They played a crucial role. Without them, there would be no modern world.

CAHIERS: The Encyclopedists were revolutionaries working toward the destruction of feudal society. Could it be that your work's goal is the destruction of today's capitalist world?

ROSSELLINI: The *Encyclopédie* provided us with a global vision of the world, only later did we start perceiving some solutions, which also happened to be revolutionary. I cannot tell you what's going to become of my work. I don't want to play the role of the revolutionary.

On the other hand, it is simpler to find solutions today than it was then, in a world that was dominated by very restrictive systems such as that of monarchy by God-given right. Today, we live in the century of science, which greatly reduces the dimensions of the struggle, because science is accepted by everybody. Logically, a scientific world must produce scientific solutions.

CAHIERS: Cinema has brought along a new understanding of things even from this point of view. There is a film, for instance, that tells you better than anything else what America is: it is *Citizen Kane,* whose educational value is in no way inferior to its artistic value.

ROSSELLINI: On the other hand, in order to be able to appreciate *Citizen Kane* one must already have a few well-established general ideas. Which is precisely what I was saying: one must always start by establishing a few general ideas.

CAHIERS: Nevertheless, you will go on making movies?

ROSSELLINI: It won't be my main activity. I'm going to film *Pulcinella* in May or June and then . . .

CAHIERS: Didn't you want to film a chapter taken from Castro's *Geopolitics of Hunger* within the context of a film encyclopedia?

ROSSELLINI: Yes, but I've been fighting for it for the last four or five years without getting anywhere. People don't seem very interested in it. I had taken it for granted that they would be, but I was wrong.

Film should be a means like any other, maybe even more valid than some, to write history and to preserve the traces of the societies that are about to disappear. Because, besides and beyond all the means to transcribe reality we have already had, today we also have the image, which shows us people as they are, along with what they do and what they say. History's protagonists are photographed along with their voices, and it's important to know not only what they say but also how they say it. These cinematic resources have at times been used for propaganda reasons, but never in a scientific way.

Besides, to photograph one man is nothing, one ought to be able to photograph an entire world.

I bought the rights to a book (but how am I going to turn it into a film?) whose author is Olivetti's psychotechnician.[1]

Olivetti has built a factory in one of the most beautiful places in the world. It's a truly Homeric Italy, a place of great historical and geological beauty. The Roman emperors had their villas there.

Its present inhabitants are underemployed. They either fish or guide

---

1 *Donnarumma all'assalto,* by Ottiero Ottieri.

tourists around. . . . Then, suddenly, there is a factory. Its aim is that of solving the problem of industrialization in southern Italy, and, indeed, people believe it's going to solve all their problems.

But the factory can only employ people who can do a certain type of work, and the role of the psychotechnician is that of testing all the prospective employees. All these people have their private dramas, their needs, they cannot understand why some of them are rejected. This gives rise to all sorts of conflicts in which everybody is right because the people have the right to demand a job and the factory has the right to demand that its employees be able to do a certain type of work.

This is an extraordinarily dramatic subject which allows one to tackle all sorts of problems, including those posed by the customs and traditions of the place.

For instance, there is the case of a woman who cannot get married with her fiancé because they have no money. So they get married in a civil ceremony, which will allow them to improve their situation from a financial standpoint, but the union cannot be consummated because in the south of Italy modesty, purity, and honor are things to be reckoned with.

So, she lives with her brother, her fiancé lives with his own family, and they will not be able to live together until after the religious wedding, which will take place only when they have the financial means to set up home.

This is when the fiancé fails the psychotechnical exam. The brother, on his part, refuses to take his. He claims he has the muscles to work, that he can and wants to work, and that's that. It is his right. No way to talk him out of it: he refuses to bow to the rule.

In the end, it's the woman who passes the exam. But, for the locals, a woman working in a factory is almost an outrage. The honor of both the brother and the future husband is put into question. What are they going to do? Are they going to be able to adjust?

This is an extraordinary subject that would allow me to deal with all sorts of problems in an exemplary fashion. Why in the world doesn't it interest anyone?

To get the public interested in something it might be necessary to teach them how to make the most of their free time. We go back to

Aristotle's idea. We have more and more leisure time every day but no one has taught people how to fill it.

CAHIERS: What about sports?

ROSSELLINI: When an entire humanity repeats the same rhythmical movements from right to left and from left to right according to the whims of a ball, then I will say we have reached the bottom of imbecility.

They should spend their time trying to discover something else! There are so many other ways to have fun. A fisherman at least learns something about the behavior of trout, after which he ought to get interested in that of snails. Ideally one thing should lead to another.

If the aim of filmmakers were to bring people face to face with important issues, cinema could become really useful. But in fact, today cinema has only one aim: to kill time, and so no wonder it has nothing to offer. In fact, it does offer something, but what it offers is an ersatz humanity, and people identify with that rather than with their own realities: so they end up being conditioned by abstractions. And this crime against humanity takes place every day!

We must rediscover the fundamentals of dialectic and see work as the end of free time and not free time as the end of work.

"Entretien avec Roberto Rossellini," in
Cahiers du cinéma, *no. 133, July 1962, pp. 1-15.*

AN INTERVIEW WITH *CAHIERS DU CINÉMA*

BY FEREYDOUN HOVEYDA AND ERIC ROHMER

This interview is divided in two parts. The first one exposes Rosselli-
ni's grievances against "cinéma vérité." The second one picks up and
pursues, while widening their focus, all the remarks gathered exactly
a year ago, in the 133rd issue of Cahiers. *Though our respective*
opinions concerning Jean Rouch's La Punition *(with E. R. definitely*
in favor and F. H. decidedly against) and the future of contemporary
art seldom coincide, we have joined forces against our interlocutor, so
that all through this discussion both of us will emerge as his most
determined antagonists.

CAHIERS: *L'Express* has published a few of your opinions about
cinéma vérité, and, in particular, about the films of Leacock, the
Maysles brothers, and Rouch. Would you mind telling us more
about it?

ROSSELLINI: The article published in *L'Express* correctly sums up
what I said at the Unesco film society without any distortion.[1] On the
other hand, I would very much like to ask you a question. What do
you think of that kind of film? As you are professional critics your
opinion is certainly more important than mine.

CAHIERS: *Cahiers* is open to every trend. It believes none should be
rejected a priori.

1 See "Entretien avec Jean Rouch," in the previous issue of *Cahiers du cinéma.*

ROSSELLINI: I couldn't agree more. But this doesn't mean you can't express an opinion. Besides, to say that *cinéma vérité* is a trend is no proof of its value.

However, since you seem to care, I will go back to what I said the other day at the Unesco. I find it very odd that one should give such importance to something that is not even an experience. I can't understand it, but I would like to.

CAHIERS: What is happening to *cinéma vérité* is very similar to what has been happening to the Nouvelle Vague, here and abroad. These are trends that cannot be accepted or rejected outright: one must take into account the different personalities involved in each movement. Now, almost all of us, at *Cahiers,* have liked *La Punition,* even in spite of what the film wants to be. Forget Rouch's theories, what matters is that he is an artist.

ROSSELLINI: . . . That he is an artist, yes. But I do not understand how he is an artist in that film.

You compare *cinéma vérité* to the Nouvelle Vague. But the label Nouvelle Vague was tacked onto the movement by outsiders. It conveniently grouped together a certain number of film directors with different ideas, whose only common goal was to produce films according to new techniques. Each of them remained what he was, with his own ideas, his own personality, his own aesthetics, etc.

But when we speak of *cinéma vérité* we are not using a label invented by outsiders: it is a flag that's being brandished by the directors themselves. At which point I can't but wonder where the truth is, what it means, and what it wants to accomplish. These are all questions to which I already have an answer that I'll give you later. In any case, I still fail to see where you can find any artistic intention in all this.

CAHIERS: It would seem it is a rather modest intention, at least insofar as Rouch is concerned. Let's say that—taking the first example that comes to mind—just as turn-of-the-century painters decried the use of artificial light, so does Rouch decry the actor's role and prepared dialogues.

ROSSELLINI: We have been doing it for the last twenty, thirty years.

CAHIERS: Not to such an extent.

ROSSELLINI: Exactly. Not to such an extent. Why? Your comparison with painting isn't appropriate, I don't think so. Painting is the firm intention of someone who, instead of opting for a meticulous reproduction of what he sees, oleograph or photograph, makes an interpretation of it. This gives you someone with a very precise stance, an artistic dream of his own, a personal emotion, someone who tries to reproduce the emotion he has received from a particular object at all costs, and who is going to try to convey this very emotion to someone less sensitive and less subtle, even if in order to do so he has to deform the object that originally aroused it. You can easily see how the author is very directly involved in all this, how his choice is determined, and how his language becomes the essential element of his expression. But in the case at hand there is none of this. We have a camera. As far as I am concerned, this camera has one quality: it's a machine, nothing else. Film is film. It's good today, it will be bad in six months or in two years when a new kind of film comes out. It will be good again in thirty years, when we realize that this film that photographed so badly bears the imprint of its time. Anyway, this has nothing to do with the personality of an artist, of a man who claims to be, who wants and must be a human being who sees things and tells them to others, thereby becoming a link between his emotions and theirs. Here we are in the presence of a strictly technical executor who reproduces what anyone with an eye can see.

Now, it is a dogma in *cinéma vérité* that the author must not intervene at all. I have even heard people declare: "We do not want to write a script, because we are unable to." I find such a declaration rather shocking.

CAHIERS: Who declared such a thing?

ROSSELLINI: Rouch and the Maysles. They are the ones who said it, not I. This means that Rouch does not want to involve his personality in his films. Now, I happen to know that he has a personality. I have seen some films of his where his personality shows. But here he renounces it. At which point I am totally bewildered.

CAHIERS: He doesn't want to intervene in the construction of a traditional script; nevertheless his intervention in *La Punition* is quite significant. Besides, he has written one page and has given certain directions to the interpreters. There are a thousand ways of directing actors!

ROSSELLINI: Yes, we know how to do it. But you've just told me a few things that Rouch has never told me. I thought he drastically refused to intervene in his films. But if he has intervened, it's another story. You tell me that he has written one page: one page, even only three lines, are more than enough to write a script. In this case, it's a different story.

CAHIERS: Unfortunately Rouch is not here to settle the matter. In any case, he told us that he had asked himself the following question: "There is intervention, that's a fact, but on what grounds and at what point?" Insofar as he is concerned, it is in a certain preparation. It is also in the editing.

ROSSELLINI: In this case everything changes. Then we are asked to judge a work that's intended by someone, even if the author has deliberately limited his intervention. As a result, our judgment must be quite different.

CAHIERS: We must judge the work itself, not the intentions.

ROSSELLINI: I can't express any judgment about that film for a very simple reason. It doesn't interest me at all, it bores me to death, and it angers me terribly because it was made by a friend. I don't understand it, it's boring, it's lazy, it's useless.

CAHIERS: So you think it's bad.

ROSSELLINI: Rouch is too dear a friend and a man I respect too deeply for me to enjoy saying something bad about him behind his back. If I was so angry—I can assure you that evening I was shaking with fury—it's because I am very fond of him.

CAHIERS: Let's broach the subject from another side. What difference do you see between *cinéma vérité* and your own documentaries?

ROSSELLINI: A huge difference. *India* is a choice. It is an attempt to be as honest as possible, but with a very clear judgment. Or, at least, if there is no judgment, with a very clear love. Not with indifference, in any case. Things can either attract or repel me. But I cannot say: I am not touched. It's impossible.

CAHIERS: Do you accept the principle of the film interview?

ROSSELLINI: No. I think it may be interesting for someone who wants to gather some scientific documentation. But not at all if I want to make a work of art. To make a work of art you have to respect certain rules. If you want to become a professional cyclist you have to be able to ride a bike.

CAHIERS: Except that no one knows where art starts and where it ends. At the beginning we used to say: cinema reproduces reality, so it is not an art. Art hides elsewhere.

ROSSELLINI: Art hides elsewhere. Yes, but there is no art that can be done by everyone. The only way this movie could be artistic is if, by chance, down the street you run into an artist!

CAHIERS: No, because the way in which Mr. X. or Mr. Y film the same thing will be different. For instance, if you compare *La Punition* and *Le Joli Mai,* you'll see that people in each of these films do not speak or act in the same way.

ROSSELLINI: Obviously, it is difficult to define art. Nevertheless we know full well what art is and know how to recognize it. And this, there is no doubt about it, is not art.

CAHIERS: Are you as critical of Rouch's earlier films?

ROSSELLINI: No. For instance I liked *Jaguar* very much. But I couldn't care less about seeing a man with a hat in one shot, without a hat in the next shot, and then again with a hat in the next shot, and other such nonsense. What was there was alive, important, full of emotion. Rouch was an ethnologist studying Africa: he approached people in the street, filmed them, and, starting from there, created for himself a conception, a point of view that he would later reintroduce into the film. His was a true creative process.

Do you really think there can be art without the intervention of a personality?

CAHIERS: No, not at all. If we like *La Punition* it's because we believe there is the intervention of a personality.

ROSSELLINI: I stick to what Rouch tells me: "I take someone and give him a suitcase in which I have placed a tape recorder. He can say anything he wants. I don't know him. I know nothing at all, and don't want to know anything at all. Nothing is organized, etc."

CAHIERS: Rouch hasn't told us anything of the sort. He has told us: "I have wanted to make a film on the theme of the meeting, which is a surrealist theme."

ROSSELLINI: It is a matter of knowing where one starts. I went to that screening telling myself: All right, here is *cinéma vérité*. On the floor there was a camera,[2] and everybody adored it—and it was just a camera. A camera is a camera. It's an object. It doesn't excite me. The mere idea of a camera exciting someone absolutely infuriates me. It's unconscionably stupid. This camera, which so excited the senses and genital organs of the people gathered around it, left me absolutely indifferent. If I can't get excited over a camera, I can't understand those who do. There are also pederasts in the world! But I am not a pederast, and I can't understand them. You have no idea how ridiculous that whole evening was. Supremely ridiculous!

CAHIERS: Still, technique is a necessary tool. You are a technician yourself. You have invented a new type of zoom lens.

ROSSELLINI: Technique is necessary but one doesn't need to talk about it. It is something that must come naturally. No need to get all excited about it. "See this camera? Look at this camera!" I don't feel like looking at it. It doesn't interest me. It's unbelievably childish. This sort of mythomania is infantile.

I was the first one to defend Rouch. Whereas you, at *Cahiers,* were rather hostile to him. All I can say about him, even if he is not here, and though I might say it with rage, will always be the expression of very friendly feelings. The other evening I thought he was touched by what I told him, and quite grateful for it. I hope I was useful to him and that my criticism will lead him, I am not saying to adopt my views, but at least to improve what he is doing, to return to his earlier premises. Something very good might yet come out of it.

CAHIERS: In any case, Rouch has always introduced his films as pure experiments. He tries to attain artistic creation through roundabout

2 The camera of the Maysles brothers.

means: "When you film with no preconceived idea, something happens," he says.

ROSSELLINI: What I am going to tell you will explain why my reaction is so violent. You know how I liked that kind of expression. I used to say the same things. But I used to say them without working at the total destruction of everything. I used to say: "I start with an idea that's clear in my head. I must express it. I refuse to use an actor because I have to prepare his lines beforehand. Since I am looking for something absolutely sincere and absolutely true, I try to do away with too much preparation. I take someone who seems to have the right physique for a part to bring my story to an end. And since he is not an actor but an amateur, I examine him in depth, I appropriate him, I reconstruct him, and I use his muscular abilities, his tics, to turn him into a character. The character I have imagined might change along the way but only so as to reach the same goal. I'd never do anything to change my initial idea and get to something completely different, otherwise I wouldn't feel I have done a thing."

At the same time, I wanted to gather as much human documentation as possible, to study certain spontaneous attitudes in man, etc. All this supplementary material was going to help me in my discovery of the truth. Because what I was aiming at was the honest discovery of the truth. However, in order to find the truth one must also have a moral stance. A critical judgment. I can't let myself be led by chance and, wanting to go to Orly, find myself at Le Bourget.

CAHIERS: What do you call a *moral* position? The advocates of *cinéma vérité* use the same term.

ROSSELLINI: First of all it is a position of love, and therefore of tolerance and understanding. And of participation. You see how things mix, complicate each other and always become tighter, closer to who you are, what you want. But the moment you stand back from any judgment, any participation, any sympathy, any tolerance, and say: "Be as you are, I don't give a damn," then we are no longer speaking of a moral stance but rather of a very cynical attitude.

CAHIERS: As far as we are concerned, we do see a moral stance in *La Punition*. A poetic one, if you prefer. There is a way of filming people that makes them look ridiculous, stiff, that reduces them to a state of animality. And then there is another one that makes them look free. In *La Punition* the characters are ridiculed, no doubt about it, but only superficially. The idea of freedom (which was the first title of the film), shows through their behavior.

ROSSELLINI: As far as I am concerned it doesn't show at all. What you say is right. There are all sorts of ways to show a person, that's true, but I do not believe that an artistic event is really such if it doesn't involve any affection. You can ridicule someone and at the same time show him some affection. You can even treat him in a way that's apparently quite cruel. But affection remains the only real moral stance. I cannot recognize anything lacking affection as artistic. In the case at hand there is no affection since everything depends on chance.

What irritates me, what infuriates me in today's world? Today's world is too gratuitously cruel. Cruelty means the violation of someone's personality, the forceful extraction of a total and gratuitous confession. If it were a confession aimed at something specific, I would accept it: but it is the practice of a voyeur, of a pervert. In other words: it's cruel.

I react very strongly to all this because I firmly believe that cruelty is always an expression of infantility, always. Today's art gets more and more childish every day. Everyone seems to have a mad yearning to be as childish as possible. I don't mean naïve: childish. From infantility we have fallen to the bottom of the human scale. We have become anthropomorphic monkeys: we'll soon move on to the stage of the frog or the eel. This is what angers me. This total lack of decency.

This infantility, we have seen it in the *nouveau roman*. We see it in an absolutely unbelievable form in painting. We have gone as far as total vanity, sickness. And all this in a world that's daily becoming more serious, more complex. Now, since this world has been made by people, I must always accept it, in spite of all the moaning and groaning that goes on, such as : "We are heading toward total destruction, the atomic bomb, etc."

Today, art is either moaning and groaning or cruelty. There is no other measure: either you complain or you devote yourself to the gratuitous practice of petty cruelty.

CAHIERS: It would seem you are attacking all the contemporary art of the last hundred years. There is no affection in Flaubert's *Éducation Sentimentale,* or if there is, then you can find it also in contemporary art.

ROSSELLINI: Take, for instance, the way in which everyone is speculating—it has to be called by its real name—on incommunicability and alienation. I find absolutely no affection in all that, only an enormous complacency. But maybe there is some affection there and I am the one who's unable to see it. Maybe it eludes me. As I cannot perceive colors this side of red or that side of violet, it is as if there were none. I must be a physicist to know that on this side of red there is infrared, and on that side of violet there is ultraviolet. If I am not a physicist, if I judge with my own senses, I am unable to perceive any affection.

Today it's enough to complain to be part of the avant-garde. But to complain is not to criticize, which would already be a moral stance. When you find out that people may drown if they fall into the water, and keep on pushing them into the water every day to confirm the awful and abominable fact that indeed they may drown, I can only be disgusted. On the other hand if, the moment you discover that people who fall into the water may drown, you start taking swimming lessons so that you can jump after them and save them, then it's another story.

This is what, as I told you last year, has made me decide to stop making films.

CAHIERS: But then, what are you going to do?

ROSSELLINI: I am going to do something else, which you will soon see. I know someone will tell me: "How come, you were boasting that you had given up cinema, and yet you're still making films!" However, what I will be doing will in no way fit within the usual scope of cinema. I intend to film a certain number of things that will above all have a didactic value. I believe that's what has to be done when we have fallen so low.

CAHIERS: Didacticism and art have never been good bedfellows.

ROSSELLINI: I couldn't care less about making art. It means giving up lots of things. It is a moral stance, which I would even define as—if you allow me to use this word—heroic. What everybody seeks instinctively is to illustrate himself. I am trying not to. I want to become useful.

CAHIERS: You say "useful." How useful?

ROSSELLINI: Useful from a human standpoint. To return to my example: if I see that people who fall into the water drown, and the world is suddenly flooded, I think it is my duty, since I am aware of what is going on, to learn to swim and become a swimming teacher.

CAHIERS: Other artists have conceived of their duty in a completely different way. For them, art has no immediate practical use.

ROSSELLINI: Let me explain myself. For art to be art, it has to have a language, it has to express things in a way that can be understood by average people. Without this it becomes totally abstract—by which, however, I do not mean to say that one must make commercial films: let there be no misunderstanding.

I firmly believe we lack the basic elements. Today we lack something more than ideas, and language: we lack a vocabulary, an alphabet. I think it is necessary, to do worthwhile work, to reestablish the letters of the alphabet. It is not a matter of transforming art but of rediscovering it. To rediscover art—an art that has been completely corrupted, that has dissolved in abstractions, that has made us forget how to use not just language but the very alphabet on which language rests—we must do our best to reestablish language, and, once we have reestablished it, to make sure that each word regains its meaning, its value, and, becomes again the fruit of some profound thought, so that language may be again a real language and not just a collection of labels stuck on samples of things of which we barely know the existence. At that point it will be possible to salvage all the forms of art. This is what seems most important to me.

CAHIERS: Don't you think that the evolution of art may be irreversible?

ROSSELLINI: Do you think that in the world there have never been periods of darkness, along with the collapse of entire civilizations? It's a historical fact that keeps recurring. Once a civilization collapses, so does art, language, etc.

CAHIERS: Even admitting that today's art is an art of decadence—or, at least, that it is heading toward an end—it is quite possible that it will not be reborn until after this civilization has disappeared.

ROSSELLINI: A civilization always bears its art as a fruit. Only its great monuments remain with us: for instance, the works of poets who, in their times, had only a very minor role in the civilization they have illustrated. But when a civilization no longer exists, or is going through a crisis, art dies with it, and often before.

So, what shall we do? In order to exist a civilization needs art. And art, in order to exist, needs clear ideas. Today, we all look at this world of science and technology with scorn. We think it is pure vanity, something disastrous that will lead us to total ruin. So, I am going to ask you another question. What have we done to understand this phenomenon—which nevertheless belongs to our world and our civilization—morally, to understand it, to participate in it, and to find in it the emotional sources necessary to create an art? There is a huge gap between, on the one side, the evolution of humanity, a technical evolution, and on the other, the artists who were once able to participate in this evolution, assimilate it, integrate it into their own consciousness, and turn it into something even more wonderful. That's when we can give a very precise meaning to strictly technological discoveries, and when they can truly become part of our civilization.

This is what the artist's function should be. If he is unable to fertilize things—which in themselves are fatal, irreversible—he has failed to perform his duty.

A bee flies over a flower, takes its pollen, and transforms it into honey. At the same time, it fertilizes other flowers. Its activity is multiple, complete: this is the real function of the artist. If an artist stops flying, stops moving, and keeps on complaining that the flowers around him are not to his taste, nothing will change, the flowers will no longer reproduce, and they will die. We are heading for the aridity of death. Now, I believe that art is not death but life. Art is life. It is a way of perpetuating life, a way of giving a reason to things, a way of firing up enthusiasm, of provoking emotions. When art revels in killing emotions, in depriving life of what is vital, then it is no longer art.

CAHIERS: Yes, but a contemporary artist will tell you that he has the feeling he is doing precisely what you are advocating.

ROSSELLINI: The highest moral stance contemporary artists have taken has been to speak of incommunicability and alienation, that is to say, of two phenomena that are absolutely negative. I would understand a modern artist perfectly if he said: "Technology has produced the alienation of a great number of men and has rendered them unable to communicate, but it is possible not to be alienated, just as it is possible to communicate." This is the function of the artist: to conquer things, to find the new language.

This is why I have decided to devote myself to strictly didactic things. Because we don't know anything at all. For instance, in Italy Vittorini has published a text investigating the possibility of communication between art and the world of science. The upshot is that four hundred pages have been written to prove that there is absolutely no possibility of communication between the two. This is what I call total lack of affection. If you look at any human phenomenon with affection you will inevitably find something vital in it. The mere fact that it is human is enough to make it vital.

CAHIERS: Some painters as well as some musicians affirm that there is communication between their art and modern mathematics. Rightly or wrongly, that's what they say.

ROSSELLINI: A little too wrongly, if you ask me. Let me give you an anecdote. Last year, in Spoleto, I directed *I carabinieri*. Musicians from all over the world come to this festival. I needed three minutes of music for a transition. Nobody could do it for me. At the eve of the general performance, I still did not have my three minutes. So, I placed myself in front of a tape recorder and with a fork produced a "tock tock," and with a piano a "twang twang," and then I asked a guy with a violin to come and add a small "dzin, dzin." And so I recorded my three minutes of music and everybody took them very seriously. Appalling, isn't it? On the billboard I wrote: *Music by Johann Pach*. This is how easy it is to fool people today. I find it amazing. . . . On the other hand, did I really fool them?

CAHIERS: It's an old criticism. People thought Van Gogh's work was childish.

ROSSELLINI: We cannot compare our times with the last century. At the end of the nineteenth century we were still living in such an artistically rich world, that any experience could be useful. But today, since these riches no longer exist, we must at least try to reestablish the elements of understanding.

Our technological evolution is on a completely different scale from what has happened until now. Humanity has put together something quite extraordinary, I have to admit it since I have the greatest respect for technology. But it is something that we can't fully comprehend. That's the tragedy. The real problem. Today's people are unable to avail themselves of the very civilization they have built.

How was the Renaissance born? The Renaissance was born at the moment artists became aware of the enormous step forward humanity had taken in the field of science and technology. What did they do then? They became scientists. They studied anatomy, perspective. Their preparation was strictly scientific, but it was so tied up with their nature, and enthusiasm was so much a part of it, that they have given us great masterpieces. The Renaissance is such a tremendous event in the history of humanity! Its artists were able to delve into a scientific reality, appropriate it, rethink it, and turn it into superior art.

I was in Pisa recently. The old cemetery (*Camposanto vecchio*) was bombed during the war. The lead roof melted, fell onto the thirteenth-century frescoes below, singed them, and seriously damaged them. To fix and restore the frescoes the first layer of paint has been peeled off and has been set up on large frames. All that's left on the walls are the red drawings over which the frescoes were painted. But what's most striking is that, when you see the frescoes themselves, you realize that everything there is reduced to the essential: there is no hint of anatomy in the figures, the lines are amazingly simple, there is no trace of perspective. Yet all this exists in the drawings. You can see all the muscles in the legs of a figure, all perfectly detailed, you can see what was done by the master and what by the artisan who was working with him—one drew the model, the other completed it. This is the sort of simplicity those people had attained! They could cast off everything they knew to get to the essential. Quite an extraordinary achievement! In those times, frescoes played the role cinema plays today. They were large messages. The words of the characters were inscribed on long ribbons.

Now, take the ninety percent of our painters and tell them: "You can paint whatever you want, but first you must make a good drawing." If the painter cannot do it, anything he will do later is cheating. If he can do it, whatever he'll do after, even if it is totally abstract, is a conquest.

Do you know the book: *The Biology of Art?* Some Russian and English researchers have taken a few chimpanzees and a few gorillas and have let them paint. Kongo, the Picasso of the chimpanzees, is an extraordinary abstract painter. But if you take him away from pure abstraction, he is absolutely unable to do anything even remotely suggesting the mechanics of thought—thought is at the basis of analysis, of consciousness, and therefore an exact science of all the things you want to express. You say: "But it is the expression of an artist!" All right, but of a monkey artist. Man has intelligence. What does intelligence mean etymologically? To understand the inside of things. If you show me a group of men who cannot read into things, then you might as well show me a group of chimpanzees. Personally, however, I'd rather see a man who can understand and read into things, and who, therefore, has an absolute awareness of things. Because if he has that, then with just a stroke of his pencil he will be able to give you the full emotion he gets from his knowledge.

CAHIERS: Jean Paulhan says that "informal" painters are mystics.

ROSSELLINI: Yes, but it is a childish mysticism. I am a man solidly anchored in reality. What does "informal" painting give me? The representation of the torment caused by a skin disease? The contemplation of skin diseases bores me! The world is so large, and has become so complex, that the artist is forced to know a lot of things. For years now I have been reading only science books.

CAHIERS: How does this help you in your work as filmmaker? What relationship is there between these two activities?

ROSSELLINI: There is a very strict relationship. You will see it when I have started my next film—but I cannot give you an example because I am determined not to say anything about it in advance. You can find extraordinary sources of emotion where you would have never suspected they could exist. The next film I am going to make . . . but I do not want to call it a film since it must not be cinema. So, let us say that I am going to "put on film" the history of iron. Do you find it ridiculous? Someone who is going to film the history of iron is bound to be ridiculous. And I intend to be not an artist but a pedagogue. And there will be so many extraordinary things in it, eliciting such a quantity of emotions, that, even though I am not an artist, I will succeed in drawing somebody to art. I am sure of it.

"Nouvel entretien avec Roberto Rossellini," in
Cahiers du cinéma, *no. 145, July 1963, pp. 2-13.*

AN INTERVIEW WITH ROBERTO ROSSELLINI

BY ADRIANO APRÀ AND MAURIZIO PONZI

APRÀ/PONZI: *Voyage in Italy* has been criticized a lot, but you have said very little about it. What do you think of it now?

ROSSELLINI: I have hardly ever talked about it—what is there to say? You can't go around defending yourself, though if you could that would have been the time to do it, because the critics were so aggressive. . . . But you see, this is a job in which you have to take all kinds of risks.

APRÀ/PONZI: What was the meaning of the finale? Many people thought—wrongly I believe—that it was mystical.

ROSSELLINI: Look, it's difficult to remember these things ten years later—they're all water under the bridge now, and once things are over and done with you have to forget about them. That finale—there was a lot of argument about it, but I thought it was really simple. There were these two great big figures with a lot of little figures around them, all of them smaller still because they were kneeling down. What the finale shows is sudden, total isolation. You could say "it's not clear"—I remember at the time they said things to me like, "well there you should have had a long shot showing such and such . . ." But I didn't want a long shot in it. You see, these things are implicit. Unfortunately it's not as if every act of our lives is based on reason. I think everyone acts under the impulse of the emotions as much as under the impulse of intelligence. There's always an element of chance in life—this is just what gives life its beauty and fascination.

There's no point in trying to theorize it all. It struck me that the only way a rapprochement could come about was through the couple finding themselves complete strangers to everyone else. You feel a terrible stranger in every way when you find yourself alone in a sea of people of a different height. It's as if you were naked. It's logical that someone who finds himself naked should try to cover himself up.

APRÀ/PONZI: So is it a false happy ending?

ROSSELLINI: It is a very bitter film basically. The couple take refuge in each other in the same way as people cover themselves when they're seen naked, grabbing a towel, drawing closer to the person with them, and covering themselves any old how. This is the meaning the finale was meant to have.

APRÀ/PONZI: And does.

ROSSELLINI: Perhaps I was wrong not to make it completely obvious, to show it as a discovery. But that wouldn't suit me. I think it is a fairly normal thing in modern society that many marriages are limited companies under another name. People get married because one of them has a job to do, the other has a number of connections, so the wife acts as a public relations officer while the husband is an economics official, to describe it in terms of actual jobs. There is more to life than that. And the couple in *Voyage in Italy* are that kind of couple—people who have nothing to say to each other outside of their work, their job, their daily routine. A vacation, more than anything else, is the death of them. Owning a lovely villa in one of the most beautiful places in the world counts for nothing, because they no longer know what to say to each other: if they don't talk about quotations on the stock exchange or making this or that deal, their relationship is finished.

APRÀ/PONZI: The film reveals their secret feelings . . .

ROSSELLINI: Yes, but it shows Italy as well, which is also a feeling, and an important one at that—Katherine looks at all the documentary stuff and scarcely sees it. It's a different kind of life, a different ethnic group—there's an ethnographic encounter too.

APRÀ/PONZI: You know that many people took the miraculous ending as the dramatic centerpiece?

ROSSELLINI: But it's scarcely there—there is a miracle, but there's confusion and hysteria surrounding it. In fact it's also a human sign, a sign of good faith. What do these two characters aspire to be? Banal as they are, they want to be perfectly rational beings. They're not geniuses, but the most 'normal' beings you can imagine. They are rational because their life is based on things they have to believe in at any cost.

The woman is always quoting a so-called poet who describes Italy as a country of death—imagine, Italy a country of death! Death doesn't exist here, because—it's so much a living thing that they put garlands on ʳhe heads of dead men. There is a different meaning to things here. To them death has an archaeological meaning, to us it is a living reality. It's a different kind of civilization.

APRÀ/PONZI: The ending of *Stromboli* has also been criticized a lot.

ROSSELLINI: And for the same reasons as *Voyage in Italy*. A woman who has been through the war, through both collaborationism and the concentration camps, and has been clever enough to find all the right answers, comes to a point where she finds herself lost in a maze. What she does is to sit down and cry like a child, and it's the only sane thing left she could do, the only tiny spark of something human and alive. If a child is crying, if he's banged his foot, he makes just the same noise—"Oh mommy," "Oh God"—it sounds just the same.

APRÀ/PONZI: Doesn't the ending of *Vanina Vanini* depend on the same kind of fear, on not knowing what to do?

ROSSELLINI: *Vanina Vanini* has a different setting. It's a different moment in time. There's more mysticism. There's a certain element of mysticism in all of us. The most atheistic man on the face of the earth finds some reason for transcending himself, even in his atheism. These things too are a part of man.

APRÀ/PONZI: In your view, is Karin leaving or going back?

ROSSELLINI: I don't know. That would be the beginning of another film. The only hope for Karin is to have a human attitude toward something, at least once. The greatest monster has some humanity in him. In *Monsieur Verdoux*, when he is about to go to the guillotine, they offer him a drink and he refuses it. But before he is marched off he needs to screw up his courage, so he takes the glass, sips at it and is off: and then he feels the taste of it, turns back and drains the glass—and then away he goes to have his head cut off. It shows an extraordinary human side of him. There is a turning point in every human experience in life—which isn't the end of the experience or of the man, but a turning point. My finales are turning points. Then it begins again—but as for what it is that begins, I don't know. I'll tell that another time, if it has to be told. If things haven't happened there's no point in going on and getting involved in another story.

APRÀ/PONZI: What do you think of the cinema today?

ROSSELLINI: I'm not interested in the cinema as such. You can't proceed by allusions. So much is now urgent in life that it's useless just to allude to things. The arguments have to be explicit now. We have to have the courage to admit that in the past hundred years all art has been reduced to complaints. An artist is lesser or greater depending on how much he complains. They call it "denunciation." The fact is that it's complaining, because if it was protest it would be carried out differently, more aggressively, and what's more, if you become aware that something's wrong, you have to be prepared to break away from it and put it right. But this eternal moaning and protesting about how much is wrong is something quite different. Anyway it's not true that everything is wrong, some things are and some things aren't. The fact is that the main reason for things being wrong is that men are incapable of living the lives they have made for themselves. Real alienation, in the strict sense of being alien to something, is when man feels alienated from his own life. Unhappily today life is very complicated, and to understand it you would need to make an enormous effort, and above all get down to studying it. And because there's more and more idleness in the world this is never done, and so there comes a point when you are living only on feelings and sentiments, and you moan about it. I agree that there are a lot of people with cause for complaint, but on the other hand there must be many who don't complain. Complaint, as a rather irrational attitude, doesn't seem to me to get you anywhere, when you have extremely concrete things to struggle for. The concrete things in life are pushed aside at every point. We know nothing of them because we don't get down to examining these problems.

APRÀ/PONZI: Don't you think that *Voyage in Italy* was a film on alienation *ante litteram*?

ROSSELLINI: Yes, it was about alienation. But that's why I say that I don't even like my own films, because when I began to make those kinds of films it was of course in a search for an orientation, but when you realize that everyone has the same orientation, or is engaged in the same search, it becomes an attitude, an attitude of complaint.

APRÀ/PONZI: But neither *Voyage in Italy* nor for example *Europe '51* are complaining films. And they were made ten years earlier . . .

ROSSELLINI: That's just the problem—I feel a great responsibility for it. Everyone else has gone the same way since. How can you justify the attitude of art in general today? Leaving aside the cinema, look at painting, which is so obviously an art. Look at the deformation that has taken place there. It's not just breaking away from formulas, it's not just a revolutionary movement. It was, but it's gradually become a kind of escape, a refusal to look at the world. It's a dramatic change. Now, the world has a right to expect something of intellectuals, and artists in particular. If the artist can't in some sense act as a guide to point the way, if he is unable to take his bearings and say, "today, at this point in time, these are our horizons," then the function of the artist disappears. For the artist to be an artist only for himself may be very pleasant indeed, but from a social point of view it offers us nothing. It's useless to go and see an artist's work so that you can say, "Look, how interesting, this man feels so rootless and alienated. . . ." You can go and look at such phenomena if you want: if you are really interested go and visit a mental hospital. You'll find much more interesting and important cases there, things you'd never imagined.

APRÀ/PONZI: What you're saying is that the artist should have a realistic outlook.

ROSSELLINI: Yes. He should be aware of the world he is living in. I think the artist has a very definite function in this world—it is to clarify things. When culture involved little knowledge, even if it was of an elevated kind—as in Greek thought, classical history and mythology, and the Bible—artists gave of themselves as much as they

could, they brought this knowledge to life and made it comprehensible to everyone: it was their civilization. But tell me, does modern art
try to concern itself with everyday things like the motorcar? The
movement of art knows no repetitions: this is why I have had to take
my distance from that world, why I could only remain a part of it by
working in a completely different way. If you make a change it must
be a total change. In a period like this there are facts that only the
sciences of biology, physiology, and demography can supply. Men
have taken a billion years to become three billion. In thirty-five years,
in the year 2000, they will be six billion, if mankind goes on repro-
ducing at the present rate—these are amazing facts. What does
anything else matter? Men must be strong enough to come to terms
with this fact. It arises from their conquests in the fields of medicine,
food production, science and technology. The result of affluence has
been that life expectation has risen from twenty-seven to almost
sixty-seven years. Alexander the Great was a little boy who would
have been soundly spanked today if he tried to do what he did then.
Now the world is inhabited mainly by old people, because life is
longer. These are the facts: once you become aware of them, there
must be some artistic response, and it may be genuine and capable of
making such an impression that everyone will be made more sensitive
to these great problems. In a very few years, if these things aren't put
right—and however much people complain they aren't being put
right—the time will come when hordes of men will come like locusts
to eat us because we have more food than they, or we will be going to
kill them because they have taken the food out of our mouths. Well,
this is not much of a prospect for *homo sapiens,* and for good or evil
we belong to the species of *homo sapiens.* We have to find out
whether we are *sapientes* or not: at least we should try to be *sapientes.*

APRÀ/PONZI: What do you think of improvisation?

ROSSELLINI: If the ideas are good you can allow yourself the luxury
of any improvisation. When you come to make a film and it has to be
specially striking, when it needs an air of authenticity which it
couldn't have if it was premeditated. Then improvisation comes in,
but it must be the improvisation of civilized man, not of the savage.

APRÀ/PONZI: I think that is what you said about Jean Rouch's
La Punition.

ROSSELLINI: Yes.

APRÀ/PONZI: And was *Voyage in Italy* improvised?

ROSSELLINI: We never knew one day what we'd be doing the next. Things came together on the spot—there's a certain logic to things that can't be calculated in advance. You're on the set, you have the scene and the actors, and they dictate the course you have to follow, they almost give you the characters themselves. But this doesn't mean you stand there and toss a coin to find out which way to film.

APRÀ/PONZI: *Europe '51* is a typical example of "character-experience."

ROSSELLINI: All my films are. I advocated this so much in France, where I have always spent a lot of time; and the young directors there, who were emerging in the right atmosphere and had had the right kind of education for it, caught on to it at once.

APRÀ/PONZI: Do these ideas still hold for you?

ROSSELLINI: Yes, but they still belong to the "complaining" school, and this gives me a horror of them. These feelings crystallized in me in the period of 1953–55, the period of *Voyage in Italy* and *Fear,* when the word "denunciation" was being bandied about so much. That was what made me think. What use is "denunciation"? It's of some use if you have a very definite philosophy and want to carry out a very definite action. If you want to do something useful, you have to be aware of all sides of the problem, and therefore of the positive sides as well as the negative. You have to go back to Jules Verne to find the positive side. The great turning point of the Industrial Revolution, a transformation involving so much social injustice, and so many ideas which are now strongly denounced, came about from the moment that man developed science and put it into practice with technical means unthought of before. This was the biggest discovery of all. Man had been a slave: energy had always been supplied by men, with some help from the animals, and then from windmills and watermills: but this was a great advance. Now, energy, steam energy, and electrical energy, were invented. It was a fantastic advance, introducing a completely new dimension into men's lives, and transforming their prospects. Prometheus's discovery of fire, which had begun it all, has been sung by thousands of poets, good and bad, and depicted by thousands of painters and sculptors. But who has tried to describe anything of what has happened this time?

It is an extraordinarily uplifting experience to seize something from nature and make a tool of it. It's out of proportion to complain because of course energy had made it possible to have factories, and factories have brought machines to make things that are quite useless, or of relatively little use; and that man is somehow subjected to these things . . . It's of course quite right that there should be protests, but what I don't understand is that people have nothing else to say. Knowledge is the most human thing there is, nothing is more human than to know things, and we no longer know anything—I think that's a basic fact of our life today.

APRÀ/PONZI: Where does your return to history fit into all this?

ROSSELLINI: Why is there nothing but protest today, if not because we have forgotten everything that went before? To put things to rights you have to put history to rights too. *L'età del ferro* [The Iron Age] shows history in this way.

APRÀ/PONZI: You show history, but in the present tense rather than in a historiographical perspective.

ROSSELLINI: History has been written, in all good faith, in order to educate. Education is both a beautiful and an ugly word. It comes from *ducere*, to lead—in other words to grab someone by the scruff of the neck and drag him off wherever you please. This is how many of our history text books are written. At one time, for example, it was necessary to uphold the monarchy, and everything was done to that end. Propaganda isn't an invention of this century by any means. It's because we can see this today that it's possible to try to rewrite some parts of history in a way that's much closer to the truth. Mommsen wrote his histories, which are a storehouse of knowledge, to show that the Germans were the only real Aryans in Europe. One person comes out with an idea which looks original—or even is original—and everyone buzzes round it like bees around a hive. And then it gets hacked about and falsified, and that's how so many mistakes arise. So even to look at or reexamine history is something of the greatest importance. What we should go back to history for is to rediscover man, and man at his humblest at that. What do the exceptional men matter to us? I'm quite unmoved by the myth of the superman. *Viva l'Italia!* is a documentary made after the event, and trying to deduce what had happened: it was made with great precision with regard to the facts, using a diary kept by Bandi, who was close to Garibaldi. He was no poet, but he wrote down everything that happened: you have only to read it and you can see what Garibaldi was like. I didn't make any of it up. Read Bandi. Garibaldi was expecting the arrival of the Bourbon generals to negotiate the surrender of Palermo. They entered his room as he was peeling an orange, and he divided it up and gave a segment to each of them. Someone was there to see it and write it down. You only have to do a little research. All Bandi says about the meeting with Mazzini is what they said to each other outside the door. We don't know what they said when they went inside as no one wrote it down, but it was not very difficult to reconstruct: it was only necessary to read Mazzini's letter to his little friend in England. *Vanina Vanini* is very like *Viva l'Italia!,* with elements of pure Stendhal. That's to say, it has a certain critical content, it's not exactly a straight version of the novel. I borrowed from many other things: *Les promenades dans Rome, De l'amour, Napoli Roma Firenze,* etc., using whatever fitted, and I made the film as a work of historical research. Being a Roman, I could easily understand a character belonging to the period of the rise of romanticism—an intense girl, who has only to give her hand to someone to feel herself swooning . . . Stendhal's character is so cynical—a Roman noblewoman who believes in absolutely nothing and satisfies specific instincts, so this is where there is a substantial change in the character. With a different actress the character would have been different.

It is highly significant that one of the many regulations at the Congress of Vienna was a ban on wearing long trousers, because trousers were not just a matter of dress . . . The *sans culottes* had become a revolutionary movement. When men are capable of such meanness it's not something you can ignore, it needs saying. It seems incredible, but these are things humanity is made of. It is the little things that strike one, much more than any theories. You have to say things so that everyone can understand them immediately. But again I should make clear what I mean. It is possible to become popular by going along with what is fashionable, but you should instead try to sow the seeds of ideas which are to become popular.

APRÀ/PONZI: You once said of *Stromboli* that Karin is a character "imprisoned in a geographical situation."

ROSSELLINI: Her geographical situation is a trap. She finds herself in a maze, not because she chose to enter it but because there comes a moment when the very structure of the world she lives in turns into a maze. I think this is the point which most closely ties in with the needs of the story. It all has a definite logic. If Karin had not ended up on an island, it would have been quite a different kind of story, with a different twist to it.

APRÀ/PONZI: What can you tell us about *Europe '51?*

ROSSELLINI: As far as the world is concerned Irene is mad. She is someone who wants to make her life profoundly moral and does everything possible to achieve that, but it isn't what the average person would do. And so she ends up behind bars in a lunatic asylum, with people looking up at her as if she were mad, while she gazes down at them as if they were mad. The unfortunate fact is that what the world lacks today is heroes.

APRÀ/PONZI: How about *India?*

ROSSELLINI: It was the discovery of another world, and I've learned a great deal from it. I felt a need to go in search of something completely new, to venture into a world I already had a mental image of. The Indian view of man seems to me to be quite perfect and rational. It's wrong to say that it is a mystical conception of life, and it's wrong to say that it isn't. The truth of the matter is this: in India, thought attempts to achieve complete rationality, and so man is seen as he is, biologically and scientifically. Mysticism is also a part of man. In an emotive sense mysticism is perhaps the highest expression of man. As all expressions of humanity are respected, so too are these. All Indian thought, which seems so mystical, is indeed mystical, but it's also profoundly rational. We ought to remember that the mathematical figure naught was invented in India, and the naught is both the most rational and the most metaphysical thing there is. India has a much more complete view of all human leanings, and attempts to preserve them all. This is what's so fascinating. In a world like ours, where everything is black and white, intermediate shades and colors don't exist: but the world, and still more the men in it, are made of such shades.

APRÀ/PONZI: And hadn't you discovered this before *India?*

ROSSELLINI: In my own personal attitude towards things, yes I had. But I didn't go to India to find this out or to get confirmation of it. I went so that I could see a world at the end of one period of history and the beginning of another; perhaps still more dramatic. That's what drew me there, and when I was there, it was this very complete conception of man that struck me most. I felt the need to break out of the restrictions and limitations here. It was there that I understood the need to embark on a new search and gain a wider consciousness: to be in the fullest sense you have to become conscious, you need to study. And I began to do so systematically.

APRÀ/PONZI: What do you think of the Nouvelle Vague?

ROSSELLINI: I haven't seen much of it. For a time I was very close to these young people, and we were very friendly, and then they went their own way. Basically, if I did make any contribution to what they have done it was through stressing again and again that above all they should not regard the cinema as something mystical. The cinema is a means of expression like any other. You should approach it as simply as you pick up a pen to write with. What matters is knowing what you are going to write—everyone should write what he enjoys writing. Writing to please someone else would only be insincerity. The absolute freedom these people have with the camera arises from this demystifying of the process of making films.

APRÀ/PONZI: What have you to say about your experience in the theater?

ROSSELLINI: You know what it is to have a chance at something? Well, this is a chance I've happily seized with both hands. Every new experience counts—they're invigorating. In the theater there's no work of creation, it's all a matter of polishing up and putting in order, trying to make the script come over clearly.

APRÀ/PONZI: What relationship do you have with the actors?

ROSSELLINI: It's a question of the individual personality. George Sanders would cry all the way through the film. He moaned terribly and I used to say to him, "What are you getting so depressed about, at the worst you'll have made one more bad film—nothing worse than that can happen. I don't see anything to cry about in that, there's no cause for despair. We've all made good films and bad films. So we'll make another bad one. What can you do? There's no need to tear your hair out or kill yourself over it." No, to be frank, you have to make them work for you. You can use anything, even an actor's temper. You see something, in a moment of temper, a certain expression or attitude, that you can use, and so of course you use it. I don't in the least believe in collective art, I can't believe in it. I don't claim to be an artist but I've always hoped that my work is artistically acceptable. It's no good descending to compromises: you have to get somewhere at any cost, at the cost of quarrels, fights, bad moods, insults, and coaxing, anything you think will work.

APRÀ/PONZI: Why did you choose Sanders?

ROSSELLINI: Don't you think he was obvious for the part? It was his bad moods rather than his own personality that suited the character in the film.

APRÀ/PONZI: How did you come to film the Indian material for TV?

ROSSELLINI: They were making a documentary and I shot the material for the documentary.

APRÀ/PONZI: Do you think the optics are different in cinema and TV?

ROSSELLINI: I don't think there are very big differences. The aim is different, that's all. If you're making a documentary, you're making a documentary; if you want to make a film you make a film. Whether you're doing it for television or for the big screen is of secondary importance. . . .

APRÀ/PONZI: So you don't think that the spectator is psychologically conditioned by the means of transmission?

ROSSELLINI: Of course not. What conditions him is who it's made by. If it's made by a fraud going round doing scandalously false things, that does affect him. If *India* was a documentary, it was thought up with the intention of making a psychological discovery, going deep into things and not just looking at the surface. When you make a straight documentary it's more journalistic in tone, but there is a purpose to that too. A documentary is for giving information, a film is more exploratory, and that's the real difference.

APRÀ/PONZI: How did it come about that you made *L'età del ferro?*

ROSSELLINI: It didn't start out as such. It started from the need to make a different kind of film. I have said this before.[1] There came a time when I felt really useless. I think this is what's wrong with all modern art. It's all moans and protests, but never takes account of what the real problems are. It seems obvious to me that these protests are made without knowledge of the world. The truth is that we protest because we are confronted with a world whose structure we haven't grasped, and that seems to me to be the basic problem. There's a point at which it's necessary to have a clear picture, a definite horizon. This is the only way to get one's bearings and see where we stand in time and space. No figure in geometry can be drawn, and so no space can be enclosed, without some points of reference. This is why I have gradually begun to work and study to try to understand how things are. Everyone knows that cars exist, but there are reasons for them apart from their being vehicles you lease and then drive along a road. In my investigations I've begun to find out things which are not only amusing and interesting but which I think can be a stimulus to the artist. What I have been trying to do is to pass on to others an awareness of this cultural need, of the experience of learning and teaching, without detracting from the content. My project has been to research new things and new sources. When you become aware of these things everything develops in a different way. Art has basically always had the aim of understanding as well as expressing things. But what does the art of today learn or teach? It is the expression of a certain malaise, of a state of unhappiness and incomprehension but no more. I don't think that real human problems are just problems of the impossibility of communicating or anything so subtle—such things belong to psychiatry rather than to man, to be frank they are extreme cases viewed by dilettantes. Man

1 See "Conversatione sulla cultura e sul cinema," in *Filmcritica,* no. 131, March 1963.

has discovered artificial energy—electricity, steam, thermodynamics, etc. It's such a great gain that today men travel through space and from continent to continent in vehicles driven by this energy, catch airplanes, light their homes at the flick of a switch, use electric irons—it's an overwhelming victory of man over nature. But tell me who has been moved by it, what artists have dwelt on this amazing fact, which is at least equal to the discovery of fire, in fact greater. We have been indifferent, we have even begun to complain about it. Now if we don't really develop our awareness of it, how can we have a feeling of the world we live in, the riches this world can have. Above all you have to take the reins of this civilization and be able to drive it toward ends that have to be thought out quite clearly and precisely. But instead, strangely enough, as science and technology advance— and I mean science and technology in the highest sense, the sense of knowledge which is human in its very fibre—art abandons itself to daydreams in the most irrational way imaginable. You build a rational world and the whole of art takes off into fantasy, fantasy which is always inward-looking because then it becomes a protest, placing a restraint on fantasy itself. Why did I choose the Iron Age?—our historical epoch is known as the Iron Age. It was one of the first things to be dealt with. If you have to start writing an alphabet, you must first work out what are the vowels. If you like, *L'età del ferro* is there to establish the vowels, and I shall go on from there. These projects must be developed with the utmost rigor of method, if they are to have their proper educative effect. I have drawn up something of a plan, which closely follows my own study program. As this program was useful to me in putting my ideas in order, it may be of use to others. This is what my system of pedagogy amounts to. I don't put myself on the outside or go and think about things in an abstract way. I just recount the experiences I have had.

APRÀ/PONZI: It is then a plan which has been tested and corrected against reality.

ROSSELLINI: Yes. Another serious mistake of our times is to try and summarize everything: things can't be summarized. It's possible to find a clear and comprehensible way of saying things that might be obscure, but you don't understand anything through summaries and digests. It's a real attack on imparting knowledge as it is understood in the modern world. It is based on a false view of consciousness, examining things at a distance and fitting them into theories which remain no more than theories and bear no relation to historical reality. It's a strange way of expressing a theory, a way which commercializes what should be a very different kind of endeavour. One of man's great struggles has been to subjugate man—there have been endless attempts, with recourse to everything from grace to eloquence, rhetoric, and history, to subjugate man to man. Every effort has been made to make this enslavement so far as possible a voluntary act, and this was the least difficult part of it. The best way to keep a slave is when he has voluntarily become a slave, in the belief that he is performing a duty. It's what in modern terms would be called conditioning. Today this has been rationalized, it has become scientific.

APRÀ/PONZI: In this state of things the very aim of art ought to be to free men from their conditioning.

ROSSELLINI: This should of course be the great mission of art. But art has also always had the opposite objective. Virgil, you know, was an "agitprop" man for the Roman Empire. This aim is clear in all Virgil's work—of course he believed in it, but it's all done to extol a definite world. It's quite clear to me that this was the case. And at the same time he was a very great poet. He worked in absolute good faith, he admired his civilization and designed all his work to further it. Today, when we can perhaps see things in more scientific terms, and the spirit of democracy has made some advance, much more choice is needed, choice of a genuine kind, with the possibility of choosing true knowledge. But instead choices are always made on the basis of slogans or stereotypes.

APRÀ/PONZI: You yourself tend toward rationality, though not in a schematic way.

ROSSELLINI: What's schematic is to limit the realm of knowledge to rationality. Arithmetic is highly rational but it's not rational 'as compared to mathematics, if you understand me. It's all a question of the level of development of thought.

APRÀ/PONZI: The striking thing about *L'età del ferro* is the way the sequences you have made alternate with existing film or newsreel.

ROSSELLINI: You have to use everything that can make a point firmly and with precision. If you are making a bridge you need so many supports. There'll be one on the bank, one in midstream, but there's sand and mud there so you put it a bit further across the stream but resting on rock, and then you come to the far bank. So you can't make supports, the supports for the span of thought and knowledge, in a completely pedantic way. I always run away from preconceived ideas. I don't fix a style in advance. You have to use everything that will help to carry out your aim. So I jump from film taken from the archives to reconstructed scenes.

APRÀ/PONZI: What criterion did you use for choosing the extra film?

ROSSELLINI: I have a lot of film that's exactly right for editing up.

APRÀ/PONZI: Film you've made yourself?

ROSSELLINI: A detail is enough for a particular kind of montage. If I haven't got it, I just have to do the montage with pieces made for something else. I use them as I want, do the montage leaving some parts blank, and then go and shoot the little bits I need to put the thing together as I want.

APRÀ/PONZI: But why did you use existing film and not original footage?

ROSSELLINI: Look, I did very little. My son Renzo did it all, he's the director—I only thought the idea up . . .

It was all found in newsreel film, he used newsreel for the things he needed at that point of the story. Again, I advised him not to look at things with preconceived ideas. You should see the films from which he took the frames he used—they were quite different.

APRÀ/PONZI: What does the fifth episode mean to you?

ROSSELLINI: The fifth episode is an attempt to end with a poetic comment on this civilization of ours, made as it is of iron and steel and machinery. There's a lot of our own film in it but a lot of material from the archives too. There's documentation of every kind in existence. If there's material you can use by way of illustration, why not use it?

APRÀ/PONZI: What's the relation of this kind of montage to what you talked about in your interview with Bazin?[2]

ROSSELLINI: It's not montage in that sense. There are some things I need to have which it would take months and months of work to make—I can find the same thing on the market, so I take it and use it in my own way—by putting my own ideas into it, not in words but in pictures.

APRÀ/PONZI: Don't you think that even before montage the pictures have a meaning that montage can't completely destroy?

ROSSELLINI: They don't. You have to give them it. The pictures in themselves are nothing more than shadows.

APRÀ/PONZI: For example, what about the shots of that strange flying machine in the second episode?

ROSSELLINI: All right, you still have the curious appearance of the machine. But if you take a detail away in touching up the film, the significance of the picture changes, doesn't it?

APRÀ/PONZI: But it can't take on an opposite meaning to what the picture represents.

ROSSELLINI: Of course it can. You don't do this just by selection, but by working on it. Anything you look at is reality for one person but not for another. If I instinctively see a certain reality, without working it out in great detail I place the camera at a certain angle, and film reality in my own way—you see? But if instead I'm using existing film, it's as if I had the picture before it was put on film: I have to rework it as with any real object.

APRÀ/PONZI: Often, even in *L'età del ferro*, you have been reproached with being too slapdash.

ROSSELLINI: If you make a film in a very finished way, it may have a certain intellectualistic value, but that's all. What I am trying to do is to search for truth, to get as near to truth as possible. And truth itself is often slipshod and out of focus.

2 See in this volume the interview with Rossellini and Jean Renoir by André Bazin, pp. 90–99.

APRÀ/PONZI: In the fourth episode, why do you have an "uncommitted" hero?

ROSSELLINI: It's a true story, I haven't embroidered it very much. The main character is a Piombino worker. The story is very significant for me. The war takes away Montagnani's living. Like everyone else at that time, he's looking for work. He goes with the rest. It's no longer just a question of the factory you work in, and all the exploitation that involves. The factory regains its importance as a source of employment, fulfilling the dreams of centuries: in that part of Italy they've worked iron for three thousand years.

APRÀ/PONZI: The fifth episode has been compared to some futuristic experiments. What do you think?

ROSSELLINI: Why, because of a few parallels? The similarity is only technical. The voice offscreen is only a commentary, expressing the need to look at things in a different way. I want to arouse interest in certain ideas. The synonyms, for example, were used not just to explain the action but to express thinking about it.

APRÀ/PONZI: You seem very involved in the fifth episode, unlike for example in the first two, where you take your distance.

ROSSELLINI: The standpoint is different. What belongs to history has become simple, manageable. But we aren't masters of the world in which we live, you can see that every day. We must make ourselves masters of it. The idea of progress hasn't really spread very far: the "denunciators," for example, have a retrogressive position.

The pictures in the fifth episode, anyway, are never grand or celebrative, they simply analyze the phenomenon.

APRÀ/PONZI: The last shot has been taken as meaning that you are inviting us to a general reconciliation.

ROSSELLINI: The last shot only shows men who are able to be in each other's company. It's a fact you can test out against reality. They're coming home from work, and each of them goes off to his own house, they don't exactly break into song. This is how things are.

APRÀ/PONZI: What's the meaning of the refrigerators which are shown at such length?

ROSSELLINI: It used to be the case that to show something grandiose you would show a cathedral, not a refrigerator. It's a statement of fact, I wouldn't generalize about it. It's true there is something absurd about the refrigerator: it's a luxury, it's superfluous, but it's also of practical importance. You have to be able to look at things without preconceived ideas to know what's right and what isn't. You have to be able to state things. This is exactly what I've tried to do in the fifth episode, bringing together a lot that can perhaps point to a clearer way forward.

"Intervista con Roberto Rossellini," in Filmcritica, *no. 156-157, April-May 1965, pp. 218-234. Translated by Judith White.*

AN INTERVIEW WITH *CAHIERS DU CINÉMA*

BY JEAN COLLET AND CLAUDE-JEAN PHILIPPE

CAHIERS: During your last interview with *Cahiers*, we sensed in you a certain bitterness toward both the world and contemporary art.

ROSSELLINI: I feel no bitterness. Whatever the culture and whatever the civilization, art has always played a very important role: that of giving a meaning to the historical period in which we live, and what's more, a meaning accessible to everyone. From Homer to Giotto, that's how it was: the real sense of things. Besides and beyond any didactic concern. Today's art has lost that role, I think. All the arts.

CAHIERS: You greatly surprised us years ago when you said you were going to leave fictional cinema to turn toward a didactic cinema. Seeing *The Rise to Power of Louis XIV*, all these distinctions seem idle. Maybe it is a didactic film, but first of all it is an admirable work of fiction.

ROSSELLINI: One must always try—as one would say in French—to make all the ingredients of a given subject "rise." And not just passion or sex. My film is a good example. It is rigorously historical: an essay on the technique of a *coup d'état*. If it "rises" emotionally it is because it deals with a human enterprise.

CAHIERS: Do you feel that at a certain moment there was a break in your work?

ROSSELLINI: I don't know. I don't care. I only care about being coherent with myself day by day. The past doesn't interest me. One should never rest on one's laurels.

CAHIERS: It would seem that one element all your films share is a certain attitude of patience. You wait for things to reveal themselves. Is this what you call neorealism?

ROSSELLINI: I am not very fond of classifications since their only use is to make one forget their contents forever. Ultimately, what is really important? To see people as they are. It is the most moving thing in the world. So, one should always set out without preconceptions.

CAHIERS: You had no idea of what you were going to do in *Louis XIV?*

ROSSELLINI: I knew something about the character. That's all. When you have a preconceived idea you're doomed to produce a thesis. That's a violation of the truth, and a violation of instruction.

CAHIERS: Could your cinema be defined as "a cinema of attention"?

ROSSELLINI: Attention and acknowledgment. When we look at a human being, what do we see? His intelligence, his desire to do things, and then his enormous weaknesses, his poverty. In the end this is what makes things magnificent. I was quite struck, as a boy, when I learned that at the siege of Toulon, Napoleon was so scared he shook like a leaf. An officer who stood next to him noticed it: "But you are shaking with fear!" he said. And Napoleon answered: "If you were as scared as I am, you'd be gone!" It's this double dimension in man that moves me, in all its infinite variations. He is small, lost, stupid, naïve. And he does great things.

CAHIERS: You have dealt with Louis XIV the way you once dealt with Saint Francis of Assisi: focusing on his lesser qualities, his shyness. He looks like a child.

ROSSELLINI: What moves me most in man is his weakness, not his strength. In modern life people have lost any heroic sense of life. They should rediscover it because man is a hero. Everyone is a hero. Our daily struggles are heroic struggles. To show this well one must start from the bottom.

CAHIERS: As in *General Della Rovere,* who, at first, is an obnoxious person and then becomes a hero?

ROSSELLINI: Yes, he dies like a hero. And it is possible because there is a welcome touch of madness that drives him to it. I always hope for such a touch of madness.

CAHIERS: The heroism in *Voyage in Italy,* does it come from within the characters or is it a force, a sort of grace that transforms them?

ROSSELLINI: I can't answer you. To do so, I'd have to support one thesis rather than another—and "thesis" isn't even the the right word since your question bears on a matter of faith. My only answer is the humble discovery of humanity. This is my main concern, which may be compared and identified with Christianity.

CAHIERS: The notion of civilization seems to be another one of your main concerns.

ROSSELLINI: What strikes me is that we live in an apparently—and from both a scientific and technological vantage point really—developed civilization. But our human civilization has not been able to keep up with this development. So, are we to think that this technological/scientific civilization is bad, or that it is man who has not been able to adjust to it? In either case, it is important to get people involved in it so that they can be the judges. If civilization is not what it should be, people should be aware of it and do their best to change it. If, on the contrary, people believe it is right and does not need to be changed, then they have to get a hold of it and control it entirely.

CAHIERS: In your recent "Manifesto" you claim that you want to resituate man within his horizon. Isn't "modern anxiety" an effect of uncertainty, of the fact that people no longer see that horizon?

ROSSELLINI: Of course. Let's examine things rigorously. School, for instance. What's its purpose. School provides young children with the first general ideas. As they grow older, and their comprehension increases, they get more and more specialized. At the university, they learn everything there is to learn about bridges, roads, concrete, and nothing else. Every day we are invaded by information: the press, radio, television, cinema, all the arts. What do they tell us? Nothing about our civilization. They only tell us about our feelings of anxiety in relation to it. It is an important observation. But it has been made. Let's move on. Up to a certain time, up to the end of the eighteenth century, that is to say until the scientific and technological evolution started moving at an absolutely overwhelming pace, our civilization, extremely slow in its evolution, had very firm bases: the Bible, history, and Greek and Roman mythology. All the arts grew out of them. In the eighteenth century things started moving with a very accelerated rhythm. Man took control over the natural forces, but without being fully aware of it. Art failed to play its role. What happened then? No more horizon: just fog all over. We no longer know where we are going. We are filled with anxiety.

CAHIERS: Do you believe in ideologies as working hypotheses? For instance, in Marxism as a method of historical knowledge?

ROSSELLINI: No. I believe we must know things outside of any ideology. Every ideology is a prism.

CAHIERS: Do you think we can see without the help of one of those prisms?

ROSSELLINI: Yes, I believe so. If I didn't, I wouldn't have made my life so difficult. There is only one starting point, which might be either right or wrong: either you have faith in humanity or you don't. If you do, then you must believe it is capable of all the possible good. If you don't, then everything I've been saying is useless. I believe man is capable of all the possible good—if he knows.

CAHIERS: To go back to your films, *Voyage in Italy* already expressed such a faith. At the beginning, the characters don't see anything of what is happening both inside and around them. Then they become anxious. Then they begin to see.

ROSSELLINI: They have opened their eyes. They were very respectable beings, a couple who had come together with the intention of doing their best in the world: work, make money, have a bank account, a decent life. It's a rather widespread dream, isn't it? But they were not real human beings.

CAHIERS: That's what you say now, but when you look at them, when you film them, you don't seem to judge them at all. Your characters seem totally free.

ROSSELLINI: I go back to what I was saying about ideologies. Every ideology has something good and something bad about it. But it always limits you in your freedom. And freedom is the center and the mainspring of everything. If you make a discovery while you are free, it is wonderful. But if you manage to achieve perfection in conformism, there is nothing heroic about that. My main concern is to bring this heroic sense back into our lives.

If man has some ability, it must be that: the discovery of morality. Take Hitler: he makes people obey. They are within the boundaries of morality since they obey. The dangers are quite serious. If man can make a choice, he becomes a real man. But his choice must stem from total freedom, and assume all the risks of error, and adventure.

CAHIERS: And even the risk of getting lost?

ROSSELLINI: This is where he becomes a hero. What is a saint? Someone who has run the risk of losing himself, who is always about to get lost. Just a tiny false step and he can topple over. The only faculty belonging to man and man alone is that of judgment. The rest of his behavior you can find in any animal, in different degrees: obedience, habits, etc. An animal's directions come either from instinct or from tropism: it moves toward things that are simply convenient to him, very practically so. But life cannot be just a matter of practicality. Today, practicality has become the myth of our lives. What has happened to morality? This is a serious question.

CAHIERS: In your films heroism is never a purely individual event. Generally it is connected to a collective adventure, a community.

ROSSELLINI: Each individual personality must live in harmony with the rest of the world. How? Through tolerance. A virtue that's born out of immense wisdom. Being tolerant means to get out of obedience, and arrive at something that's born out of your own consciousness. Unfortunately, in today's world we rely on classifications. Classifications don't lead to consciousness, and therefore they can't lead to the heroic need to improve.

CAHIERS: Godard used to say of you that in pushing realism as far as it could go, you rediscovered theater. At the end of *The Rise to Power of Louis XIV*, the king's life becomes pure spectacle: hence the king's meal.

ROSSELLINI: Yes, he lives on stage. He lives for others, but also to be above them. Until the final scene when he demands to be left alone and gets rid of his costume. There, he redeems himself. His victories have led him to bitterness. He speaks of the sun and of death, neither of which can be looked at. He doubts. That's when Louis XIV reacquires a very human dimension. What's important, in his case, is that bitterness brings about judgment. "I want to be left alone and rest," he says. There is no pride in him at that moment. By undressing he gets rid of the masquerade where the others have followed him out of stupidity. He redeems himself completely. What I like in that character is his daring. In the scene at the tailor's, for instance. He is even insolent. At the same time, we are aware of his terrible shyness.

CAHIERS: He's fighting against himself.

ROSSELLINI: That's the double dimension that makes his character so extraordinary.

CAHIERS: This may well be the first time that, in your work, you deal with a character who seems unable to love. Only the dying Mazarin is capable of an enormous generosity.

ROSSELLINI: The main character is a king who exercises his power. So, what do you expect? It's a considerable premise, don't you think?

CAHIERS: Since *General Della Rovere,* you've been using a great deal of zoom shots. In your other films the characters were followed by the camera.

ROSSELLINI: In *General Della Rovere* as well. Before the zoom shot, to follow a character was no mean deed. Now, thanks to this new technique, I can make a film like this one—which is quite a big film—in twenty-four days. And working less than six hours per day. At the ORTF [Office de la Radiodiffusion et Télévision Française], there was a strike against overtime. We couldn't put in more than five-and-a-half hours of work a day.

CAHIERS: What were your work conditions like at the ORTF?

ROSSELLINI: I was given total freedom. I didn't want any stars, I just wanted someone. They let me do what I wanted. Which in today's cinema is no longer possible.

CAHIERS: Godard manages to get that freedom working with tiny budgets.

ROSSELLINI: Yes, but you have to stick to certain themes. Even with a little budget, you can't get out of those themes, and they are always the same. With the exception of Godard, Resnais, and a few others, the *cinéma d'auteur* is a thing of the past.

CAHIERS: What do you think of the way in which you have influenced Italian cinema?

ROSSELLINI: Maybe I have had some influence on young French cinema. But I wouldn't say this of the young Italian cinema. My relationship with young French filmmakers have been very warm and human. But I haven't had anything similar with young Italian filmmakers. If I have had any influence on Italian cinema, it has happened through my films. There have been no man-to-man contacts otherwise. Whereas I have had such contacts with French filmmakers. The last time I saw Truffaut, for instance, I told him that my daughter had had an operation. He felt ill, there and then. It both distressed me and moved me very deeply. Then he told me. "You know, you are part of the family." See, this is a great conquest. In Italy, I have never found such a warm relationship with any of my colleagues.

CAHIERS: Lyricism in your films has always had a dazzling quality. We wait for it, and then we are struck, as if by a lightning bolt, illuminated.

ROSSELLINI: Just a few minutes ago you used the right word: patience. Patience is also a virtue! Then there is the spark.

CAHIERS: What do you think of today's audiences?

ROSSELLINI: Today's audiences are so accustomed to getting no respect that when they finally get it, and genuinely so, they feel lost.

"Roberto Rossellini: La prise de pouvoir par Louis XIV," in Cahiers du cinéma, *no. 183, October 1966, pp. 16-19.*

A PANORAMA OF HISTORY

ROSSELLINI INTERVIEWED BY FRANCISCO LLINAS AND MIGUEL
MARIAS, WITH ANTONIO DROVE AND JOS OLIVER, MADRID,
JANUARY 1970.

LLINAS/MARIAS: Can you tell us about *Socrates?*

ROSSELLINI: I try to make films which give general information and
a general sense of direction. We made a twelve-hour series, *La lotta
dell'uomo per la sua sopravvivenza* [Man's struggle for survival],
which is a sketch of the history of man from the time he appears on
earth to when he lands on the moon. It's a history of new ideas, of the
difficulty getting them accepted and the painfulness of accepting
them. The whole of human history is a debate between the small
handful of revolutionaries who make the future, and the conserva-
tives, who are all those who feel nostalgia for the past and refuse to
move forward. The film gives an outline of history—I think it's useful
as a start, because school study programs have degenerated so and
don't meet modern needs. It gives me a kind of core around which I
shall take certain key moments in history and study them in greater
depth. I made *Atti degli Apostoli* [Acts of the Apostles], for example,
because I think the arrival of Christianity was an important turning
point, changing man's relationship to nature and thereby putting him
in a position to act. The result was Western civilization. This happened in the specific historical context of Greece, Rome, and Jerusalem. *Atti degli Apostoli* is about Jerusalem. For Greece, I've chosen
Socrates, who may have been much earlier, but represents in embryo
everything that was to come. Greek civilization was based on fate.

Destiny plays the principal role throughout all Greek tragedy. Socrates introduced the idea that man must use his brain, and he was condemned for it. His starting point was magnificent: "All I know is that I know nothing." And from the idea that it's necessary to use reason, came science. My next film will be *Caligula*.

LLINAS/MARIAS: Do you write your scenarios on the basis of actual fact?

ROSSELLINI: I don't write scenarios. I'm incapable of it. But I have fairly definite ideas. For one thing I have read all the documents about Socrates, though there are few enough of them. The basic source is Plato's writings, but even there you have to be careful: some modern critics raise doubts about them. But they are important works. And then it's possible to reconstruct the life of the period on the basis of documents. For example, everyone talks about Athenian democracy, but we know nothing about it. No one dreams what it was really like. There were continual elections, which were really tantamount to drawing lots—they weren't proper elections. They drew names and then black or white voting balls, and if a white ball was drawn at the same time as a name, that person was elected to public office. Another interesting point concerns the tribunals which judged Socrates and others. There was a jury of 515 people. They drew lots in the morning and they had to give the verdict before dark, as they didn't dare let them sleep. History is full of things like that—it makes it more spectacular and more accessible to the public. I am very strict in this respect, and don't allow myself to make anything up. I perhaps allow myself some interpretation of the psychology of the character, but none of it is invention.

LLINAS/MARIAS: What will *Caligula* be like?

ROSSELLINI: It will be a proper film, because it's a difficult thing to deal with for television—for example, Caligula and his sister were lovers, and if you cut that you lose all the historical feeling and authenticity. I make him into a rather special character. If you have read *The Lives of the Caesars*, you'll know that Suetonius thought all twelve Caesars were a bunch of madmen. But Suetonius was writing long after the event, when these families were no longer in power, so I think it's rather a facile view, I've adapted the story of Caligula to the psychology of a modern Roman. He was the son of Germanicus, who had been a great hero and a champion of the republicans. The birth of the Roman Empire was a gigantic paradox: after a hundred years of war between the republicans and the monarchists, the republicans won and proceeded to build the Empire. Germanicus was almost certainly poisoned by Tiberius, after giving him the support of his legions in the election. Caligula's brothers and his mother were also assassinated by Tiberius and Caligula himself was deposed by his grandmother Julia and his younger sisters, one of whom was to be the mother of Nero—nice little sisters for a man to have. My stories are strictly historical but there is always some room for interpretation of character. In my opinion Caligula, as the son of Germanicus, is a republican. His grandmother knows it and so do his sisters, and Tiberius is soon informed. He decides to adopt him and make him emperor so that he won't stand in his way. He couldn't kill him as he had killed his father and brothers, as public opinion would have rebelled against him. This probably is what happened, for Tiberius did say, "Thus shall I rid myself of the serpent in my breast." Later Caligula joins forces with Tiberius and becomes his heir. This is all true. He began with extraordinary acts of justice—for example, he ordered the burning of all documents concerning Tiberius's trials of his mother and brothers, which meant that they were rehabilitated. He called elections, to find out what public opinion was, but no one would take part. Gradually he realized that the corruption ruling in Rome was so great, and the people so insensitive, that there was nothing he could do. And suddenly he began to do insane things, going so far as to make his horse a consul. In my view he did these crazy things in order to debase the idea of the Empire in the eyes of the Romans. He did quite incredible things, but Rome could take incredible things. For example, he declared war on the North Sea, and marched from Rome with his legions, a hundred thousand men in all. I'm not making this up, and it isn't some scriptwriter's fancy—he got to the shore of the North Sea and ordered them all to start gathering shells. In Rome, the Senate hailed it as a great triumph. It's all highly paradoxical.

LLINAS/MARIAS: When you choose these key characters, do you take their contemporary significance into account?

ROSSELLINI: I think it's enough to know what happened, there's no need to think up fables. The world is always the same because it is shaped by men. It's easy to find parallels with things that happen today—it's a matter of chance, and I have no interest in picking them out. *The Rise to Power of Louis XIV* describes the technique of taking power—which is a useful thing to know. What Caligula shows is how corruption can reach such a point that people can no longer identify their own interests. I think that's a serious matter. But the thread that runs through all these films is the reconstruction of daily life. If you've seen *Atti degli Apostoli* you'll have noticed how meticulously it's recreated. It's important because it shows a recognizable side of man.

LLINAS/MARIAS: Can you tell us about *L'età del ferro* and how it is related to *La lotta dell'uomo per la sua sopravvivenza?*

ROSSELLINI: It's a matter of looking at history from different angles. *La lotta dell'uomo per la sua sopravvivenza* is much more concerned with ideas, which are always related to technology as well. The agricultural revolution was a great advance for mankind, the first great revolution carried out by man, because from then on man was not so completely at the mercy of nature and began to use it to strengthen himself. He no longer feared nature and gradually embarked on the decisive conquest of it. *L'età del ferro* is more concerned with the development of technology. The technology of iron brought advancement, and changed men's way of looking at things. It began with the Etruscans. Etruscan civilization spread from north of the Tiber into Tuscany and across Italy to Venice. In that period, the Iron Age, about 1200 BC, the great metal-producing centers of Europe were Etruria and Spain. The metal production of Etruria was a possible focus of development within Italy. The Greeks, who had established themselves in the south of Italy, went up to central Italy in search of iron ore, which was already indispensable to them. They built roads for this and it is possible that Rome was built at a junction in this road system, since it lay at a point where the Tiber could be forded. The adventurers and prostitutes who were living there eventually began to levy a toll. This is a different, much more concrete way of looking at history.

LLINAS/MARIAS: All these films are very concrete and at the same time very meaningful. Can you tell us how you achieve this?

ROSSELLINI: I don't know, it's part of my way of doing things. The scenes are very faithfully reconstructed. I always begin with the things of daily life. For example, when coins began to circulate in Greece tunics had no pockets. So people carried the coins in their mouths and when they had to speak, they spat them out into their hands, and put them back in their mouths after they'd finished speaking. It's very concrete, but highly significant. It's a way of making the film interesting and saying something original at the same time as giving real information.

LLINAS/MARIAS: In *L'età del ferro* there are fragments of other films, such as *Austerlitz, Scipione l'Africano*, etc. Was this because of economic difficulties?

ROSSELLINI: It's very important to make the film spectacular, because above all you must entertain people. These are films which should be of use not just to intellectuals but to everybody—if they were not it would be pointless to make them. They have to be spectacular and that means spending a lot of money, which you can't do for TV. These are cultural programs and so they come furthest down in the television budget. If you try to fight to change this you don't get any films made, and the important thing is to make films. So we took some sections of other films and reused them in a different context, and in this way we got the spectacular effect for much less.

LLINAS/MARIAS: What role do you play in the series your son has made?

ROSSELLINI: I write what you might call a scenario, though it isn't really, it's more a series of suggestions and bits of information, and the series is made from that. I virtually produce them—I certainly follow them very closely, but I leave him complete freedom and responsibility.

LLINAS/MARIAS: Is it true that your son directed some scenes in one of your films?

ROSSELLINI: When I was making *The Rise to Power of Louis XIV*, one of my daughters was having a very serious operation, and on the day I left Paris for Florence. As production couldn't be held up, my son shot the sequence in the kitchen and the dining room.

LLINAS/MARIAS: Your son directs the series and you make the films. Why is this?

ROSSELLINI: Because I'm older and can't work as hard: but it doesn't make any difference.

LLINAS/MARIAS: Is the series you are preparing on the Industrial Revolution at all like *L'età del ferro?*

ROSSELLINI: It's more like *La lotta dell'uomo per la sopravvivenza.* It too will be twelve hours long. It shows the beginning of a complete transformation of the world, and the origins of the modern world. It starts with short scenes from the Middle Ages, as you always have to have a definite starting point. The Middle Ages saw the establishment of a completely vertical kind of civilization, with very strictly defined values, and a clearly established way of thought. We had to show the normal everyday life of the artisans, the guilds, and the corporations. The film goes on from these brief scenes to the discovery of the technology which gave rise to the Industrial Revolution, and therefore to a related series of phenomena like colonization, new forms of social organization, and the new political ideas.

LLINAS/MARIAS: What other series or individual films do you intend to include in this panorama of history?

ROSSELLINI: A number of key points come out of the series on the Industrial Revolution, for example the period of the French *Encyclo-pédie.* We shall show developments of modern time as well; recently there have been extraordinary phenomena such as youth movements which begin with very great energy, and then disperse because they encounter so many obstacles. And then there's the problem of men taking on more and more responsibilities, needing to make themselves better and better as men. Then I want to make a film of the history of colonization, which is very important, and arises directly out of the Industrial Revolution. And for western countries I am thinking of making a history of Japan, which could be very interesting, as it's a highly developed country, scientifically and technically one of today's four great world powers, but appearing in a much less advanced part of the world. I think it's very important to study it closely. These plans are enough for three or four years' work.

LLINAS/MARIAS: Will it take you very long to make *Socrates?*

ROSSELLINI: Four weeks—I never take long to make films. It will be two hours long, so that it can be shown on TV as well as in the cinema, and it will be in color. I do everything in color now.

LLINAS/MARIAS: Do you think your work will be affected by being shown on TV networks which still don't have color, as in Spain?

ROSSELLINI: You will have color soon, and there's always some delay in showing these films. But it wouldn't matter very much if you saw them in black and white. Externally it would not look so good, but internally it wouldn't change. What matters is not seeing the film in the best possible conditions, but the film itself, and you can't do much harm to it by showing it on a small screen instead of a big one, or in black and white instead of color.

LLINAS/MARIAS: What is your attitude toward color?

ROSSELLINI: Quite simply realist.

LLINAS/MARIAS: Aren't you making these films in chronological order? Why did you make *L'età del ferro,* which covers the whole span of history, before *The Rise to Power of Louis XIV?*

ROSSELLINI: These were the first two, and they're experiments trying to show what could be done in this field. After that the real educational operation began. I have a better order now, but the problem is there are hold-ups. It can happen that I have difficulty in making a particular film, and have to alter the order. *Caligula,* for example, has been a great problem, as I can't make it for TV, and to do it for the cinema I'd have to accept production norms, use well-known actors, etc., and this would make it impossible for me to make the film I want to: I can't make it in such conditions. Perhaps I'll leave it until later to make it, but I must make it somehow.

LLINAS/MARIAS: Does it matter to you what order the public sees these series in?

ROSSELLINI: It ought to matter, but I don't mind as long as they are shown soon. If they see *Atti degli Apostoli* first and then *La lotta* there's no harm done, though it would be better to see them in the order in which they were made. We have a production problem as well. They're not easy to produce—they're fairly expensive for TV, though they're cheap in terms of the cinema. To make a good film which will reach the widest possible audience, you have to make it spectacular. TV has great potential but at the same time it is very restricted. The tendency towards this kind of program is still not very marked: the need for it is felt but it's not yet clearly expressed.

LLINAS/MARIAS: When did you first form this interest in making educational films? For example, were *Vanina Vanini, Viva l'Italia!*, and *The Flowers of St. Francis* a part of this plan?

ROSSELLINI: I've always had an inclination for it—less definitely, of course, and instinctively rather than consciously. Then I gradually realized that the cinema wasn't up to much, because there was so much to be said and at that time it was saying things of very slight importance—so I began to work on this program of study and explanation.

LLINAS/MARIAS: But don't you think the aim of *Europe '51* was as laudable as that of your recent films?

ROSSELLINI: Yes, but I had to make it then, in 1951, because when it was released, all the political forces hated it, they felt exposed. In all honesty I must say that in 1947 or 1948, I don't remember when exactly, a French friend of mine interested me in a book by Marcuse, and I read it. It's not that I based myself on the book, but it obviously made me think in a certain way about things—and so I thought it very important to make a film about the situation in Europe. It was an attempt to show contemporary history, and I think *Europe '51* even predicted things we have seen happen since.

LLINAS/MARIAS: In 1965, you published a manifesto[1] about educational cinema along with [Bernardo] Bertolucci, [Vittorio] Cottafavi, [Gianni] Amico, [Tinto] Brass and others. Did it have any practical repercussions, apart from Amico's *Tropici,* which was also made for TV?[1]

ROSSELLINI: I don't think so, but I don't really know. I didn't see

1 This *Manifeste* was published in *Cahiers du cinéma* (no. 171, October 1965, pp. 7–8), and signed—besides Rossellini—by Gianni Amico, Adriano Aprà, Gianvittorio Baldi, Bernardo Bertolucci, Tinto Brass, and Vittorio Cottafavi.

Tropici, but in Pasolini's latest film, *Medea,* all the first part, on barbarian civilization, is very educational. It's a good sign.

LLINAS/MARIAS: Pasolini admits to being influenced by some of your films, especially *The Flowers of St. Francis.*

ROSSELLINI: I can't give you a critical judgement. Pasolini is someone very important, very tormented and involved—an extraordinary man.

LLINAS/MARIAS: You wrote a very enthusiastic piece about *Hawks and Sparrows.*[2] Do you feel close to Pasolini in some way?

ROSSELLINI: When Pasolini made the film it seemed very likely that it would be a complete failure commercially. So I defended the film because I thought it was right.

LLINAS/MARIAS: Do you think your ideas about educational cinema should be adapted to the cultural level of the people who will be seeing these films?

ROSSELLINI: I don't think so, because you have to be very direct, and find out what stimulates people's imagination: and what's more I think that while people may have different levels of culture, they don't differ in their ability to understand things. There is really nothing beyond men's understanding: all it takes is to say things comprehensibly, in as entertaining and interesting a way possible.

LLINAS/MARIAS: But for example, the kind of subject to be dealt with will vary from country to country.

ROSSELLINI: I follow what I believe in. For example, we give *La lotta dell'uomo per la sua sopravvivenza* free to the underdeveloped countries, and let them use it as they want, with complete freedom. If they want to make an introduction running down our civilization and what it has brought them, they can do so—because in this way you can carry out useful educational work. So far I've only made films about things that happened around the Mediterranean, because that's what I understand best. But these films can be used by people as they like, even to criticize us if they want. The important thing is to open the debate and start a discussion.

---

2 Although Rossellini sided with Pasolini's film during a press conference at the 1966 Cannes Film Festival, he is not known to have written any article in this sense.

LLINAS/MARIAS: Everybody still talks of you, even today, as a neo-realist, though that seems to us to be an oversimplification.

ROSSELLINI: It's just a label.

LLINAS/MARIAS: It's said there's a break between your earlier films and your more recent work for TV. It seems to us that your way of looking at things is still the same, and your aim is still the same: to understand reality. The only difference we can see is that your early films had contemporary subjects, and now they are more historical. Your early characters suffered things passively, while Louis XIV and Caligula are people who act. Can you tell us how this change of perspective came about? Why is the outlook different, when the vantage point is the same?

ROSSELLINI: I accept what you say. Of course, one matures, one's own experience deepens. Man is in struggle with himself, a struggle between his animal and human sides. Anatomically the result is that the cerebellum is the oldest and strongest part of the brain. If a man dies and is put into a resuscitation chamber, this is the first part to recover, followed by the heart, lungs, etc. But the cortical area, which is the newest and the most delicate, as well as the most advanced— since this is where thought arises—does not recover. Man in a way feels the responsibility this part of the brain lays on him and often tries to put it to sleep. Alcohol, and certain inhalants found in all civilizations, are ways of evading this responsibility. This tendency is more violent in the modern world, because man's responsibilities are greater. He feels afraid of them, he either confronts them or runs away. When he runs away he becomes an animal. We are in a period of great progress. Should we reject it and hold ourselves back, or go along with it and master it? This is why we must constantly raise our consciousness. For example, I have never reseen any of my films, because I'm afraid of the temptation they offer to stay tied to things that are over and done with. It leaves me free to go in search of new things. I undertake the search because of what I am. I don't change: my age changes, but not my nature. I now think that what's important is to show man that he can be completely human, and that responsibilities too can give him exceptional happiness.

LLINAS/MARIAS: What do you think now of films like *Voyage in Italy* or *Stromboli?*

ROSSELLINI: I don't think about them. Things that I've completed are finished with for me, they concern me very little.

LLINAS/MARIAS: That's strange, because they are more intimate, personal films, perhaps more autobiographical than the others, which take a distance from things.

ROSSELLINI: Yes, but for all the appearance of taking a distance, they're always a little autobiographical in the end, I can't fail to feel involved. And when I make a film it's not something I want to see again. I'm interested in things that are to be done.

LLINAS/MARIAS: It's well known that you're in favor of informing people and opposed to "educating" them, but we'd like to know how you think the teaching of the cinema should be organized.

ROSSELLINI: As the director of the Rome Centro Sperimentale, I have done some things in this field, and I hope they've been right. In particular, I reduced the number of students to the financial capacity of ·the school. We accept only as many students as can really do everything in the two years they spend there. There are twenty-eight, nine of them foreign, and they form one group, while the nineteen Italians are split up into four other groups. Apart from the studies they do over two years, they make their first films in the television studio, because the eye can adjust with the Ampex and they can check what they have filmed at once. Then they go on to 16 mm, and those who are able to, go on to make full-length films, but on their own account, not ours. They are quite free to do what they want. This is how the school is organized today. We don't have our own professors, but we call in people who are highly qualified in a wide variety of fields. The course is designed to give a thorough knowledge of technique which enables the students to get to grips with the cinema and also to experiment with new things. Together with this, as well as three months' practical work, we organize seminars sponsored by the school. For my part I think it's highly relevant to hold seminars on economics, psychology, and sociology, so that they'll talk about things they know about, not what they've been told. We also organize what seminars the students think necessary—if two or three people want a seminar on the history of the cinema, we hold it; if a few, or even one, want one on advertising, we do that as well.

LLINAS/MARIAS: Are there classes in cinematographic theory or the grammatic rules of the cinema?

ROSSELLINI: No. All the students who come to the school know much more about it than we do. What could we teach them? Such things can't be taught, methods of that kind have entirely disappeared. If someone thinks it necessary, he asks for a seminar. But don't you think they all know these things? Who could teach them? What's important is to have a technical medium. If the student is an artist, that's all he needs. If he's not, I think it's absurd to imagine that someone else can make him into one. All the students have a study grant of 75,000 lira a month, and food provided. So they don't have subsistence problems, which I think is very important. The students are also on the Administrative Council and have a consultative vote. I think it all works very well. They are completely responsible for themselves and we don't have to worry about discipline at all, as they see to it themselves. The important thing is for the school to be as efficient as possible. I should add that the overall curriculum is adapted to the type of student we have: the courses are determined by their needs.

LLINAS/MARIAS: Are the films made at the school shown to the public?

ROSSELLINI: We can't show them commercially because the school is a state institution. This year we presented a student's film at the Locarno festival, and last year we entered one at Venice. We can do this kind of thing, and we also show in cine-clubs.

LLINAS/MARIAS: Does the school produce the students' films when they've finished?

ROSSELLINI: Never. We have three well-equipped miniature studios, planned a long time ago. The students can experiment in them at times. The school also has a rather good film library, with some eleven thousand films.

LLINAS/MARIAS: Why do you have so little interest in fiction, and in the narrative mechanism used to create emotions in what is usually called fictional cinema?

ROSSELLINI: Because reality is much more fantastic than fiction.

LLINAS/MARIAS: It seems to us that a high degree of confidence in reality is the cornerstone of your filmmaking.

ROSSELLINI: Above all I have confidence in man. Man is everything. What interests me most is to see him operating, in any circumstances.

LLINAS/MARIAS: But isn't your confidence in reality, which goes together with a rejection of fiction, also a way of avoiding personalism? I mean, you always have a very clear moral viewpoint about what matters, but at the same time you don't want to point it out, because you have confidence that things will speak for themselves.

ROSSELLINI: I try to intervene as little as possible. My work is scientific: I observe things and bring them into contact—which of course has to be done in such a way that they stand out and express themselves. I restrict myself to doing that, always staying close to the reality of the world and the reality of man, which is the basic thing.

LLINAS/MARIAS: This confidence in man is expressed also in the fact that you don't underline a point, placing your confidence not only in the reality you film, but in the viewer.

ROSSELLINI: If I have confidence in man, I must have confidence in the viewer. If I didn't believe in man, I would no longer be a man myself, and if I set out to doubt man, I would be a monster.

LLINAS/MARIAS: Your films tend to be less and less dramatized.

ROSSELLINI: Dramatization and the search for effect take you further from the truth. If you stay close to the truth, it's difficult to go looking for effect. To make a film well it's necessary to eliminate all falsification and try to free ourselves from the temptation to falsify reality.

LLINAS/MARIAS: Is this why you don't like *General Della Rovere?*

ROSSELLINI: It's an artificially constructed film, a professional film, and I never make professional films, rather what you might call experimental films.

LLINAS/MARIAS: The advantage the cinema has over literature is that reality is always so rich that it can overcome any schematism on the part of the director a hundred times over; whereas when you write, all you have before you is the paper—you have no immediate point of reference and no guarantee of objectivity.

ROSSELLINI: What's important in literature is to lay bare the personality of the writer—it's a more concentrated form of work, whereas if you make a film, you have to give general impressions, as it's very difficult to analyze. You have to do so where it's unavoidable, but if you make a completely analytical film, you lose the spectacular element and you lose everything. The cinema has the advantage that, if you know how to look at things, you can put so much into one picture that the result is quite complex, while writing is analytical work, consisting of putting one idea down after another and organizing them.

LLINAS/MARIAS: It's as if you were looking for some kind of communion between man and nature. For example, at the end of the first chapter of *Atti degli Apostoli* the camera pans around the upper table from one to another, showing the community among them.

ROSSELLINI: All these things come about in a completely instinctive way, not as the result of forethought. If they were planned they would appear cold and mechanical. They must arise from natural impulse. For example, the very long pan from the hands of these real workers and peasants to their faces, is a form of microscopic discovery, it's like watching a cell. Even more than being in harmony with nature, man must be conscious of it, and also dominate it. But the relationship between man and nature can never be eliminated, even if it is artificial, as it is in the city. Many traumas arise from this relationship with nature, and with the universe too—we are only just beginning to realize what the universe is.

LLINAS/MARIAS: I suppose that the experience of India strongly influenced your attitude of confidence in man.

ROSSELLINI: It did. You are in contact there with an enormous mass of humanity. Going down the street is like swimming through a river of men. Countries are underdeveloped basically because they lack the right technology, but they aren't really because they live within a clearly defined civilization. We in the advanced countries live in a less clearly defined civilization, which has not yet stabilized: we are on our way to a new civilization. In the underdeveloped countries the roots are deeper—the basic ideas may be backward, but they allow for an exceptional human equilibrium. India is a moving place, because of both the great drama it is living through in its vast population explosion, and the heroic struggle it is making to face up to the problem. What makes it heroic is the method of struggle. It's moving to think that Gandhi, who originated nonviolence, was born in a country which is in fact very violent—though "nonviolence" is an imprecise translation of the term he actually used, which was "not harming anyone." It is an amazing concept. Gandhi took a stand and said, "between violence and cowardice, I choose violence"—and yet he did everything possible to avoid it. Gandhi is the product of his civilization. And we shouldn't forget that India also gave us the "naught." There's nothing so concrete and at the same time so abstract as the figure naught—it's very profound as a concept, making it possible to keep the two dimensions together.

LLINAS/MARIAS: When you went to India, did you intend to make a film?

ROSSELLINI: I didn't have a ready-made plan, I thought I'd do a lot of filming. I wanted to make both a film and a documentary. India is a very interesting country to film. It was the first country to be decolonized. Once Gandhi came to Rome. As early as 1931 or 1932, at a London round table, I had told him that I should like to go to India to see the new world emerging there. Then later I saw Nehru when he was on a visit to Europe, and spoke to him about it again.

LLINAS/MARIAS: Have you seen other films about India, like Renoir's *The River* or Malle's *Calcutta*?

ROSSELLINI: I didn't see *Calcutta* so I'm only going by what I've been told, but I think he had the wrong attitude to go to an underdeveloped country with. You have to go with the intention of seeing what's positive—it's much easier to see the negative side. I don't think it's a very compassionate attitude. It's very easy to give people a one-sided impression. Renoir's film is fantastic, but it's of quite a different kind to mine.

LLINAS/MARIAS: Did Godard really have that interview with you about *India '58*,[3] or did he make it up, as it's been suggested?

ROSSELLINI: I think he made it up. Godard is an exceptional person, and astonishingly talented. He is really one of the most honorable people I know, he's exceptionally upright.

LLINAS/MARIAS: Did you have anything to do with the early Nouvelle Vague films? It's been said you supervised the scenario of Chabrol's *Le Beau Serge*.

ROSSELLINI: No, what happened was this: when I met these young men for the first time they were critics for *Cahiers du cinéma*. I had a great exchange of ideas with them and we became very friendly. They were all very eager to make films. I strongly advised them to remain independent—that's my only contribution. At a time when there was a big crisis in the cinema I thought I could get them money to make their films. A law had been passed in France to aid experimental cinema. For a while I tried to convince a producer who was a great friend of mine, a very intelligent and unusually good producer, to help them—I tried for nearly a year but when the time came to start work it all fell through. I had discussed a lot of ideas for films with these young people—but soon after this I went to India.

LLINAS/MARIAS: What do you think of the way these directors have developed?

ROSSELLINI: I'm very friendly with them but I don't know about all their films because they only tell me about the ones I like best. For example, I'm sure I'll see Truffaut's *L'Enfant sauvage* soon, because he wants me to see it. But there are some films they think won't interest me. We have a fraternal and friendly relationship still.

LLINAS/MARIAS: How did you get into the cinema?

ROSSELLINI: Partly by chance and partly by vocation. My father was very rich, we had no financial problems. He built the first "modern" cinema theater in Rome in 1918. I had free access to it and saw a great many films. What's more my father was a great patron of the arts and our house was always full of artists: when my father was alive,

3 Article in form of interview published in *Arts*, 1–7 April 1959.

Sundays were marvelous because the most interesting people would come to the house. So I always had a great interest in art. This, together with the fact that I knew a great deal about the cinema, which was fairly rare in those days, meant that when my father died and our fortune vanished, I could go to work in films, taking advantage of the fact that I knew a lot of people in the business. I began by doing cutting and editing for a short time. Then I did a lot of work writing scenarios for other people. This is why I have such contempt for scenarios: I know how they're written. Then I began to practice making shorts.

LLINAS/MARIAS: We saw one, *Fantasia sottomarina,* and I believe you made another one about fish. Why were you so interested in fish?

ROSSELLINI: I have always loved fishing, I knew the sea but at that time it was thought impossible to film underwater. In 1929 three Japanese had come to the gulf of Naples for underwater fishing, though at that time there were no underwater masks or rifles, let alone cameras.

LLINAS/MARIAS: I've been told the fish were moved on strings.

ROSSELLINI: They sometimes were because we were filming in an aquarium and some fish died very quickly, so that for some scenes we had to manipulate them like puppets.

LLINAS/MARIAS: Your early films, such as *La nave bianca,* already show the characteristic way of approaching reality that came out in *Open City.*

ROSSELLINI: I think that's true, though it should be said that half of the copy of *La nave bianca* now in circulation isn't mine. My name isn't even on it, because they took the film out of my hands and changed it. The whole of the naval battle is mine, but the sentimental part was done by De Robertis, who was director of the Navy Film Center—he had asked me for a short about a hospital ship. The style was the same as in *Open City.*

LLINAS/MARIAS: And the same as in your recent films.

ROSSELLINI: The method doesn't change. Perhaps I have improved it now—at that time my steps were faltering. In *Open City* we were just emerging from the horrors of the war, and it was necessary to look at it clearly and objectively. I didn't for instance want to make the German out to be just a demon—I tried to give him a psychology and show him as corrupted and drugged, in order to explain his behaviour and make him understandable as a human being.

LLINAS/MARIAS: But in *Open City* the Germans are shown in a different way from the other characters: they're shown more schematically, because your own ideology is imposed on the film.

ROSSELLINI: I know that there is that weakness. I tried to explain the Germans—but at that time they were an intangible entity ruling over us, who would come along every so often and beat us up and pull our nails out. They were like a terrible accident that happened over and over again. We had no other contact with the Germans, and this is the reason for the disparity with the rest of the characters. I wanted to carry out a psychological reconstruction, but I didn't know enough to do so—the conversation between the three Germans, when one of them gets drunk and says that the end has come, was an attempt to do this. I don't know whether it was accurate, but I imagine that from time to time they must have felt a prick of conscience. You have to have some compassion for the enemy.

LLINAS/MARIAS: In *Era notte a Roma* [It was night in Rome], the informer, Tarsizio, is a cripple. Was this an attempt to explain his behavior?

ROSSELLINI: This was someone that I knew in real life. I had to hide from him for months. He was crippled, and that gave me some insight into his psychology, which gave rise to the character in the film.

LLINAS/MARIAS: The character played by Ingrid Bergman in *Europe '51* is intriguing—coming so soon after *The Flowers of St. Francis* she seems almost Franciscan.

ROSSELLINI: That's right—they're necessarily linked, it's not just coincidence.

LLINAS/MARIAS: The character played by Fabrizi in *Open City* reminds me of Brother Ginepro in *The Flowers* and there was something similar in the episode with the monks in *Paisan,* too.

ROSSELLINI: Yes, there is. That episode of *Paisan* began in a very interesting way. When I was making the film and needed equipment,

I came across an American regiment posted in Rome and they gave me an armored car, two or three jeeps, a few arms and three German prisoners with an escort of Americans to guard them. But the guards were always slipping off and were never there when we were shooting the film. These poor devils, being German, needed precise orders, and when there was no guard on them they didn't feel like prisoners. They went off to a monastery to find somewhere to sleep: at least there they had rules to comply with and they would not be in danger if they spent the night there. And that's how I found the monastery. When I went there to collect the prisoners I met the monks, who moved me in their simplicity, and so I thought up that episode.

LLINAS/MARIAS: How did you achieve such a tone of comedy?

ROSSELLINI: It was the way the monks played themselves. Perhaps you remember the scene where one of them goes into the kitchen, lifts the lid off the pot and says, "Ah, that smells good!" That was Brother Raffaele, who was very old and didn't understand much that went on. I told him to go into the kitchen, bend over to sniff at the pot, and say the phrase. "All right?" I asked and he said, "Yes, signore." So he stuck his head so far down into the pot that I had to sit on the floor and pull him back so that he wouldn't burn himself. He was so ingenuous. Fellini was my assistant at that time, and he had to instruct the monks to come one by one into a cell where I had the camera. When it came to Brother Raffaele he stood back for Fellini, because he didn't want to go through the door before the director's assistant. It came out as a comedy quite naturally. The same thing happened with *The Flowers,* in which all the monks were played by real monks, except of course for Fabrizi who played a tyrant, and the very old monk, "Giovanni il Semplice," who always goes around with Ginepro.

LLINAS/MARIAS: He was in *The Miracle* too.

ROSSELLINI: He was a local beggar, an extraordinary character. At the end of *The Flowers* all the monks decided to spin themselves round to determine what direction they will go in, and as he was lame he turned round very slowly and it took him half an hour to fall down. When he fell he was supposed to say "I'm pointing to Embolo," but he couldn't understand it however much we tried to explain. When he fell, St. Francis asked him where he would go and he said, "After that bird," because there was a bird flying by. It was a priceless phrase and we kept it in. This beggar had a very red nose and so he was called Peparuolo, which means pimento. He was a very gentle person, and so old that he didn't understand a thing. At the beginning, I explained to him, "St. Francis says such and such to you and you reply such and such. All right?" "Yes, signore." So he went on and repeated all my instruction. I told him not to say anything but his own lines—he answered that he understood completely and then he went and did the same thing again. I decided it was useless to explain things so I sent him for a long walk while I got the scene ready, and I put him in it without saying a word to him. The scene came out of what he did.

LLINAS/MARIAS: You can tell that, because he always repeats what St. Francis says.

ROSSELLINI: Giovanni il Semplice was supposed to repeat what St. Francis said but if I explained it to him he didn't understand it at all. Doing it the other way it worked perfectly, and it was funny too.

LLINAS/MARIAS: Anna Magnani's character in *The Miracle* is very similar.

ROSSELLINI: Yes, in the poor areas in the South, along the Amalfi coast, there are many beggars, some of them mad, and the good thing was that these characters really lived there. I once asked Brother Raffaele if he had ever had visions. "Yes, always." "What do you see?" "The saints." "Which saints?" "All of them." "And the Virgin Mary?" "Yes, signore, from head to foot." From head to foot, not just in close-up! That's how I thought up Anna Magnani's part.

LLINAS/MARIAS: Would you tell us something about that very strange film, *La macchina ammazzacattivi*? It seems to be about the cinema.

ROSSELLINI: It's rather a game, an attempt at comedy, and once more it's about the Amalfi area.

LLINAS/MARIAS: This film and *Dov'è la libertà?* [Where is freedom?], both have a tone of fantasy which is unusual in your films. Do they represent a tendency or are they just isolated cases?

ROSSELLINI: They are experiments. *La macchina ammazzacattivi* is an isolated experiment, but *Dov'è la libertà?*, which is like it in some ways, is much more a side-product of *Europe '51*: it's related to it because it's an attempt to investigate the same situation. Then there's the extraordinary character of Totò. The film as it stands today is very much hacked about, it was much more cruel. The softening up was done by the producers and it makes it more lightweight. But they're not very important films, just experiments.

LLINAS/MARIAS: Can you tell us about the sketch in *Siamo donne* [We, the women]?

ROSSELLINI: That was just a piece of fun. It was almost all improvised. It's not something that really happened, but it's true to life.

LLINAS/MARIAS: In *Stromboli* there is a scene with Ingrid Bergman and a volcano erupting, which was done without any special effects. Did you take advantage of a chance eruption or was it part of the scenario?

ROSSELLINI: The volcano started erupting—it was very good to me. The finale was supposed to be like that, though it was difficult to see how it could be made. But it started erupting quite happily. I always have confidence that these things will work out.

LLINAS/MARIAS: In *Germany Year Zero* and in *Europe '51* there are child suicides.

ROSSELLINI: They are very different kinds of suicide. The child in *Germany Year Zero* kills himself in a moment of despair. *Europe '51* shows a typical child suicide, an attempt to attract attention which goes wrong and the child is really killed. But the problem of children is there, it's very serious in modern times. I have children of my own and so this has always made me think a lot about children.

LLINAS/MARIAS: Many of your films are about a woman.

ROSSELLINI: That's only natural. I'm a man and I have a natural interest in women. Women are so easily men's victims.

LLINAS/MARIAS: There is a degree of similarity between *Germany Year Zero* and Buñuel's *Los Olvidados*.

ROSSELLINI: I'm quite incapable of giving you a critical judgement.

LLINAS/MARIAS: It's a shame we have never seen your films before. I think you would have had a positive influence on the Spanish cinema.

The two men we needed most were Buñuel and yourself, and it's only now that we're able to make contact.

ROSSELLINI: Thank you for saying that.

LLINAS/MARIAS: What do you think of *Jeanne au bûcher* and *Fear,* which we haven't seen?

ROSSELLINI: It's difficult to remember. I think *Fear* was quite an effective film, along the lines of *Voyage in Italy. Jeanne au bûcher* was more of an experiment. It was a Honegger opera and all Joan's lines were sung. It had often been produced with great success, and it offered a way of using all the techniques I now employ as a matter of course. It was the technical side of it which most attracted me.

LLINAS/MARIAS: Do you regard *A Human Voice* as an experiment too?

ROSSELLINI: Everything's an experiment. It did have some importance at the time, because the idea of microscopic cinema made it possible to observe things scientifically in a way which had never been attempted. It was a worthwhile experience for me, and in one way or another I've used the same method ever since. The subject was the pretext for making a particularly interesting experiment. Today the American "underground" cinema has taken this to the point of insanity, filming a man sleeping for seven or eight hours.[4]

LLINAS/MARIAS: Do you find that interesting?

ROSSELLINI: Everything is interesting.

LLINAS/MARIAS: Then how do you explain your polemic with Rouch over *La Punition*?

ROSSELLINI: It was the distortion of *cinéma-vérité* which started the argument. Rouch set off in an attempt to find truth in people. But the upholders of this school had developed theories which distorted what had been a good principle. *Cinéma-vérité* is an absurdity. You can't trust to chance, because even if it does make it possible for you to observe immediate, day-to-day things, the film has to be worked

4 The allusion is obviously to Andy Warhol's *Sleep* (1963).

on—if not it turns into the lowest kind of documentary. Where it's scientific it's worthwhile, but there it began to turn into dramatic cinema. Its value in terms of scientific investigation makes it possible to develop new dramatic techniques and observe things in a new way. My polemic with Rouch was quite friendly: what I was opposed to was his making a myth of *cinéma-vérité*. I recall that shortly after I came back from India he invited me to a UNESCO *cinéma-vérité* session. When I walked into the theatre I saw that everyone was bending down and looking at something underneath the screen. I could only see their backs and I thought they must be looking at a crocodile or an iguana or some other exotic animal. But then I realized it was nothing but a hand camera. That was the end; you can't get much crazier than that.

LLINAS/MARIAS: Don't you feel an affinity with this near-documentary approach to fiction that you object to in Rouch?

ROSSELLINI: I do. But that was the other extreme. At first all films were fictional, and then there was an attempt to break away from this. That requires a careful study of psychological confrontation. From this to the purely coincidental was far too big a step. These films may have had some scientific value, but they were not themselves scientific, because the people who made them knew very well what had to happen. It was an ambiguous, worthless formula.

LLINAS/MARIAS: In this polemic, you said that the truly moral attitude is affection. Do you think that this attitude is valid at all times and in respect of all people?

ROSSELLINI: Yes, because you can look at even the most terrible criminal in the world with compassion as well as hatred. I think it's right to look at people with affection and to make an effort to understand what goes on inside them.

LLINAS/MARIAS: If you gain an understanding of such a man, aren't you obliged to form a judgment, and say that he is a criminal for some specific reason?

ROSSELLINI: I try to see things, never to make judgments. I try to show things as they are. Everyone is responsible for himself, and I don't feel I have a right to judge. What I am interested in is studying a phenomenon and trying to get into it, but I leave people at liberty. I don't want to act as a moralist, or say what people should do. My position is one of complete objectivity.

LLINAS/MARIAS: Sometimes that's very difficult. For example, you said yourself that in *Open City* you were still too close to the events shown in the film, and that made it less objective.

ROSSELLINI: But I did try to be objective. I tried to find out why the Germans acted as they did, and that in itself was a compassionate attitude.

LLINAS/MARIAS: You have often said that ideology is a prism. Do you not think that any religion is also an ideology, and therefore itself a prism?

ROSSELLINI: Of course. I think that men must try their hardest to be themselves. This is another of the great lessons of India. All Indian thought is thought that can be called materialist and scientific. The Veda and the holy texts are scientific works. But just as science is made of concrete, direct observations, we know that man also has a metaphysical dimension. Does God exist or did he arise in the minds of men? I don't know, but the phenomenon of religion does exist. It's therefore very important to examine it scientifically. You should see how gently, and how freely as well, the Indians confront the problem of religion. The temples are open to everyone and anyone can go in and celebrate in any way he likes. There isn't a standard ritual. I remember that one day we were on our way to Tibet along a mountain road 4,000 meters high. Because of the heat of the engine and the high altitude our petrol evaporated, and we had to stop every few hundred yards to wait for the petrol to cool down. We saw a man carrying an enormous weight—he would catch up with us when we stopped and then we would leave him behind. This happened seven or eight times. At about dusk I saw him leave his load by a tree. He started looking around him, and went over to a stream, looking for something. He took a stone from the water, came back to the road, put the stone in the hollow of a tree and began his prayers. I realized that he was looking for some means of contact and found it in a stone.

LLINAS/MARIAS: Is your film about Sicily in some way like *India '58*?

ROSSELLINI: It's a one-hour film. There are so many legends about Sicily—when you hear about Sicily what you hear about is the Mafia, and people imagine that everyone in Sicily is in the Mafia. No one makes an effort to see Sicily as it really is or to understand the behavior of its inhabitants. Sicily has been invaded time and again: first by the Greeks, then by the Romans, and by all kinds of people from AD 500 on—the Arabs, the Normans, and so on. Sicily has on average had a new master every 117 years. So it's obvious that each of them has had to impose ethics and laws which are quite out of keeping with the country. The Sicilians have turned further and further in on themselves. To have an idea of the tragedy of Sicilian history, you only have to know that not a single plant on the island today is a native one: everything was imported. The Arabs brought the orange trees, the eucalyptuses were brought from Australia in the late nineteenth century, the Romans planted the pines, the Greeks brought the olives. Sicily has been devoured—and so of course the Sicilian people have developed a tendency toward secrecy as a form of defense. Women are always the first victims of invaders, and this is the origin of the distorted view of women Sicilians have, as "flesh of my flesh," and their pride in saving their women from the invaders. So their psychology is quite out of the normal run, with a secret hypertrophy of the "ego." The bandits made secrecy their method. But Sicily is far from being a land of bandits. My film was a kind of defense of Sicily.

LLINAS/MARIAS: How do you decide on your scenes? What are your criteria for what interests you?

ROSSELLINI: It's all based on logic. It's like writing—you choose certain adjectives, you form the phrase in a particular way.

LLINAS/MARIAS: There are scenes that any other director would have that you don't.

ROSSELLINI: It's just a matter of my style. The way forward is always that of logic, and of the greatest effectiveness for the least expenditure of energy. It's a fairly basic rule.

LLINAS/MARIAS: In *General Della Rovere* you experiment with a moving lens for the first time.

ROSSELLINI: I had used one before, but here I was taking it seriously.

It's now my usual method. *Atti degli Apostoli* and *The Rise to Power of Louis XIV* were filmed entirely with moving lenses. I always defended the hand camera as a means of demystifying and de-dramatizing the cinema. You have to make films simply and directly, and use the clearest possible language. I chose hand cameras to free myself from big industrial organization. Since then they've been so much abused that going to the cinema is like boarding a ship, you come out feeling seasick. To avoid this but still have the same mobility, I made a camera that could be optically mobile but still remain in a fixed position, which would make these eccentricities impossible. I began by thinking out how to transform the zoom camera, in particular the controls. My system has two interlocking motors, and one of them acts as a counterweight to stop the lens from oscillating as it moves, so that you don't get a zoom effect. This gives me great mobility—for example, I can zoom from an angle of 25° to one of 150°, and this opens up enormous possibilities. I operate it myself, it's a very easy thing to use and you can improvise with it during shooting. If an actor isn't quite in the right spot, for example, you can follow him with the zoom lens. It saves a lot of time and it may improve the actor's performance—if he loses the rhythm during the scene usually it's much less convincing. These slight adjustments show him more closely. The camera works more like an eye, and so you can develop a system of constant direct participation, because when you have organized the scene and begun shooting, you can see if it's going well, and if not you can stop.

LLINAS/MARIAS: You sometimes use the zoom to give distance.

ROSSELLINI: That shows how varied its potential is. We always shoot in sequences, which reduces montage to a minimum. This optical mobility makes it possible to base it all on organizing the scene, and this means you have to know the set very well. You have to establish it. Normally you take a shot showing the set as a whole, then the actor comes on, you cut in nearer to the actor, follow him, etc. With the travelling lens you don't need to alter the distance. It's all linked in the context of the scene, which has to follow a certain pattern and bring over a particular meaning. I have to know exactly where the actors are and make the meaning very clear. With this kind of mobility I can do that. I was tending to do this even before: in *Europe '51* there were many very difficult moving sequences, which had to be shot with the camera on a dolly following the actors around the whole time. In Hitchcock's films the moving shots are very important and he has to have special sets built that the actors can appear and disappear in, which is extremely complicated. But the travelling lens simplifies all this enormously.

LLINAS/MARIAS: Do you shoot film for TV with direct sound?

ROSSELLINI: It depends. It's a problem of technique. *The Rise to Power of Louis XIV* was made entirely with direct sound, because they are extremely good at it in France. Nothing is done in the studio, it's all done in natural settings. So it takes a great deal of skill to record the sound track. You may remember hearing far-off noises of horse-drawn carts passing from time to time: in fact they were airplanes and we covered the sound over with the other noises. At other times all the sound is dubbed in. It's a technical problem. In Italy so little importance has been given to sound, in order to speed up production, that there are very few technicians who are able to do direct sound, whereas in France it's often used and the technicians are extremely good.

LLINAS/MARIAS: Were *Germany Year Zero* and *Fear* made in German or Italian?

ROSSELLINI: In German, because practically all the actors were German. The Italian copies are dubbed. Whenever I can I direct the Italian dubbing myself—I did it for *Voyage in Italy*, for example.[5]

LLINAS/MARIAS: Do you have anyone working with you on the research for your films?

ROSSELLINI: I use books, not people, because otherwise it would create enormous confusion.

LLINAS/MARIAS: Are you interested in the theater? I know that you have directed *Jeanne au bûcher* and *I carabinieri*.[6]

5 Almost all Rossellini's films with Ingrid Bergman were made in English.
6 *Jeanne au bûcher* is an opera by Arthur Honegger based on a book by Paul Claudel. *I*

ROSSELLINI: Not really, because I'm too busy with other things: apart from the Centro Sperimentale, I am involved in other kinds of teaching too. I go to Houston, Texas, for two months, for example, to lecture at Rice University, which is one of the big American technical universities, to stimulate the interest of technical students in artistic expression. I try to show them that they can be artists. If a biochemistry graduate can find something artistic in his work, biochemistry can be made clear to everyone, wouldn't you think? It could be very useful, it could make all kinds of things understandable to the mass of people. These are things worth devoting one's energies to. I also have films to make—it's a lot of work.

LLINAS/MARIAS: *Anima nera* [Black soul] is going to be shown in Spain . . .

ROSSELLINI: I think it's an awful film. It was based on a comedy by [Giuseppe] Patroni-Griffi, which I changed a little. After that I gave up films altogether.

LLINAS/MARIAS: Did you give up films just because producers were not interested in the films you wanted to make, and because of the time problem?

ROSSELLINI: The producers didn't seem to be interested in my plans. And I already had fairly clear ideas about making these educational films. This was out so far as the cinema is concerned so I left. It's not exactly been easy with TV, but it's been less difficult.

LLINAS/MARIAS: So you're not saying that the cinema is finished.

ROSSELLINI: There are two points I must make. Firstly, the cinema was no use for what I wanted to do, and secondly, it's now obvious how badly things were going: the film industry is dying on its feet and there's an enormous crisis. It's pointless to pretend otherwise, because it's the undeniable truth. In England, Japan, France, the United States, and everywhere else, aid to the cinema has been cut enormously in recent years. These are the symptoms of crisis, and it's not surprising, as the film industry has never acted very sensibly. It's only ever got

---

carabinieri is a play by Beniamino Joppolo, which Rossellini told Jean-Luc Godard about, and was taken by the latter as the basis for *Les Carabiniers* (1963).

temporary deals. It's a good sign that the public has deserted the cinema when it's proved itself so useless. The industry is trying to save itself now by producing for a special public with sexual complexes and repressed violence. So it goes in for sensation, to capture this small section of the public. It's a good thing that not many people are attracted by that. The cinema must live on, but to do so it needs to be much more conscious of its duties. I think the division between cinema and TV is a false one, and a fusion of production could be a real solution. They're two media for diffusion, but in reality they're one. There isn't one set of aesthetics for films and another for television. They must be united and develop together, with a clear view of what has to be done. The world is convulsed by the need for knowledge. The men of today suffer because they are not told enough. We are living in a period full of discoveries and new ideas, but we know absolutely nothing of them and we end up with the anguish of living in a world which is being transformed without being able to observe the transformation. An American scientist conducted an experiment with children on the basis of a very important hypothesis. He believes that the basic impulses which have always motivated men are desire and fear. I would add another, the impulse to show knowledge. The desire to know is innate in man, and this desire goes together with the *need* to know, because we are victims of a civilization we have built without virtually any participation in it, and we must make ourselves masters of it. This is the great problem. If this impulse does exist in man, he should not be humiliated, and there is no call for teachers to speak down to him and tell him, "You know nothing, listen to what I have to say . . ." Things have to be said as if everyone knows them. This is the real problem today, and it's one the cinema should he aware of too. I think these are the great objectives of your generation, because it is yours that can carry them out, not ours.

LLINAS/MARIAS: So these films are an attempt to explain how and why we have reached this point? Will they also explain the situation we are in now?

ROSSELLINI: Yes—we have reached the point we are at through a very special civilization, unique I think in the history of man, the civilization of specialists. Their mission has been accomplished, but only in one sense.

There has been no coordination, things have worked out by pure chance. I think the time has come to change this situation: the real question is to transcend the specialist and come back to man, because if man is made more complete, he will be able to participate in what he has created, and give it a real meaning. Many years ago Ortega y Gasset wrote about the anguish of specialized man. Defining some idealist suppositions, he goes on to describe exactly the anguished awareness man has of horizons which move further off and become more and more nebulous. This is quite obviously the point we have reached today.

LLINAS/MARIAS: Don't you think it is in a sense necessary, then, that the world should be made up of specialists?

ROSSELLINI: There's a lack of professionals, but that's another matter. When I went to school in Italy, the early classes taught very general ideas, to children who were too young to synthesize them. As you went on with your studies, teaching became specialized and general ideas were left behind. You got to university and there you dealt with only a small portion of man's knowledge: and it was always out of date at that. Education produced for the market of the professions.

I don't know whether or not this was right. We don't yet have the historical facts that would enable us to say. The fact is that we have made enormous technical and scientific conquests which have changed our horizons completely. We must be aware of this, and realize what it is that men have been able to do: we are not victims, but masters. This is the meaning of my educational films, and so I try to work at pedagogy rather than philosophy, and to have the endless patience necessary to put back into order the whole of the alphabet of knowledge which has been scattered in a hundred and fifty years of parcellisation.

LLINAS/MARIAS: You view the cinema in a sense as showing the inner value and emotions of things, leaving the discussion of general ideas to more analytical media. This is consistent with the way you showed the heroism of daily life in your early films, and it reveals a confidence

in mankind which requires a very sane-minded outlook quite un-
alienated from this reality of the world. It would be impossible to be
so confident if you were alienated by reality.

ROSSELLINI: It requires a great awareness. It's very uplifting to have
this sense of value.

LLINAS/MARIAS: The most interesting thing you have said is about the
need to stop complaining and do something.

ROSSELLINI: We can't just resign ourselves to weeping, there's been
enough of that already. We must move on to action of a different
kind. I think that's what's important. Look at all the confusion that
has been created in the world—we see it more every day. Where can
men find a salvation of any kind? They adopt one orthodoxy or
another. We are confronted by a paradox: we live in an extraordinarily young world, because at every second we are changing, and we are
governed by dead men through these orthodoxies. There shouldn't be
orthodoxies, there should be just men who at a particular moment in
time have meant something as part of our culture and our civilization.
Merely observing orthodoxy takes us nowhere. It serves for a given
moment, it doesn't allow us to know everything. If you live in an
orthodox way, following a political ideology, you freeze in a certain
mold, it becomes impossible to move forward. We must try to become
masters of ourselves, and not let dead men be our masters, however
great our respect for everything they have given us, and the visions
with which they illuminated the future—it was for them the near
future, not eternity.

LLINAS/MARIAS: Do you think that when one is alienated from the
situation, trying to make films in the way you see it could remove this
alienation?

ROSSELLINI: What is alienation, if not being a stranger to reality? It's
an absurd situation. Instead of being alienated from reality, you have
to participate in it. If you want to change something, you must be a
part of it. Not everything that is, is good. Some things are not and
have to be corrected. Moaning about it will put nothing right—one
only despairs and becomes unable to act. And action is what counts.

LLINAS/MARIAS: But for example, in a situation like that of Italy under

Mussolini, I imagine there must have been some good things and a great deal of bad. How would it help to concentrate on the positive side?

ROSSELLINI: You have to be aware of the whole. I know because I have lived through it. The years of Fascism were twenty years of total darkness: it was like being kept in a state of ignorance. The wildest political ideas were born in Italy, out of ignorance: for example, Catholic communism, a contradiction in terms. We were tormented, wounded, confused—we didn't know what was happening. The motto of Fascism was "To believe is to fight": to believe in what existed and nothing else. There was not the least trace of dialectics. It exists today, a debate has born fruits. But to believe full stop had nothing dialectical about it, it was a living death. This is the great difference. Even among those peoples which claim to be the freest in the world, freedom has its limits. With faith in man, such as I have, one has faith in logic and rationality too. We know that however long it takes, we shall achieve it. To destroy everything means throwing away the whole of our cultural inheritance: it would not be a very rational thing to do. There are no limitations on man if change can be carried out not in a passion but rationally. When action becomes passionate, there is naturally a defensive reaction, because passion is not rational, and defense against it is built on the basis of a fear of irrationality. If you refer back to human reality, it is impossible to imagine anyone capable of saying, "Today I am going to act like a scoundrel and a criminal." I don't think such people exist. We all have aspirations towards justice, but we apply them badly. Very few men have adopted a method of criminal action in pursuit of an ideal. They have rather been wrong about things. Human intelligence knows no bounds. An animal, always acting by instinct and testing out the ground, isn't able to make such errors. Intelligence is magnificent, but it can also be very dangerous, because it gives the possibility of making very serious mistakes. Nothing in the world can hold back irrationality. There are men who can't understand what is the rational thing to do, and so divisions arise. We must constantly come together with each other. Our great historical destiny is to be men together. It is the most beautiful thing there is.

LLINAS/MARIAS: Do you agree with the Marxist theory that behavior and superstructural phenomena depend on the economic system?

ROSSELLINI: Yes, of course. Such ideas are very important, but I think we have entered a completely new period of history. Particular methods of observation and research are valid at a particular moment. Huizinga once said something very enlightening, to the effect that up until a certain point in history, the ruling sin was pride. When greed came to rule in its place, the world was transformed. Adam Smith marked the beginning of the whole of modern economics, and the opening up of a world based on greed, and on principles which religion and high ideals had condemned. The structures of this world were transformed into what they are today. Karl Marx, living at the time, saw this world through the prism of the thirst for gain. Today something quite marvelous is happening in the world. The youth of America, for instance, have been born into a pragmatic world, and therefore in a place where the object of life is to take as much as possible, where there has been no class struggle, where a man of a lower class is permitted to rise to a higher one, where belonging to the upper class means having money, and it is money that buys power. And yet it came about, and I saw this happen in 1967, that they took poverty as their ideal. All the hippie movements and so on have the same staggering significance of a rejection of wealth. It's a very positive sign, a return to the moral ideals which have basically always ruled the world. What had been certain until then, no longer is. We must base our struggle on this new truth. The world of today is full of ideals and I think that we may be entering the period of mankind's greatest fulfillment: what the prophets, the moralists, the various religions have always advocated, has never been put into practice. There is another, very important saying of Huizinga's: the sin of pride was metaphysical, but greed is only physical, material. I think that today we stand on the threshold of a marvelous epoch. I am convinced of it, and so all I am trying to do is to try to bring it into being as easily as possible. I don't know whether we shall succeed or not. You must forgive my idealism.

LLINAS/MARIAS: It's a little like that of St. Francis.

ROSSELLINI: I feel very close to him. Believe me, I spend a lot of my time with people of your age, and I know how much there is about you all that's marvelous. I never in my life felt more emotion than I did at the time of the confrontations in Paris; but then it was all gone within a few days, all that great explosion of extraordinary feeling was lost, became confused, because it gave way to passion. We must stay within the orbit of what's rational, it's the only way to begin again. You must forgive me for ending up with a sermon.

"Una panorámica de la historia. Entrevista con Rossellini," in Nuestro cine, *no. 95, March 1970, pp. 44-60. Translated by Judith White.*

AN INTERVIEW WITH ROSSELLINI

BY JAMES BLUE

ROSSELLINI: You have always to know: what are the meanings of the scenes? We can talk approximately: first of all you have to establish where you are. That you can solve by making a long shot, from far away. And then you know where you are.

Immediately after that you must go to the character, the actor, and explore him deeply, but because he does and he says such kinds of things those things affect the others. So you have to analyze also the others. That's the way to proceed.

Now: if you do it with a camera still. It was like that at the beginning of film. They hadn't invented the travelling movements, etc., etc. Just the long shot. One starts to talk. To him, close-up. Close-up of all the others who are listening. And again a medium shot so that—there's not much of the ambiance but—now they are looking. And again and again. That sort of analysis.

Using that sort of technique and again using that technique when the film was silent, the main language was the cutting (editing).

Now you have many other kinds of possibilities. You can use very freely the camera, you can move, you can come back and down, it is only a question of not doing "*morceaux de bravoure.*" Not to "show off." As if to say "look how capable I am of moving the camera." No—and again it is my point—we have to *cancel* the camera. The camera can do the most complicated job and you could not realize that job the camera is doing—if you invent a lot of little transitions.

See, for example, I like to do a complete scene in a single take. But in that single take I know that I need everything. I know I need the close-up. I know I need the reaction of the others. I need to know the angles where the scene is placed. Those needs are always the same, you see.

So you have to invent a lot of little things to give the camera the possibility to move without realizing that the camera is doing that. I think that outside of a classroom people in general move a lot. If you sit in an office and have a discussion, after a while you need to get out because you are attracted by something else. A noise from outside, or because you don't want to follow any more what's going on. Because in that moment you feel impatient.

So you see in developing movement, you can develop it for a lot of reasons which can add to the meaning of the scene and to the emotion of the actor. Am I clear?

BLUE: In inventing the transitions you develop that which adds to the emotion of the scene and the character of the actor.

ROSSELLINI: Yes.

BLUE: Mechanical transitions for enabling close-ups can also be used for . . .

ROSSELLINI: They *must* be used, they *must* be used for that . . . there are a thousand things that you have to put together, one after another because, more or less, not more than three or four seconds can you stand with an image. That image must mutate continuously. This is the kind of thing that raises interest and involves you in the film.

If you calculated, if you made a bet with yourself, saying: "Well, every situation—I mean every frame—(*shot*) in the camera must not be longer than, say, four or five seconds. Try an exercise like that. *You* have to invent *something* every five seconds. It must oblige the camera to do another movement, to go to discover another kind of thing. If you do that exercise, obliging you to change the angle every five seconds, you will see how many things you have to invent, and you will see what kind of good exercise it is for inventing things. Because that is the whole secret for example. If you want to work with nonactors, you have to invent what a nonactor can give to you. What he can give you is physical presence, and certain kinds of movement.

No more than that, than what he is used to doing. If you study it and survey him a little bit and you give him the occasion to do all those kinds of things, he becomes a very good actor. Otherwise he is not.

BLUE: If you just give him his movements to make.

ROSSELLINI: Always. Even very little movements. If it's natural for him. Even just put his finger in his nose, I don't know. Any sort of thing . . . but *his own* way of doing, you know?

Each one of us has a way to say things. The nonactor has a way of making a gesture, let's say you focus on those kinds of things and you can synthesize those kinds of things in your mind, you can ask him to redo what you have observed him doing.

The muscles of the man are trained so he feels immediately at ease.

BLUE: And you know that if he scratches his head, that will mean something at that point in your film even though the nonactor doesn't understand the meaning in that context.

ROSSELLINI: Yes. See, for example,— let me give you an example— look at him (*refers to a student in class—very tensely seated*). See how he keeps control of himself. He is the one who has made fewer gestures than anyone else here in the room. Now. How can you utilize that? You can see thousands of examples in a film of those kinds of things. If you utilize his own attitude in the *contrary situation for that attitude,* then immediatedly that attitude becomes dramatic!

If you use that way of being so immobile, and you made of him a character that was tremendously violent, you have immediately a character! Many qualities must be played in contrast, you see. In one of my recent films, the contrast was used in many ways. The man who played the king was ashamed all the time. He did not have the courage to say the line. He was timid. He would forget the line. So I had to utilize that, because physically he was exactly the type of man I needed. So with a little bit of shrewdness you could utilize that. Because he was so stiff, he turned out to seem very strong. He appeared to have a great will.

He couldn't remember the line. It was totally impossible for him, he was totally blind. When he was in front of the camera he was trembling and could do nothing. So I realized I had to play everything on the stiffness of the man, no? Always more stiff. How can you do (*something*) with a man by making him more stiff? It's quite easy! If you put on a blackboard at the right distance what he has to say; — and if you have it at the right distance his eyes won't move at all, so that the man tends to be very stiff. Those were the kinds of shrewdness needed to make him play.

BLUE: When you have it all rehearsed how many takes do you make?

ROSSELLINI: One. (*laughter*) One. Yes. If something is wrong technically you repeat it. It might be interrupted. Sometimes the camera stops, there's a noise. Someone feels completely lost. But otherwise there is just one take.

BLUE: Do you speak to the actors during the take?

ROSSELLINI: Yes. Some of them need that. But others don't.

BLUE: Do you sometimes ask them to adjust their speed?

ROSSELLINI: No. Because when you have done the rehearsals enough they already have the rhythm. But if they do make some mistake like going to the wrong point—because there are a thousand little movements to make, you know—I may speak to them.

BLUE: So your work is to organize detail and physical movement within the set to give the impression of emotion, etc.?

ROSSELLINI: Surely. For example: if you have somebody facing toward the camera and the other one in the scene is talking, and that person is to appear moved, surely that's difficult. But if the person is turned slightly from the camera and just a little he lowers his eyes and then turns, if he does that it's a great emotion. Only that great emotion is nothing at all. Everybody can do that—even the dog that's here in the classroom. Everybody can do that.

BLUE: I find it interesting that you who are so intent on obtaining an impression of realism use what essentially could be called "tricks."

ROSSELLINI: But to get "realism" you need tricks. Otherwise you never will get the reality. If you begin to depend on "feeling" and "acting"—feeling and acting are never *real*, you know—it's something a little above the line, no? So it becomes impossible to get a realistic thing.

    In the theater you can get tremendous emotion, but you know very well that everything is a little bit above the line. Above the truth. It's always the exaggeration of the truth. It's an *emphasis* of what you think is true. And in films you have to go in reverse, in the other sense. Because the camera is a microscope you always have to be "under" and not "over."

BLUE: Would your reason for using the nonactor be that he would not object to this treatment?

ROSSELLINI: Surely. That is one of the great reasons. I started with nonactors because I had no money. I still have no money, but now I know that it is much better that way.

The job of the director is to achieve significance in the work and a full domination of the medium. When you know everything about the medium you worry no more.

A mistake to avoid when you teach technique, is thinking that technique is something magic. It's nothing. It's a stupidity. But it's something you need. The alphabet is the most stupid thing in the world but without the alphabet you could not express yourself. So you need the knowledge of technique and the training in it.

I never go to see the rushes of what I am doing. Sometimes I have the temptation to go see them, why not? But if I get used to seeing the rushes I know the danger that I am happy because I reached a certain result. I think it is much better to take the risk. For when you take the risk. It means that you are obliged every day to be there at the maximum of your effort. You have to run that risk. So that is the reason why I *never* go to see the rushes of my films. I never see a film of mine in a projection room, when I finish totally the shooting, I get all the material at the moviola. I number it and divide it up, and I start from the first scene to cut the film, to put it together. It goes very quick. It's a very little job.

BLUE: How did you keep this up for long takes?

ROSSELLINI: It's very difficult to work with a nonactor in little pieces. Because his expression is bound up to the physical movement.

When you use his physical movement a great deal, it's easy. A person walks in a certain way. So if you put him in a certain situation, that walk gets a certain kind of significance.

You have to use properly the significance of the walk or gesture— properly or improperly, that's the question.

I don't know if you realized it or not, that he was so ashamed that for him it was absolutely impossible to walk straight. He was always walking like that—not putting his heels on the floor.

Just for a joke I left a few frames of that in.

It was absolutely impossible for him to walk naturally in front of the camera. So if you use that awkwardness properly that will come out as a character.

BLUE: So you use the nonactor's difficulties to your own advantage.

ROSSELLINI: Yes. You remember, when he has the scene with the mother and they go down in the corridor, if you have the occasion to resee the film, see how I ended that scene, he does that (*Rossellini imitates*)—tiny little steps like that! But I left that because it was very important. Immediately afterwards he goes to the stairs. You remember the scene where he cries? He was lying all the time to his mother pretending to cry. Then he goes to the stairway and begins to go down it like a little kid (*stomping his feet*) just for a second.

So if you utilize all those kinds of things, it's easy to get a result.

D. TERRY: Did you want those physical characteristics when you chose him?

ROSSELLINI: No, because I didn't know him. I chose him first of all because physically he looked like the character I wanted. And when you see somebody, you can make a certain judgment about him. The physical aspect of somebody is always greatly tied with his own psychology. No doubt. It is a rough estimation, but he is *that*. So you choose the person physically because that physique corresponds to a certain kind of psychology. So that's the way I choose people to play a certain kind of part.

D. TERRY: Do you have to do something to get him to participate, to be involved?

ROSSELLINI: No! No! Why does he have to be involved, poor thing? If he gets involved he suffers all the time. He's not an actor. Why must he be involved? He must not be involved *at all*. He has only to be capable enough to attract our attention.

While you are waiting for the lights to be arranged you can play cards with him, just talk about the weather, world events, news in the paper, that sort of thing. But if you look at these people you see immediately how they move. How they behave also. Those are the two things always tied together. So you recollect in your mind all of those kinds of things and you reconstruct him as he *is*, not as you want him to be. It's a very simple process in a sense. It requires only a little exercise to observe things. That's all. And to exercise your ability in remembering things. So that after two days or three days of work with somebody you know everything about him. Everything. And then he can do everything you want.

BLUE: How about when you need from a character an emotional quality?

ROSSELLINI: But I don't need *his* emotion. I need an emotion in the film. That's another kind of need. I can build that emotion. Why don't you *build* the emotion you need? I'll just give you a silly example to simplify the thing to the maximum.

If you have the person move very slowly, or say things slowly, and suddenly just for a short section you accelerate, you have the emotion. You accelerate the action. It's mathematical. That is absolutely mathematical. If you have somebody who says: "Yeah . . . yeah . . . I see, I see" and suddenly something happens, then you have the emotion.

It's a question of the rhythm. The rhythm is very important. It's very important, because if you start with a very high rhythm, it's impossible to go up. But if you start with a slower one, and suddenly you change the rhythm, you have immediately the emotion.

BLUE: In *Open City*, most of the people talk very fast. And they are always moving. Suddenly something happens. Anna Magnani is shot for instance almost without warning. Is this what you mean?

ROSSELLINI: Yes. When you make an abrupt change, believe me you have the dramatic point.

BLUE: But how would you obtain from a nonactor the emotional quality of Fabrizi in *Open City*? Or would you not attempt it?

ROSSELLINI: No. I'll tell you a story about Fabrizi. You remember the scene when he realized that the engineer died and he blessed him? Well Fabrizi told me: "You must do me a favor. I want to cry. I want really to cry." So I said: "O.K. cry, then." And we spent half a day waiting for him to cry. Then we said: "How can you cry?" "Well, you know I think, for example, of a white little flower." So he said: "Be ready! When I snap my fingers, start shooting because I will be crying."

And so we wait for hours. Then he says: "May I have a cognac?" "Yes, O.K., you can have a cognac." So finally after twenty cognacs, he gets totally drunk and he thought about that little white flower and starts to cry. It was absolutely disgusting you know. The tears coming out from the nose in balloons, from the mouth—it was absolutely a disgusting scene!

So I called him later into the projection room and I said: "You can see what a masterpiece you have made."

"But I really cried!"

"I know you really cried, but what does it mean to really cry? It means nothing at all!"

So, it was so disgusting. From the nose, balloons were coming out. Exploding! So we have to do the scene again. And it was very easy. With a few drops of glycerin he was crying. It was nothing at all.

So if you want an actor or a nonactor to participate at that level, you must always have Greta Garbo, Sarah Bernhardt, or someone like that—that's another kind of work.

But how can a poor actor in a studio with the lamps, the electrician around, and everybody tired of waiting—how can they get into the mood? Practically they have to prepare themselves for all eventualities. They just know two, three, or four tricks and they always play on those kinds of tricks. But if you want something else, you must invent things and you must make them at ease. To "feel," to "participate" to me means nothing at all.

BLUE: So you depend upon their natural movements?

ROSSELLINI: Natural movements and natural gestures.

BLUE: Then you articulate them in movement before the camera.

ROSSELLINI: Yes.

BLUE: When you have someone who reads the line badly, what do you do?

ROSSELLINI: I dub. (laughs)

BLUE: So there *are* people who may look wonderful but just won't work in their voice?

ROSSELLINI: Yes, but you see, if you don't ask them any sort of expression. If you say: "Please read that," or "Say that in the same way that you a read a cable," you will always find that people perform well. Read flat.

BLUE: You ask all of your performers to read "flat"?

ROSSELLINI: Right.

BLUE: How did Anna Magnani react to that?

ROSSELLINI: But she's another kind of thing. She's really a dramatic actress, but the danger with her is to act too much. You feel that she's extremely capable but in certain films it is too much. If you are fed too much cream, after a bit you don't want any more cream. Something absolutely good, good, good,—honey, etc.—is too much.

BLUE: But if you read it flatly, it isn't the way people speak in everyday life!

ROSSELLINI: But how do people speak in everyday life? We have not really a measure for that. Also the word is less important. If you build properly the images, what comes out of the mouth of the nonactor is just a "caption"—no more than that—like subtitles.

BLUE: So if the verbal language is reduced to simple information, then the eye reads the significant aspects of the gestures, of the body posture, of the movement, and of the decor, and puts it all together. The mind also understands the important facts of the scene or situation.

ROSSELLINI: Yes, that's it exactly.

STUDENT: That seems to put an incredible load on the director.

ROSSELLINI: Surely, but why not? I am a director, so they put everything on me. I think it is very, very important. I don't think it is possible to do a film with many authors. There is always only one author. The idea is over everybody. It's that kind of thing.

BLUE: What do you feel you gain by changing the camera emphasis through staging rather than through cutting?

ROSSELLINI: Well, see for example, when you cut you have a rhythm which is not natural. It's a rhythm which is completely built up. When you move the camera it's a natural sort of rhythm that comes out. And you have many more possibilities if you train yourself to invent a lot of little accidents, we can say, inside of the thing. You can feel extremely more sure.

BLUE: What do you mean by accidents?

ROSSELLINI: Accidents mean: little gestures, little things, mannerisms. If you invent and you collect a lot of those kinds of things you have solved the problem. In that little piece you must put a lot.

BLUE: When you say natural rhythm do you mean it feels more like real time?

ROSSELLINI: Surely, but what I am doing is always "realistic." It's not that everyone should do realistic things, but if you do want to do realistic things, I think it's quite difficult to escape from that technique.

STUDENT: How do you give them the dialogue?

ROSSELLINI: I give them the dialogue at the last second. The last moment when we start the rehearsal. I don't give them the dialogue before, because if they learned the dialogue before—and especially if they are "little" actors—they start to invent for themselves a lot of things. So then I first have to get rid of what they have done and thought, and start from zero to build another kind of thing. So I prefer not having to do my work over twice but rather only once simply. So they are embarrassed. They have the line at the last moment. They have only to follow what I'm suggesting.

There is time for every movement. Each aspect must be utilized for everything. A man who must go to a spot must reach it at the proper moment otherwise the meaning won't be created. Do you see? In rehearsal he has the text in his hands.

BLUE: It would be useful for us at this point to follow how you go about staging. What are the steps you take? First, you say you do not rehearse with the actors beforehand.

ROSSELLINI: Just on the set. I go on the set with everybody altogether—actors and technicians. You immediately get the feeling of where to put the camera. And what determines the choice of the first place for the camera comes because you must have quickly the idea of what the whole scene will be like. You must find the place most convenient from where you start—a place for the whole scene—even if you are going to do it with cuts, because the problems remain exactly the same. And when you have the camera, you start to look through the camera because what is outside of it does not exist, you see.

And being at the camera, you say: "Please, sit down there. Now start to say your line. Now stand up, when you say that word. And move in that direction." When he does that, I ask my second actor: "Please, you stay there so in that movement with the camera following the other I discover you. And you get out of the frame and you come here and you sit."

BLUE: Have they learned their lines by now?

ROSSELLINI: No, they have them on paper. If they memorize, it's O.K. If they don't memorize, we very often use a little radio in their ear and we tell them the line over a microphone. Or they read it from a blackboard. They get the lines on paper just when we go to the set.

STUDENT: Do you let the people discover these things? The crew?

ROSSELLINI: No. I discover by myself. And they have to follow it. I've been doing this job forty years. So I don't need . . . At the beginning, I would go to different positions to decide where to put the camera. But when you have a little training, you know immediately where to go.

BLUE: And you put the camera where you can follow . . .

ROSSELLINI: . . . The smallest movements . . . usually on a small dolly in the middle of the scene . . . and when the whole thing is fixed you rehearse two, three, four, five, six times, because you have to put together the movement of the camera, the cameraman who is focusing the lens, the grip who pushes the dolly physically pulling it up and down. Everything must be harmonized. And the sound.

BLUE: Don't you look at it once it's put together?

ROSSELLINI: No, I do it myself. I'm quicker than an editor. They take care of the negative, those kinds of things. You know, our Italian moviolas are wonderful. The high speed. I do all the cutting in high speed. I don't slow down except to check to see if the shot is right. Otherwise not. I know everything already. You know the tempo, everything. To cut the film took two or three days, no more than that, *(Louis XIV)* because every scene practically is only one shot.

When you do a film you always do a certain kind of sketch. No more than that. Why insist on little things? It's no use. Otherwise you have to do a film, to look at your film, to study your film, to criticize your film, and start again the shooting. And when you have shot it a second time you can start again to look at the film, to criticize what you have done, and start the third time to shoot. It's impossible.

There is always a sketch. And you must get from it the maximum possible. When a film is finished that experience is finished and another one begins.

Those who know a lot are the scientists. And what is wonderful is that they know that they know a lot but they know mainly that they don't know much more. And that is a very dramatic situation very simply. An extraordinary situation.

STUDENT: Are you thinking of doing a film on scientific activities?

ROSSELLINI: That's just the secondary part of it. What is the main thing is the meaning of the thing, the approach of the thing.

See, for example, now somebody said that science very clearly is going in a *third* phase. The third phase of science is to do the work with the use of abstractions. Surely, you must have knowledge before going to an abstraction. A scientist here at Rice told me something absolutely extraordinary. He said: "If I want to deal purely with speculation, working with my fancy and with my knowledge, and with mathematical language, I must draw always a caricature of the aspect I want to see. I must *exaggerate* a certain kind of thing." Through that caricature, suddenly he can see in a broader way a certain grouping of phenomena. If you go through the work of analysis it will take a lot of time to reach the same point. Instead you have to go by synthesis. So that is a new kind of aspect of science, that I didn't know before coming here: to caricature, to work with your fantasy. Exaggerate and forget the various data in the midst of it.

You build a model and you have the main picture of the thing.

Art, of course, builds models, but at present the kind of models built by art are far removed from the reality of the world. Because, you know, the reality is much more fantastic than fantasy. When you have in your hand the reality, you can go on with your fantasies.

For example, we learn that oxygen is purely toxic. If you don't know that, how can you be oriented? Life started on earth when oxygen did not exist. Little by little photosynthesis appeared, and oxygen appeared and we had to adapt ourselves to that thing which is toxic.

STUDENT: But what about carbon dioxide?

ROSSELLINI: No. Don't go through those details. If you do that . . . see, for example, a more simple thing. . . .

Let's remain with pollution. The common man has now discovered the word pollution. But, pollution has always played a tremendous role in nature. When a certain group of animals were formed, and they grew living together, immediately pollution grew. No doubt. And the pollution is the reductive factor that takes the population back to the original equilibrium.

Now, just in the interest of discovering *new, dramatic motifs*, let's look at this: we are complaining about the pollution. We know that we have to do something against the pollution. Because? Why? We want to save ourselves. Huh? But in the meantime we preach *pills* in order to reduce birth, etc., etc., which is another kind of pollution that you create. (The *pill* is pollution in that it kills.)

Now when you go just to look upon those kinds of factors, you can find thousands of conflicts inside, absolutely human. What do you want to write, that or that one? It starts to become a new kind of dramaturgy which can arise from that knowledge. That is the attempt I am making.

We have become so aware of pollution. Pollution is the same as life. Because pollution has always interfered to reduce the explosion of the population. It reestablishes the primitive equilibrium that is in all life.

Today we complain of the pollution. We want to do something about it, otherwise it will reduce the population growth. But we invent another way to reduce the population with the pills, etc., etc., and sterilization.

So if you would think five seconds about all that, you would see what tremendous new dramatic motifs you can find.

Immediately what can rise up: we consider only ourselves, that we are alive. We don't consider the future. We refuse to be polluted, but we want to pollute the newcomers. So that perhaps in a few years we will have a world of old people like me. You can imagine what a pleasure it would be. You see, if you just go a little bit with fantasy, you will find that there are thousands of things that you can work with, you know. That is the dramaturgy. Dramaturgy is the way of finding conflicts.

"An Interview with Rossellini," in Rossellini. May 1-20, 1979 *(pp. 17-19; original English text), a special publication of the Public Theatre of New York by Joseph Papp, in occasion of the Rossellini retrospective; James Blue interviewed Rossellini at Rice University in Houston, Texas, in 1972.*

ROBERTO ROSSELLINI: "WHERE ARE WE GOING?"

BY TAG GALLAGHER AND JOHN W. HUGHES

John W. Hughes and I met Roberto Rossellini in the lobby of the Algonquin Hotel. He had recently returned from Rome where he'd signed a contract to do The Messiah. *For days he'd been answering questions; for months before that he had been answering questions at various universities; for years before that he had been answering questions from reporters and critics. No doubt they were mostly the same questions and hence were receiving the same answers. We struggled, as our interview shows, to get Rossellini to talk about his films, and he did not so much elude us as confront us with a guru-like simplicity. He is not bashful in displaying his courtesy and, while everything happened as one would expect in a hotel lobby, I realized later that it had all been a koan with RR showing a way, and like so many others who have told of meeting Rossellini, I felt the experience was one of the most profound of my life.*

GALLAGHER: How do you feel your historical films differ from your previous work?

ROSSELLINI: The purpose is different, the sense is different, totally different. There is cultural information that I have to convey. There is no fiction at all.

GALLAGHER: But you've retained elements of drama.

ROSSELLINI: Everything in life is drama, too. I don't build anything. There is no invention at all, just the selection of material. That is all.

GALLAGHER: Do you feel that in your films with Ingrid Bergman you already had a style which was in some respects materialistic?

ROSSELLINI: I don't know, because I never thought of those kinds of things. I don't care about them. What I want to do is to be myself, and as true as possible as I am in the moment. I am not a critic or a philosopher. I hate all sorts of aesthetic ideas, so I have no idea, no answer to the question.

HUGHES: We're not trying to pin you down, but we want to understand your intentions.

ROSSELLINI: Anybody can have his own theories. I refuse to have theories.

GALLAGHER: You wish things to be open? Not to impose your own interpretations?

ROSSELLINI: Yes. I don't want to impose. I want to be ready to change as much as I can. You see, it is a total refusal of those kinds of things.

GALLAGHER: But you've always been open?

ROSSELLINI: Well, I think so, yes. I've become more open now but, you know, you have to *train* yourself to be open.

GALLAGHER: I've noticed that the central figures in your films, even in the later ones, are often alienated from society and through this alienation become the outstanding individuals that they are.

ROSSELLINI: Perhaps. I don't know. Anybody can be alienated. You see, these are the sort of things that it is difficult for me to answer because I don't know. I refuse to know, even. One must be absolutely spontaneous and nothing else, because if you start to think in terms such as, "I am an artist," you are immediately a son of a bitch. That is my impression, and I hate that.

GALLAGHER: John and I have been having a debate about the Bergman films and about *Stromboli* in particular. I feel that at the end of the film (in the Italian version) you were already somewhat materialistic, because in one respect Ingrid-Karin thinks she's found God but, in another respect, it's merely a human being—like us, but not someone we identify with, and maybe she finds God and maybe she's just instinctual. I like the films for that reason. The last shot of the birds is so materialistic, free, open.

ROSSELLINI: I think that you have seen the thing properly.

GALLAGHER: And that she comes to this because she's so alienated. In *Europe '51* again she's alienated, insane, or a saint, we don't know. Louis XIV is also alienated. Socrates too.

ROSSELLINI: Yes, you can say that. Well, everybody can be alienated or crazy.

GALLAGHER: But is the great man, the individual, always alienated?

ROSSELLINI: That is your point of view, but in fact each one of us in life tries to do something and has to confront a lot of prejudice, a lot of preconceived ideas, a lot of superstition, a lot of weakness, a lot of shrewdness. Each one of us deals with those kinds of things.

GALLAGHER: But each of your films seems to pose the problem of the individual trying to rise above the crowd. You always have the two.

ROSSELLINI: That doesn't happen all the time? It is our daily life! Somebody who goes out and buys a car or a camera does so because he wants to be above the crowd. Anything we do is always to try to get there, because in fact one of the main pushes in life as it is today is vanity. Vanity is such a strong behavior in man that it makes everything confused, for that reason. Because no one is really tied to reality but instead is looking at himself. He gets lost very easily. So that can be a form of alienation perhaps.

GALLAGHER: You've said you believe in the progress of humanity, but is it man who progesses or is it the single individual who leads mankind?

ROSSELLINI: You see, there doesn't exist a single individual and the human species. A single individual is part. All those things are interconnected, so if somebody makes a step, the others, because they are monkeys, will imitate that step, and they become everything, everybody. You see, it is very difficult to divide, to rationalize, to analyze properly those kinds of things. These are phenomena which are happening all the time, all the time. You don't agree with me?

GALLAGHER: I agree, and this is what fascinates me. Louis XIV is just a common everyday man, not a remarkable individual.

ROSSELLINI: No, he's a king and he does the profession of a king. He doesn't do anything else except the profession of a king.

GALLAGHER: But because of what happens to him, he is forced into a situation . . .

ROSSELLINI: Yes, he is forced into the situation, but it isn't his main goal: which is to be a little bit more of a son of a bitch than the others. But it's a goal, no? Because you are dealing with sons of bitches you want to be a little bit more of a son of a bitch than the others. It's absolutely instinctive and natural.

GALLAGHER: Your heroes always seem to be a little bit insane.

ROSSELLINI: You think that the people in life are all sane? If you look at the reality we have to face, you see that insanity is part of the reality.

GALLAGHER: Do you believe in God now?

ROSSELLINI: No.

GALLAGHER: In any sort of God or any sort of mysticism?

ROSSELLINI: No, not at all.

HUGHES: You really didn't when you made *Stromboli*?

ROSSELLINI: I am looking at people who believe in God. Should I superimpose my own thought?

HUGHES: But a year ago you told me that the attitude of the early fifties was essentially religious.

ROSSELLINI: I said that? No. Perhaps I said that the opinion of people was that my films were religious. I think that's absolutely nonsense. Religion is around us all the time, so if you have to show human beings, you have to show human beings as they are, not abstractions.

GALLAGHER: Anthropological?

ROSSELLINI: Surely.

HUGHES: Do you think there is an Unconscious, that Freud was right?

ROSSELLINI: I'm not Freudian, but Freud made an important discovery in the method of the examination of things. But if you become totally Freudian you're castrating yourself. Everything we reach, the way of thinking is important.

HUGHES: So your position is not so tragic as the film *Socrates*. He was an intelligent man who came along and was killed.

ROSSELLINI: Well, people are killed all the time, all over the world. Perhaps it's necessary that someone has the courage to sacrifice himself. The world is so trained to react emotionally, instead of with reason, that when you see there is no possibility of driving people to reason, perhaps the only way is to build up a big emotion and that will affect people.

HUGHES: In the early films there's a kind of emotional involvement which you think is sick now, commercial and outdated.

ROSSELLINI: Um, perhaps, yes. I'm more interested in thinking than in emotion. We are wrong when our starting point is always emotion, and after we try to rationalize the emotion. I think the procedure is wrong. We must be first of all intelligent, to have the capacity to read inside everything, and afterwards we can see what happens. Our training is a purely emotional training.

HUGHES: Why is the theme of sexuality so little evident in the late films?

ROSSELLINI: Because in general one exerts sexuality by himself, closed inside a room, not in the middle of the street.

GALLAGHER: In your Bergman films you did a beautiful job showing a woman as a human being. They're Women's Lib films, if you like, but women seem to have disappeared from your films.

ROSSELLINI: They will come up again. I have no preconceived ideas.

HUGHES: The "Essential Image" you talk about,[1] we know it's not a theory . . .

ROSSELLINI: It's a research.

HUGHES: . . . It's a way that you create, but it's difficult for some people to understand. As I understand it, the "Essential Image" is not just an unconscious image . . .

1 See J. Hughes, "In Search of the 'Essential Image,'" in *The Village Voice*, 10 May 1973.

ROSSELLINI: Nothing is unconscious.

HUGHES: . . . You talk about it as something beyond words, beyond preconceptions, so a lot of people interpret it as similar to, say, Brakhage. I don't see any comparison.

ROSSELLINI: No, no. I have realized suddenly that what we call images are illustrations of a way of thinking that is purely verbal. Now, if we can go back to what was for us, the human being, the image before language developed, surely the images would have another value. Because through the images you get the revelation of everything, you understand everything. The problem is to get rid of that system which is purely verbal. Our dialectic is purely verbal. We can theorize as much as we want, but in fact we are making illustrations of a mental process which is purely verbal. If we can get rid of that, most probably we can find an image that is essential. To see things as they are, that's the main point. It's not easy to reach that point. I'm searching for it. I've not found it yet.

HUGHES: Is this not very difficult to do when you're doing historical subjects?

ROSSELLINI: No, why?

GALLAGHER: Because you must choose which events to study.

ROSSELLINI: No. Anything, if you have to see a tree or a butterfly, it's a tree, a butterfly. An historical event is an historical event. It has the same value as a tree or a butterfly or a mushroom.

GALLAGHER: But you choose the tree.

ROSSELLINI: No, I don't choose the tree. I must get the tree who is there. There is not a choice of the tree. Not at all. I'm totally refusing all sorts of aesthetic preconceived ideas, totally, totally, totally. That's the point.

GALLAGHER: But you start with a script?

ROSSELLINI: No. I have ideas, quite clear, and so on. The dialogue is based on many documents, and so it's not invention.

GALLAGHER: But when you made the Medici film, I presume you did a great deal of research.

ROSSELLINI: Naturally.

GALLAGHER: And then you took certain ideas from this.

ROSSELLINI: When you want to talk about something, you must know the thing. When you know the thing well, you can say what is essential. When you don't know it well, you are lost in the middle of a lot of things which are impressive. I refuse the things which are impressive. I try to express the things which I think are essential. So you see, it's a different procedure.

HUGHES: That's the image the child sees, as Merleau-Ponty shows when he talks about how Cézanne in his paintings restructures perception. He makes you resee the act of seeing, and in a sense the child does that. I think your films do that.

ROSSELLINI: That's your opinion. I don't want to get involved there. Each one is free to think what he wants.

HUGHES: Yes. But you've sort of said that. You say you're going beyond preconceptions . . .

ROSSELLINI: Yes, I try to do that.

HUGHES: The point I'm trying to make is that the child doesn't analyze reality, whereas your images do.

ROSSELLINI: Well, we think that a child does not analyze, but he's analyzing all the time because he's learning so much faster than we.

HUGHES: In [The Rise to Power of] Louis XIV, when Louis goes into his mother's bedroom and tells her he wants more power, at that moment you have Louis and his mother in the exact same position as a painting of Christ and Mary right behind their heads. In the [Age of the] Medici, there are many relationships between images and paintings.

ROSSELLINI: You see that (laughs). I haven't seen that.

HUGHES: You didn't see the correspondence at the time you made it? I find that hard to believe.

ROSSELLINI: No (laughing). I would be a . . . a dirty cockroach if I did a thing like that. I refuse it completely. I'm looking at reality, that's all. The reality is there. Were I to refer to a painting you would immediately get the idea that now I'm showing you how capable I am, how intelligent I am, how learned, how refined. I hate all those things.

HUGHES: So essentially your films are just trying to decondition people from having theories.

ROSSELLINI: Yes, absolutely.

GALLAGHER: Yet your films seem to present a theory. You remain an individual, you choose scenes, events, what to show. And your films look as though they were made by one individual, by you.

ROSSELLINI: You would recognize my handwriting. Like anyone's, it's absolutely distinctive. If you want, I choose. But I don't choose. If you have to go from here to that door over there you have to take one step after another. There's no doubt. Those are only steps and nothing more than that.

HUGHES: But there is also spectacle in your films.

ROSSELLINI: But in real life everything is spectacular. What is very bad is to make an effort to be spectacular.

GALLAGHER: I think what we're getting at is that your films still look beautiful in a theater sense, in a photographic sense. They speak to us as art at the same time as other things.

ROSSELLINI: Well, so what?

GALLAGHER: You claim you don't try to do that, even in the death scene in *Pascal*?

ROSSELLINI: It's my handwriting, no more than that.

GALLAGHER: But the color, the soundtrack . . .

ROSSELLINI: Why not use color? We have the language of color. I use the color. I have no aesthetic problems at all. It's a research.

GALLAGHER: But all these things interpret the action.

ROSSELLINI: It's up to you to judge that, it's not up to me. It's not a creative act. I refuse to accomplish any creative act. The only creation possible is to build a child. That's all. That's a creative act.

HUGHES (to GALLAGHER):   I told you he was hard to . . .

ROSSELLINI: I'm not hard. I'm simple. It is hard because you want me to say what you want to say. I appreciate what you can say. To push me to think on your terms is difficult because I think on my terms. I try to be as simple as possible.

GALLAGHER: Have you considered eliminating dramatic action altogether?

ROSSELLINI: I think that, more or less, I have always tried to get rid of that artificial construction.

GALLAGHER: How did you get started on these ideas?

ROSSELLINI: Because I think that we are totally ignorant and we are suffering by our ignorance and our protection, so if we can start to know a little bit perhaps we can improve ourselves. It was always my feeling, and I've become more aware of that problem. I've tried to do it, more or less, in all my films. There's no rupture between my early films and my late ones. It's an evolution. You change your mind. The ideas are vague first of all, later they are less vague, someday they become more clear. It's not a decision made in a day.

HUGHES: You were saying at Yale that the main interest you have in the zoom that you've invented is that it preserves depth of field without flattening space. Yet in the *Medici* you're continually flattening space by having rectangular paintings or blocks of material in the background in a Matisse kind of effect, bringing the back toward the front. As you zoom out, space flattens.

ROSSELLINI: I don't know. I don't remember. You look at the thing through an aesthetic point of view. It's difficult to have a dialogue about this. You can say what you want and I can say what I want. I think that to begin to know anything is very difficult.

GALLAGHER: What is the focal length of your zoom?

ROSSELLINI: From 25 mm to 250 mm.

HUGHES: What is the meaning in *Louis XIV* of always zooming in on Louis?

ROSSELLINI: What do you do with your own eyes? The eye is tremendously mobile. It takes in a lot. I try to have a lens which is like the eye.

HUGHES: Does that mean that the zoom is your personal signature?

ROSSELLINI: Perhaps, yes.

HUGHES: Focusing in on history?

ROSSELLINI: Not only history. Focusing on facts.

HUGHES: Aren't the facts history? We were arguing before about whether the point of view in your films is that of the time in which they take place or that of the present.

ROSSELLINI: We are the result of past time, so if we don't know what was before we don't know our own time. We get so confused.

GALLAGHER: You said once that the important thing in art . . .

ROSSELLINI: In "art" . . . it's difficult to dimension the word "art."

GALLAGHER: . . . You said that art has always had an important role: to give the historical meaning of the time that one is living in.

ROSSELLINI: Art has the capacity of doing things, no more than that.

GALLAGHER: I mean, do you want to give the meaning of the historical period 1974?

ROSSELLINI: Yes, because we are so involved that it is difficult for us to understand. To understand ourselves today we must explore how we were formed, little by little. Evolution is always existing. It means also that we can make a lot of mistakes. There's nothing wrong with that. It's a fact. But it's a section of things. How we can understand ourselves today is almost impossible because we get so involved emotionally. It's almost impossible to understand anything. We can theorize a lot. We can have a lot of opinion, but between the opinion and the fact, the reality of the fact, there is a big difference. So we deal always with opinion and I don't like the opinion, so I try to know a little bit more than to have an opinion.

HUGHES: In the *Medici,* the scene with the machines making ammunition and so forth . . . There are a lot of emotional overtones. It's a very Blakean, horrible atmosphere. Were you trying to get that effect? Or am I reading into it?

ROSSELLINI: Surely you are. Why would I try to get another effect? That is the effect I wanted. You see, I try to put as many messages as I can in a little shot, or even a little frame.

HUGHES: The film seems to be about Cosimo inventing bourgeois society, like Louis XIV did. You have that scene where Alberti shows the factory, sort of the first modern factory. It seemed to me you were predicting the problems of the industrial revolution.

ROSSELLINI: No, I was just looking at what happened at that time. If you have a tree, before it was a tree it was a seed. So I go to the seed. You know very well that from the seed one day you'll have a tree.

HUGHES: Did you find reproductions of factories like that? It must have cost a lot of money to reconstruct it so accurately from commentaries.

ROSSELLINI: Yes, from documents. It cost a lot of money, unfortunately, a lot of money.

HUGHES: When you look at the fact of the invention of Renaissance perspective, do you see that as just an objective fact? I mean, is it totally a good thing, this invention?

ROSSELLINI: Surely, only a fact. I don't know if it's a good or a bad thing. It's a fact.

HUGHES: You think spectacle is bad? Louis tried to invent Madison Avenue.

ROSSELLINI: Yes. I don't want any sort of seduction. When you become very effective you can be seductive. You're no longer yourself, you're creating a temperature in somebody. What is important is that each one of us is himself. But to be oneself we must get a lot of information. So I supply the information.

HUGHES: But to be myself I find it necessary to relate to the idea of Renaissance perspective in all its ambiguity, as you present it.

ROSSELLINI: Surely, yes. That's the funny thing. In life each one sees the thing as he wants. And that's the intelligence of the human species, that each one of us is himself and not somebody else.

HUGHES: But you're making educational films corresponding to your sense of history and the breakdown of western culture. We have to figure out how to relate to Alberti.

ROSSELLINI: Do that. But *you* have to do it. Don't force me to.

HUGHES: I just want to make sure I'm not totally off the mark when I find these things.

ROSSELLINI: No, no. We each have our own point of view. That is the richness of life. I'm happy that you're forced to think. That's a good thing.

HUGHES: In your films, are things from your perspective?

ROSSELLINI: I try to go beyond, or before my point of view.

HUGHES: That's what makes the "Essential Image" idea so complex. It's totally simple but yet totally complicated. You're analyzing things but not in a reductive way.

ROSSELLINI: That's the point. Not to analyze in a reductive way. The moment you have an opinion you're analyzing in a reductive way.

GALLAGHER: In what language did you make the *Medici?*

ROSSELLINI: English.

GALLAGHER: Many of us thought that in some of the small parts lines are occasionally spoken rather stupidly.

ROSSELLINI: Perhaps.

GALLAGHER: You don't want to say more? This bothers me, because audiences laugh at them. This was not intentional, I presume?

ROSSELLINI: Everything is intentional. What I do, I do because I want to do it that way. Perhaps I am wrong, but I don't care. One must take the risk. I am jealous of my freedom. I don't search for success. I don't want to be seduced by vanity.

GALLAGHER: Do you rehearse the actors in their English dialogue?

ROSSELLINI: Surely, the little rehearsal that I have to do, just so they know what they have to do.

GALLAGHER: On the set?

ROSSELLINI: Yes, and even before. It's such a boring thing to work and to do the shooting.

HUGHES: Was the man who played Cosimo a professional?

ROSSELLINI: No, he's a counterman in a Rome nightclub. He takes the tickets. He's still there.

HUGHES: Is Louis XIV back in the post office?

ROSSELLINI: No, I think he left. It was the old Ministry of Colonies, not the post office. The last I heard he was doing experimental theater.

GALLAGHER: So, these lines of dialogue, it wasn't a question of time or language?

ROSSELLINI: Everything is intentional. I must be responsible.

GALLAGHER: But, why?

ROSSELLINI: Because otherwise you are not yourself.

GALLAGHER: No, I mean why do you have them speak stupidly?

ROSSELLINI: I don't know. I made them speak as I thought it right.

GALLAGHER: John theorized that you were trying to remind us that it was a film, artificial.

HUGHES: I think it's definitely a kind of Brechtian effect.

ROSSELLINI: Not an effect, a fact.

GALLAGHER: The point is that you're watching the film and you can't help but accept it in some sense as a reality, here we are in old Florence (*Rossellini nods yes*). Then, all of a sudden, some character says something in such a tone of voice that you know he's just a bad actor, and everyone laughs at it.

ROSSELLINI: I don't know how to help. That means I'm an idiot.

GALLAGHER: The mirror shots in the *Medici,* the superimpositions, the cartoon lithograph of Florence as a little sliver of gold superimposed on the real, green valley, all of these have the effect of making it seem that the Renaissance did create a sort of artificial synthetic culture that replaced the feudal culture based on nature, not money. Is that the theme of the film?

ROSSELLINI: Well, it's the theme, but outside of the images. It's the theme of the film, surely.

HUGHES: It showed the Renaissance to be glorious, but also a real problem because it introduced the synthetic into human relations, i.e., money, commerce, banking.

ROSSELLINI: Surely. There is no doubt.

GALLAGHER: How have you financed your recent films?

ROSSELLINI: Mainly making debts.

GALLAGHER: Through the RAI (Italian TV)?

ROSSELLINI: They gave me a very little portion of the money, about a fifth. The rest are debts. I am in debt to everybody.

GALLAGHER: How do you manage to go on?

ROSSELLINI: I create new debts. I am working, when I get a little money I pay a little bit.

GALLAGHER: This is amazing.

ROSSELLINI: It's not amazing. No one tries. It's a very simple operation. I'm not escaping or running away. I am here, I have debts, so what? I went to the bank the other day and said I need $100,000 in a few days. They say, "What kind of guarantee can you give?" I say, "No guarantee. If I have a guarantee it's absolutely insane to come ask you for money. I want money, because I need the money."

GALLAGHER: Has *Louis XIV* made back its production costs?

ROSSELLINI : Yes. It cost about $175,000.

GALLAGHER: And the *Medici* cost?

ROSSELLINI: More or less a million.

GALLAGHER: Somebody must have faith in you that they keep giving you money?

ROSSELLINI: Well, it's a good way to build up debts. Some people have faith. They know I'm always there. I pay a little bit and go on. If I pay a little bit it's a good reason to have more debts.

HUGHES: Have you made money on any of the historical films?

ROSSELLINI: No.

GALLAGHER: It's very difficult to see your films in America. I've heard that there was some possibility of a distribution contract coming up.

ROSSELLINI: Everybody's asking me for the films, but now I'm a little bit careful, because I don't want to spoil future possibilities. We're discussing the contract, but it's been going on for months now. I don't know if I'll reach an agreement or not, because I'm very stubborn on little points.

GALLAGHER: What is the next film you'll make?

ROSSELLINI: *The Messiah,* surely, and most probably also the one on DeGasperi [*Anno uno* (Year one)]. That will be decided soon.

HUGHES: What is *The Messiah* based on?

ROSSELLINI: On the Messiah! The idea of the film is that the tribe of

Israel was living in a patriarchal society and so there were no chiefs. They were confronting different powers, kings and armies and things like that. And they wanted also to be like that. They asked Samuel, who was the spiritual leader in a sense—a judge—to have a king, a power established like the others. Yahweh apparently answers Samuel warning them that if you want to have a king, your daughters will have to go to perfume his body, to work in his kitchen, your sons will be put in the army and you'll have to give the king your donkeys and crops, etc. But they wanted the king anyway, and so they got the king. In the period of the king started all the movements of prophets who were protesting against the kings and waiting for someone who would bring back justice, in the large sense. And finally Christ arrived who is just an expression of the human being, more simple, the most humble. And that is the reason why he was not identified with that idea of justice, like an avenging angel with sword in hand. I'll use nonprofessional actors. It will be shot in Tunisia, Yemen, and Iran, in color.

HUGHES: And the other project on the Prime Minister, DeGasperi. I hear it's to be a kind of continuation of *Open City*. What kind of style will it have, a fusion of the late and early?

ROSSELLINI: It will be didactic, but I have really no preconceived ideas about it. I'll do what I think is right.

GALLAGHER: Why did you leave the commercial cimema?

ROSSELLINI: Because it's boring.

HUGHES: Why are you going back into it?

ROSSELLINI: If I do the film on DeGasperi, I'll do it because I think that the political situation requires a revision of a moment of our own history.

HUGHES: Is the rise of neofascism part of it?

ROSSELLINI: Yes. DeGasperi created a certain kind of democracy after twenty or so years of Fascism. It was quite a peculiar conception. For example, he was absolutely anticommunist, absolutely crazy against communism. But in his purpose to create a new kind of democracy in our kind of republic, he allowed the communist party to exist, and all the time defended that existence, even though it was very menacing to him.

GALLAGHER: You wish to do a film on the American Revolution?

ROSSELLINI: I think it is the only revolution that was accomplished in the world. The original idea was the creation of the constitution, the dream rather than the reality, the conception of a power as weak as possible. It is said by Thomas Paine so beautifully, that power is a necessary evil. That's the novelty of the American Revolution. It's not a question of anarchism, but of faith in man. If you have faith in human beings, you know very well you ought not to be a shepherd, that you have to be a human being involved with other human beings, and to establish a certain kind of government in which you can survive together.

GALLAGHER: Would you see the American Revolution in Marxist terms?

ROSSELLINI: But Marx was not born. I want to see the facts as they were.

HUGHES: He mentions Marx because there is a kind of sense which is close to Marx or Engels, say, in the *Medici*, where you very scientifically analyze a change in society.

ROSSELLINI: You think that to be scientific is to be Marx or Engels? My theory is to understand. I go straight to the facts.

HUGHES: The closest thing I know to your *Louis XIV* is Brecht's *Galileo*, but you always seem rather negative when I mention Brecht.

ROSSELLINI: I've seen that play, but I don't understand the effort of trying to make a thing valuable because it looks like something else. Perhaps everything looks alike. There are not so many good things in the world. I don't know.

GALLAGHER: You seem to be concentrating on the eighteenth century.

ROSSELLINI: I am proceeding with my system. Right now I've reached the eighteenth century. Next I'll do Diderot. I want also to do Niepce and Daguerre, the inventors of photography.

HUGHES: Do you think Descartes was a more sympathetic character than Pascal?

ROSSELLINI: Less perhaps. He was a son of a bitch, a coward, a lazy person, but he was also intelligent. He was quite repulsive, of course, not *simpatico*. But I don't care about that. What is important is to look at the passage of the ideas.

GALLAGHER: Have you thought of doing a film on Kant? It would seem natural, since you've dealt with so many philosophers.

ROSSELLINI: No, not for the moment. What I'm trying to reestablish is that man is "essential." I have to try to draw that map, the main line of human development. Kant was somebody who went deeper into what was already there.

GALLAGHER: I always thought he was the most important philosopher after Plato.

ROSSELLINI: Surely, there is no doubt, one of the most significant, but in the map that I am trying to draw he doesn't fit.

GALLAGHER: So you have a plan?

ROSSELLINI: Surely, to demolish my own ignorance. I hope that I am not the only ignorant one in the world, so I will help others like me. It's a very simple theory.

GALLAGHER: Did you see [Francesco] Rosi's *The Mattei Affair?* It seemed to relate to your work.

ROSSELLINI: I know Rosi very well, but I haven't seen the film. I never go to the movies. And I've never seen one of my own projected.

GALLAGHER: Did you use to go to the movies?

ROSSELLINI: Yes, when I was young and inconsiderate.

GALLAGHER: What did you like?

ROSSELLINI: The first impression that I have were the films of Griffith, Murnau, King Vidor.

HUGHES: Renoir?

ROSSELLINI: *Toni, Grand Illusion, La Bête humaine, Rules of the Game,* many of them.

GALLAGHER: Do you feel that Renoir and others have tried, like you, to discover "men as they are"?

ROSSELLINI: Renoir has done a lot of that. We are very close friends.

GALLAGHER: Ford?

ROSSELLINI: I only saw one or two of his.

GALLAGHER: Any of Straub's films?

ROSSELLINI: No.

HUGHES: Do you see *Louis XIV* or the *Medici* as political films?

ROSSELLINI: Everything is political. Human beings are similar. Politics is similar all over. Style of dress changes, but we don't change the rest.

GALLAGHER: You said you thought our civilization is doomed.

ROSSELLINI: It's gone. It doesn't stand anymore. We're in a tremendous crisis.

GALLAGHER: Where are we going?

ROSSELLINI: I don't know. I'm not a prophet. I think the main thing is to have a new kind of conception of the human being . . . the world is full of idiots and a few geniuses. I think that is totally wrong. Everybody can be very intelligent if he's properly informed, etc. . . . and we have not exploited that natural resource which is the human intelligence.

"Roberto Rossellini: 'Where are we going?'," in
Changes, *no. 87, April 1974; original English text.*

Roberto Rossellini was born in Rome, 8 May 1906, the son of Angiolo (Angelo) Giuseppe and Elettra Bellan. He had one brother, Renzo (1908-1982), and two sisters, Marcella (1909-1990) and Micaela (b. 1922). In 1936, he married Marcella De Marchis and had two children, Romano (1937-1946) and Renzo (b. 1941). He was married a second time in 1950 to Ingrid Bergman. This marriage produced three children: Roberto (b. 1950), and Isotta and Isabella, twins, (b. 1952). His third and final marriage was to Sonali Sen Das Gupta in 1957. They had one child, Raffaella (b.1957), and Rossellini adopted Gil, the son of Sonali and Hari Das Gupta. He began working in 1932 on film dubbing and sound effects, then editing and scriptwriting.

In the years immediately following World War II, Rossellini gained international recognition as a neorealist with Paisan, Open City, and Germany Year Zero. From 1948, he moved into more personal stories, beginning with Amore, a film dedicated to Anna Magnani and dealing with the near-delusion of a woman's subjective experience. After this film, he was approached by Ingrid Bergman, and shortly after by Howard Hughes who offered him to work for RKO; the result was the much debated Stromboli (1950). Rossellini and Bergman eventually married and together made more films, such as Europe '51 and Voyage in Italy. Toward the end of the 1950s, their partnership entered a personal and artistic crisis. A long trip to India and the divorce from Bergman (1958) marked a new phase in Rossellinis's career—India, Viva l'Italia!, and Vanina Vanini showed his new interest in documentary and historical reconstruction. His last films were done primarily for television and were based on historical subjects. Drawing from his earlier experience in works such as The Flowers of St. Francis, Rossellini worked out an educational form of filmmaking, bringinig to the screen such diverse figures as Louis XIV, Socrates, Pascal, and the Medicis. He died in Rome in 1977.

FILMOGRAPHY

English title is given when released in US and/or UK; if two years are mentioned, first year is year of shooting, second is year of release

1935: *Dafne* (short; can be the same known as *Prelude à l'après-midi d'un faune*; possibly shot but not edited nor released).
1938-40: *Fantasia sottomarina* (short).
1939(?)-41: *Il ruscello di Ripasottile* (short).
1941: *La nave bianca.*
1941-42: *Un pilota ritorna.*
1942-43: *L'uomo dalla croce.*

1943-46: *Desiderio (Woman*, finished and co-signed by Marcello Pagliero).

1945: *Roma città aperta (Open City)*.

1946: *Paisà (Paisan)*

1947-48: *Deutschland im Jahre Null / Germania anno zero (Germany Year Zero)*.

1947-48: *L'amore* (two episodes: *Una voce umana / A Human Voice*, shot in 1947, before *Germany Year Zero*; *Il miracolo / The Miracle*, shot in 1948).

1948: *La macchina ammazzacattivi*.

1949-50: *Stromboli / Stromboli, terra di Dio*.

1950: *Francesco giullare di Dio (The Flowers of St. Francis)*

1951-52: *L'invidia (Envy*, fifth episode of *I sette peccati capitali / The Seven Deadly Sins)*.

1951: *Santa Brigida* (short, never edited nor released)

1951-52: *Europe '51 / Europa '51 (The Greatest Love)*.

1952-54: *Dov'è la libertà . . .?*

1952-53: *Ingrid Bergman* (third episode of *Siamo donne)*

1953-54: *Viaggio in Italia (Strangers / The Lonely Woman*, aka *Voyage in Italy)*.

1953-54: *Napoli 43* (fourth episode of *Amori di mezzo secolo)*.

1954-55: *Giovanna d'Arco al rogo / Jeanne au bûcher*

1954: *Angst / La paura (Fear)*.

1956: *Le psychodrame* (short, possibly never edited).

1957-59: *J'ai fait un beau voyage/ L'india vista da Rossellini* (documentary; 10 episodes for TV).

1957-59: *India Matri Bhumi*.

1959: *Il generale Della Rovere (General Della Rovere)*.

1960: *Era notte a Roma*.

1961: *Viva l'Italia!*

1961: *Torino nei cent'anni* (medium-lenght documentary for TV); *Torino tra due secoli* (short).

1961: *Vanina Vanini (The Betrayer)*.

1962: *Anima nera*.

1962-63: *Illibatezza* (first episode of *RoGoPaG)*.

1964-65: *L'età del ferro* (5 episodes for TV; directed by Renzo Rossellini, jr.; supervised by Roberto Rossellini).

1966: *La prise de pouvoir par Louis XIV (The Rise to Power of Louis XIV*; for TV).

1967-68: *The Sicily of Roberto Rossellini / Idea di un'isola* (documentary for TV).

1967-71: *La lotta dell'uomo per la sua sopravvivenza* (12 episodes for TV; directed by Renzo Rossellini, Jr.; supervised by Roberto Rossellini).

1968-69: *Atti degli Apostoli* (5 episodes for TV).

1970: *Socrate* (TV).

1971-73: *Intervista con Salvador Allende* (medium-lenght documentary for TV).

1971-72: *Blaise Pascal* (TV).

1971-73: *Rice University* (documentary for TV).

1972: *Agostino di Ippona* (TV).

1972-73): *L'età di Cosimo de' Medici* (The Age of Cosimo de' Medici; 3 episodes for TV).

1973-74: *Cartesius* (TV).
1974: *Anno uno.*
1974: *A Question of People* (documentary film).
1975: *Il Messia* (The Messiah).
1977: *Le Centre Georges Pompidou* (medium-length documentary).
1977: *Concerto per Michelangelo* (medium-length documentary for TV).

SELECTED BIBLIOGRAPHY

SCREENPLAYS

Open City, Paisan, Germany Year Zero:
The War trilogy, Stefano Roncoroni (ed.), New York: Grossmann, 1973.
"Rome ville ouverte" (*Open City*), in *L'avant-scène/Cinéma*, no. 71, June 1967 (in French).
Paisan, original subject, original screenplay of episodes I and III, screenplay of unrealized episode "La nurse," treatment of unrealized episode "Il prigioniero," in A. Aprà (ed.), *Rosselliniana*, Rome: Di Giacomo, 1987, pp. 93-129 (in Italian).
Paisan, screenplay of unrealized episodes "Parco di Predappio" and "I partigiani del Nord," edited by Stefano Roncoroni, in *Filmcritica*, no. 410, December 1990, pp. 567-584 (in Italian).

The Miracle:
Federico Fellini, "Le miracle," in *La revue du cinéma*, no. 14, June 1948, pp. 15-24 (treatment, in French).

The Flowers of St. Francis:
"Francesco giullare di Dio," in *Inquadrature*, no. 5-6, October 1958-September 1959, pp. 39-48 (treatment, in Italian).

Voyage in Italy/Strangers:
"Voyage en Italie," in *L'avant-scène/Cinéma*, no. 361, June 1987 (in French).
"Voyage en Italie" de Roberto Rossellini, Alain Bergala (ed.), Crisnie (Belgium): Ed. Yellow Now, 1990 (essay and frame enlargements, in French).

India Matri Bhumi:
R. Rossellini, "L'India tra il vecchio e il nuovo," in Il *Contemporaneo*, 11 January 1958 (subject of 6 episodes).
A. Aprà (ed.), *Roberto Rossellini. India*, Rome: Cinecittà Estero, 1991, pp. 18-26 (subject of 4 episodes, in French).

General Della Rovere:
Indro Montanelli, *Il generale Della Rovere*, Milan: Rizzoli, **1959 and 1975** (novelized version of the film treatment, in Italian).

Era notte a Roma:
Renzo Renzi (ed.), *Era notte a Roma*, Bologna: Cappelli, 1960 (in Italian).

L'età del ferro:
"Il ferro," in *Filmcritica*, no. 139-40, November-December 1963, pp. **699-718** (in Italian).

The Rise to Power of Louis XIV:
"La Prise de pouvoir par Louis XIV," in *Télé-Sept Jours*, October 1966, pp. 32-119 (in French).
Acts of the Apostles, Socrates, Blaise Pascal, Augustine of Hippo, The Age of Cosimo de' Medici, Cartesius:
Luciano Scaffa & Marcella Mariani Rossellini (eds.), *Atti degli Apostoli, Socrate, Blaise Pascal, Agostino d'Ippona, L'età dei Medici, Cartesius*, Turin: ERI, 1980 (in Italian).

The Messiah:
"Il Messia," in *Rivista del Cinematografo*, no. 7-8, July-August 1977, pp. 328-372 (in Italian).

WRITINGS AND INTERVIEWS BY ROSSELLINI

R. Rossellini, *Utopia Autopsia 10^{10}*, Rome: Armando Editore, 1974 (in Italian)
R. Rossellini, *Un esprit libre ne doit rien apprendre en esclave*, Paris: Fayard, 1977 (in French)
Sergio Trasatti, *Rossellini e la televisione*, Rome: La Rassegna Editrice, 1978 (anthology, with an essay on Rossellini; in Italian)
Edoardo Bruno (ed.), *R.R. Roberto Rossellini*, Rome: Bulzoni (Quaderni di Filmcritica no. 7), 1979 (anthology, in Italian)
R. Rossellini, *Le cinéma révélé*, Paris: Cahiers du cinéma/Editions de l'Etoile, 1984; Flammarion, 1988 (edited and with an essay by Alain Bergala; anthology, in French)
R. Rossellini, *Il mio metodo. Scritti e interviste*, edited by A. Aprà, Venice: Marsilio, 1987 (anthology, in Italian).
R. Rossellini, *Fragments d'une autobiographie*, edited by Stefano Roncoroni, Paris: Ramsay, 1987 (in French); Italian transl., *Quasi un'autobiografia*, Milan: Mondadori, 1987.

BOOKS ON ROSSELLINI

Massimo Mida, *Roberto Rossellini*, Parma: Guanda, 1953; new enlarged edition: Guanda, 1961 (in Italian)

Mario Verdone, *Roberto Rossellini*, Paris: Seghers, 1963 (in French)

José Luis Guarner, *Roberto Rossellini*, London: Studio Vista & New York, Praeger, 1970 (in English).

Pio Baldelli, *Roberto Rossellini*, Rome: La Nuova Sinistra/ Samonà e Savelli, 1972 (in Italian)

Gianni Menon (ed.), *Dibattito su Rossellini*, Rome: Partisan, 1972 (in Italian)

Gianni Rondolino, *Roberto Rossellini*, Florence: La Nuova Italia, 1974 (in Italian)

Edoardo Bruno (ed.), *Roberto Rossellini, Il cinema, la televisione, la storia, la critica*, Città di Sanremo, 1980 (in Italian)

Donald Ranvaud (ed.), *Roberto Rossellini*, London: British Film Institute, Dossier no. 8, 1981 (in English)

Michel Serceau, *Roberto Rossellini*, Paris: Ed. du Cerf, 1986 (in French)

Stefano Masi & Enrico Lancia, *I film di Roberto Rossellini*, Rome: Gremese, 1987 (in Italian)

A. Aprà (ed.), *Rosselliniana*, Rome: Di Giacomo, 1987 (international bibliography and dossier on *Paisan*; in Italian)

Peter Brunette, *Roberto Rossellini*, New York-Oxford: Oxford Un. Press, 1987.

Patrizio Rossi, *Roberto Rossellini: A Guide to References and Resources*, Boston: G.K. Hall, 1987.

Rainer Gansera, Rudolph Thome & Wolfgang Jacobsen, *Roberto Rossellini*, Munich: Carl Hanser Verlag, 1987 (in German)

AA. VV., *Roberto Rossellini*, Rome: Ente Autonomo Gestione Cinema, 1987 (includes screenplays of unrealized projects "American Revolution," and "Science"; in English and Italian)

AA. VV., *Roberto Rossellini*, Rome: Ente Autonomo Gestione Cinema, 1990 (same as above; in French)

Alain Bergala & Jean Narboni (eds.), *Roberto Rossellini*, Paris: Cahier du cinéma/La Cinémathèque Française, 1990 (in French)

Fernaldo di Giammatteo, *Roberto Rossellini*, Scandicci (Florence): La Nuova Italia, 1990 (in Italian)

Edoardo Bruno (ed.), *Rossellini Bergman. Europe Six*, Rome: Cinecittà Estero, 1991 (in French)

INDEX

Verne, Jules, 159
Vidor, King 41, 243
Vienna, Congress of, 161
Virgil, 167
Vittorini, Elio, 149

Weil, Simone, 54, 119
World War I, 11

World War II, 58
Wright, Basil, 20

Xanthippe, 43

Yemen, 241
Yutkevich, 17, 20

Zweig, Stefan, 57, 120–21

Among the most celebrated filmmakers of our century, ROBERTO ROSSELLINI wrote and spoke with great care and passion about his art. Here, for the first time in English, hard-to-find interviews with and scattered writings by the father of Neorealism are collected, revealing a career of true originality and insatiable curiosity. Rossellini's subjects, like those of his films, are wide-ranging: from the Renaissance to the Hollywood studios, from Neorealism to television (which deeply fascinated him), and from Fascism and World War II to St. Francis of Assisi. This volume brings to light Rossellini's revolutionary outlook on film and culture, involving the reader in the making of the landmark Neorealist films, as well as going into more provocative territory such as historical values, the Third World, and mass technology in contemporary cinema.

These original and long-unavailable texts allow us to rediscover the work and thought of a filmmaker who changed the way movies are made. *My Method* offers a fresh perspective into the exemplary and often remarkable life and art of Rossellini, whose films, in the director's own words, always tried "to persuade everyone to live adventurously."

Born in Rome in 1906, ROSSELLINI made his first films in the late thirties under the Fascist regime. With the breakthrough of Neorealism at the end of World War II, most notably with *Open City* and *Paisan,* he gained notoriety and an international reputation. In the fifties, his partnership with and marriage to Ingrid Bergman marked a series of more introspective films, such as *Stromboli* and *Voyage in Italy.* By the end of the decade, Rossellini was devoting his career to historical and documentary subjects; his later works were a highly original and ground-breaking series of films for television, including *The Rise to Power of Louis XIV, The Age of the Medici,* and *The Messiah.*

ADRIANO APRÀ was a close friend of Rossellini's. A filmmaker and scriptwriter in his own right, Aprà is a noted film critic. He was the founder and director of the journal *Cinema & Film,* and, in addition to the original Italian edition of the present anthology, he recently edited Alessandro Blasetti's writings on cinema (*Scritti sul cinema,* Venice: 1982). He is also the director of the Pesaro Film Festival.